PRAISE FOR *INTRODUCING PHILOSOPHY OF RELIGION*

'Chad Meister has written a clear, systematic, engaging introduction to philosophy of religion. There is no better single volume that covers the contemporary and classical themes and arguments with greater skill, fairness, comprehensiveness and efficiency. This is a brilliant book for newcomers as well as advanced scholars who want to take a fresh look at philosophy of religion today.'

Charles Taliaferro, *St. Olaf College, USA*

'*Introducing Philosophy of Religion* by Chad Meister is a solid introduction to the fascinating field of critical reflection on religious belief and practice. Meister draws upon the traditions and thinkers from the Eastern as well as from the Western religions as he brings the reader up to speed on the most current debates. The book is structured in a way that helps the first-time student grasp clearly the essentials of each issue. Questions for discussion at the end of each chapter aid readers in beginning their own journey of careful reflection. This book is a great place to begin.'

Gregory Ganssle, *Yale University, USA*

'Teachers want to generate capacity for critical thinking about religions. Students seek access to religions in order to understand their globalized world. The clarity and scope of this text accomplishes these interconnected requirements. This is because Chad Meister presents the philosophy of religion as something that people do. He introduces the dimensions of a practice and a history of its practitioners like a clearly arranged chorus, which enables readers to find their own voice for doing the philosophy of religion.

Meister has created a comprehensive text which concisely reviews a field that today expands beyond the exclusive study of theistic religions. Each page relates historic debates to current investigations in order to illustrate the dynamism of its topic. Key terms are situated and explained in very simple language; and the examples are oddly humorous. This effectively establishes many points of entry for further research and reflection. As such, this text's accomplishment is profound.'

Nathan Loewen, *Faculty of Religious Studies, McGill University, Canada*

Introducing Philosophy of Religion

Does God exist? What about evil and suffering? How does faith relate to science? Is there life after death? These questions fascinate everyone and lie at the heart of philosophy of religion. Chad Meister offers an up-to-date introduction to the field, focusing not only on traditional debates but also on contemporary concepts such as the intelligent creator. Key topics, such as divine reality, and the self and religious experience, are discussed in relation to different faiths. *Introducing Philosophy of Religion*:

- offers a lucid overview of contemporary philosophy of religion;
- introduces the key figures in the history of philosophy of religion;
- explores the impact of religious diversity and pluralism;
- examines the main arguments for and against the existence of God and the nature of the divine;
- looks at science and issues of faith and reason;
- explores how the different religions approach the concept of life after death.

The wealth of textbook features, including tables of essential information, questions for reflection, summaries, glossary, and recommendations for further reading make the book ideal for student use. Along with its accompanying Reader, this is the perfect introductory package for undergraduate philosophy of religion courses.

Chad Meister is Professor of Philosophy and Director of the Philosophy Program at Bethel College, Indiana. He has substantial experience of teaching in American philosophy departments and is the author of *The Philosophy of Religion Reader* (Routledge, 2007).

Introducing Philosophy of Religion

Chad Meister

Routledge
Taylor & Francis Group
LONDON AND NEW YORK

First published 2009 by Routledge
2 Park Square, Milton Park, Abingdon, Oxon OX14 4RN

Simultaneously published in the USA and Canada
by Routledge
270 Madison Ave, New York, NY 100016

Reprinted 2010

Routledge is an imprint of the Taylor & Francis Group, an informa business

Typeset in Charter by
HWA Text and Data Management, London
Printed and bound in Great Britain by
CPI Antony Rowe, Chippenham, Wiltshire

British Library Cataloguing in Publication Data
A catalogue record for this book is available from the British Library

Library of Congress Cataloging in Publication Data
Meister, Chad V., 1965–
Introducing philosophy of religion / Chad Meister.
p. cm.
Includes indexes.
1. Religion—Philosophy. 2. Philosophical theology. I. Title.
BL51.M4855 2009
200.1–dc22 2008040857

ISBN10: 0-415-40326-X (hbk)
ISBN10: 0-415-40327-8 (pbk)
ISBN10: 0-203-88002-1 (ebk)

ISBN13: 978-0-415-40326-9 (hbk)
ISBN13: 978-0-415-40327-6 (pbk)
ISBN13: 978-0-203-88002-9 (ebk)

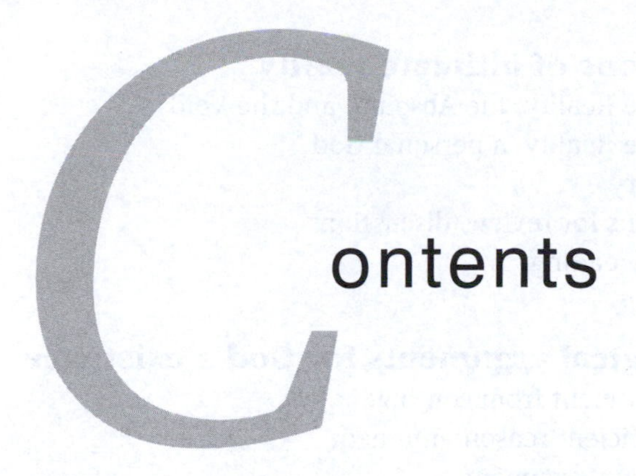

Contents

Illustrations

Figures

Table

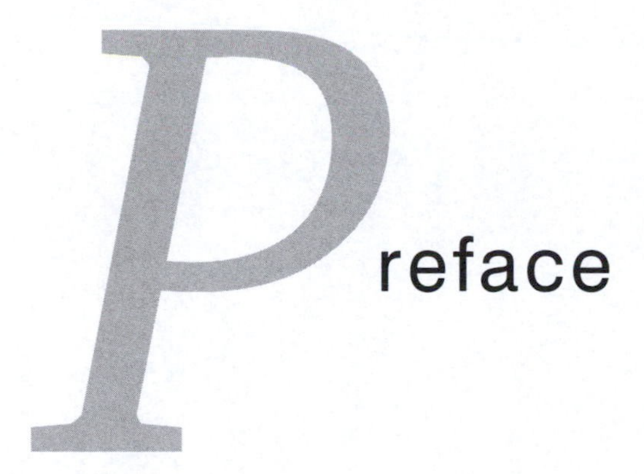

Preface

This book emerged from over two decades of personal philosophical reflection on religious ideas. My aim in writing it has not been to provide *the* answers to the diverse questions in the broad field of philosophy of religion. Rather, it has been to introduce the major issues and debates in this exciting and flourishing field and to create a thirst for further reflection on and study of them. I cannot think of any more important questions than those related to God/Ultimate Reality, faith and reason, the self and the afterlife, and how to think about and relate to those of other faiths and worldviews. If this book generates even a trifling interest in these matters, I will consider it a success.

In thinking through (and rethinking) many of the issues in philosophy of religion, and in crafting this book, I have benefited from dialogue with a number of friends, colleagues, and students. Special thanks go to Pamela Sue Anderson, Peter Byrne, Paul Copan, Win Corduan, William Lane Craig, David Cramer, Timothy Erdel, Cristian Mihut, Paul Moser, Katherin Rogers, Austin Schertz, James Stump, Charles Taliaferro, and Keith Ward. In various ways I have learned much from each of them, and I am grateful for their work, wisdom, and insights.

My wife, Tammi, was kind enough to read through the chapters, offering her own perspective on the material, style, and structure of the book. Her practical wisdom and creativity continue to amaze me. Many thanks are also due to Amy Grant for her superb editorial support and to Lesley Riddle, a first-rate senior publisher, for her expert guidance and insight.

I dedicate this book to my students, who never cease to challenge and inspire me.

C.M.
Bethel College
USA

Preface

Introduction

The field of philosophy of religion has blossomed in recent decades and is now flourishing internationally with creative, first-rate thinkers – many of whom are thought-leaders in other areas of philosophy as well – utilizing their philosophical expertise to tackle a host of religious topics. The range of those engaged in philosophy of religion is also rather broad and includes such diverse scholars as analytic and continental philosophers, feminists and ethicists, and Eastern and Western thinkers, among others. Given the breadth of the field, a number of topics could have been included in this book, and various approaches could have been taken as well. My goal in writing this book has been to construct a text which includes the major issues typically addressed in philosophy of religion textbooks and covered in philosophy of religion courses, but also to offer some atypical ones which are emerging in the field and quickly becoming notable topics of discussion. I have tried to write in a manner and style which is both accessible and interesting to undergraduate students in philosophy of religion, but which also has merit for graduate students and others interested in the field. I have sought to avoid unnecessary technical jargon as much as possible, and have defined and explained terms and ideas which would be unfamiliar to most undergraduates. Though the traditional "analytic/continental" dichotomy is not as sharply defined today as some would like to think, nevertheless the approach I take here generally follows the method and style of the analytic tradition in that I include positions, formal arguments for those positions, and objections or rebuttals to the arguments (and sometimes rebuttals to the rebuttals), sometimes without considering the history, context, or cultural milieu of the positions. This critical method was not always feasible or beneficial as some topics do not readily lend themselves to analytic style and argument forms.

There is certainly value in having an author of a work such as this one provide her or his own views, arguments, and conclusions on subjects as controversial as many of those discussed in philosophy of religion; however, that is not my intention in this work. Rather, I am striving to be non-partisan, at least as non-partisan as I can be in a work covering such exciting and contentious topics as these. I have attempted to keep from presenting my own views and conclusions to the issues and instead have presented, as clearly and concisely as possible, the major positions, arguments for, and rebuttals to, the central topics in the field today. Of course, even the selection of topics and the arguments and rebuttals chosen will reflect my own leanings and biases to some extent, but my intent has been to be impartial and evenhanded.

SCOPE AND STRUCTURE

Until recently, much of the philosophical work in religion in the West was primarily focused on the theistic traditions of Judaism, Christianity, and Islam. As a result, the diversity of religious thought expressed by those in other traditions was, for the most part, ignored. With the escalating presence and awareness of non-theistic religions in the West, however, it has become increasingly more important to include them in philosophical dialogue. I have attempted to do so in this book. While I include many of the major traditional topics from theistic discussions, I have also endeavored to be multicultural in perspective and to include a number of major non-theistic themes as well.

Chapter 1 begins by exploring the meanings of the terms *religion* and *philosophy of religion* and the important question of what religious beliefs and practices are about. It also includes an extensive philosophy of religion timeline. Chapter 2 continues this exploration by examining the growing phenomenon of religious diversity. It focuses specifically on five major world religions: Hinduism, Buddhism, Judaism, Christianity, and Islam. Each of these religions makes claims about fundamental issues, including the meaning of salvation/liberation and the nature of Ultimate Reality. These world religions, and the central historical philosophers within them, either imply or affirm that their fundamental claims are true. As a number of these claims conflict with one another, the next question explored is how one should philosophically approach such conflicts. This chapter also considers the task of evaluating religious systems, possible criteria for making such evaluations, and the importance of religious tolerance.

Philosophers of religion reflect on a variety of religious concepts, but probably none has been more dominant than the concept of God/Ultimate Reality. Therefore, it is important to examine the principal topics relevant to the nature and existence of the divine. Chapter 3 explores two unique ways of conceiving God/Ultimate Reality: (1) as an absolute state of being (as within certain schools of Hinduism and Buddhism), and (2) as a personal God (as within the three major theistic traditions). One of the major contemporary discussions relevant to the concept of God is whether the traditional attributes are logically consistent and coherent, so some time is spent on this issue as well.

Philosophers of religion are not only interested in exploring the concept of God, but also knowing whether such a concept is true – that is, whether God actually exists. Chapters 4, 5, and 6 explore three major types of arguments for God's existence: cosmological, teleological, and ontological. While each of these argument forms is quite old in nature, none of them is an antiquated relic; each one has undergone much discussion and development in recent decades. And just as there are philosophical arguments for God's existence, there are also philosophical challenges to belief in God. Chapter 7 hones in on one of them: problems of evil.

Religion is not typically a domain completely isolated from other aspects of society and culture. It includes (some would say "infects") virtually all facets of human life. One of these areas is science, and for centuries religion and science have had a knotty relationship; sometimes they are at odds, sometimes they are supportive of one another. Chapter 8 tackles several basic options for understanding how religion and science are related. Whatever the relationship, it seems evident that religion and science have unique roles in life and thought. It is also apparent that the practice of science has, on occasion at least, implications for religious faith, and that religious belief isn't always devoid of scientific reasoning. Consequently, the rest of the chapter focuses on several options for relating faith and reason.

One element of religion common to all the major traditions is religious experience. Chapter 9 explores this phenomenon in several of its various forms. It also examines the question of whether this kind of phenomenon can provide justification for religious belief and whether scientific explanations of religious experience demonstrate that such experiences are merely the result of neurophysiological causes (and thus ultimately delusory).

All the religious traditions provide an understanding of what it means to be a self, and they all offer hope for oneself – hope for this life and especially hope after death. How we understand our own nature plays a significant role in how we understand what the afterlife entails. These topics of the self, death, and the afterlife are considered in Chapter 10, the final chapter of the book.

PEDAGOGICAL FEATURES AND RESOURCES FOR FURTHER EXPLORATION

This book incorporates a number of pedagogical features to enhance your learning experience, including summaries at the end of each chapter, provocative reflection questions to clarify important points and reinforce your understanding of the material, tables and boxes to keep definitions and arguments clear and concise, a glossary of important terms that are unfamiliar to many readers, and an extensive index. At the end of each chapter I have also provided an annotated further reading section which includes many of the major works on the chapter's topic. I have tried to be comprehensive, inclusive, and balanced in choosing these selections. Relevant websites are included at the end of each chapter as well. Many of these sites include important articles, summaries, and further resources on the relevant topics.

The Philosophy of Religion Reader (Routledge, 2008) is designed to work in tandem with this text as it provides a considerable number of related seminal articles in philosophy of religion, both classical and contemporary, Eastern and Western. It would be an excellent companion to utilize as you work through this material.

My hope is that as you read this book you will engage with the ideas, diving deeply into the positions, arguments, and counterarguments; that you will sift through the further reading material and websites listed at the end of the chapters and do your own research and reflect on the topics that especially interest you; and that through these engagements you will find yourself absorbed in the kind of philosophical reflection on religious ideas which have spanned the centuries and inspired some of its greatest minds.

1 Religion and the philosophy of religion

RELIGION AND THE WORLD RELIGIONS

Sigmund Freud (1856–1939), one of the great psychologists of the twentieth century, wrote that religion is comparable to a childhood neurosis.[1] If this is so, the world is filled with something like five billion neurotic individuals. As I type these words, in sheer numbers there are roughly two billion Christians, consisting of Roman Catholics, Protestants, and Orthodox; there are well over a billion Muslims, close to 80 percent of whom are Sunni and 20 percent Shiite; there are over a billion Hindus; roughly 350 million Buddhists (Theravada and Mahayana); approximately 350 million adherents of the Chinese traditions of Confucianism and Daoism; about 300 million adherents of African traditional religions (Animists, Shamanists, etc.); 25 million Sikhs; 14 million Jews; 7 million Baha'i; 4 million Jains, and the list goes on (see Figure 1.1[2]). And the religious traditions are not limited to geographic regions. Western religions have migrated East and Eastern religions have traveled West. As a case in point, Diana Eck – Director of the Pluralism Project at Harvard University – has pointed out that the formerly "Christian country" of the United States has now become the most religiously diverse nation in the world, with millions of adherents of Eastern as well as Western religions.[3] Worldwide, nonreligious people are clearly in the minority, making up only about 15 percent of the world's population.

No doubt, religion is ubiquitous. Nevertheless, attempting to offer a *definition* of religion which captures all and only what are taken to be religions is notoriously difficult. Central to some religions is a personal God and other spiritual entities; for other religions, there is no God or spirits at all. Some religions view the eternal, personal existence of the individual in an afterlife as paramount to understanding Ultimate Reality and much more important than temporary earthly existence. Others see what we do in *this* life as fundamental, with little if any consideration of the hereafter. Other differences among the religions abound.

But as diverse as religions are, several components seem to be central to the world religions: a system of beliefs, the breaking in of a transcendent reality, and human attitudes of ultimate concern, meaning, and purpose. Given these three elements, the following perhaps captures what most take to be the essence of the concept of religion: *a religion involves a system of beliefs and practices primarily centered around a transcendent Reality, either personal or impersonal, which provides ultimate meaning and purpose to life*.[4]

While this is not a book on world religions, work in the philosophy of religion would be deficient without taking into consideration the diversity of beliefs among at least the major religious traditions. It would be an enormous task to include all of what are commonly taken to be the major religions (and I consider the list above to be fairly inclusive of the *world* religions) in a textbook such as this one, so limitation is necessary. This delimiting process was not easy, but several factors made it more manageable than it could have been.

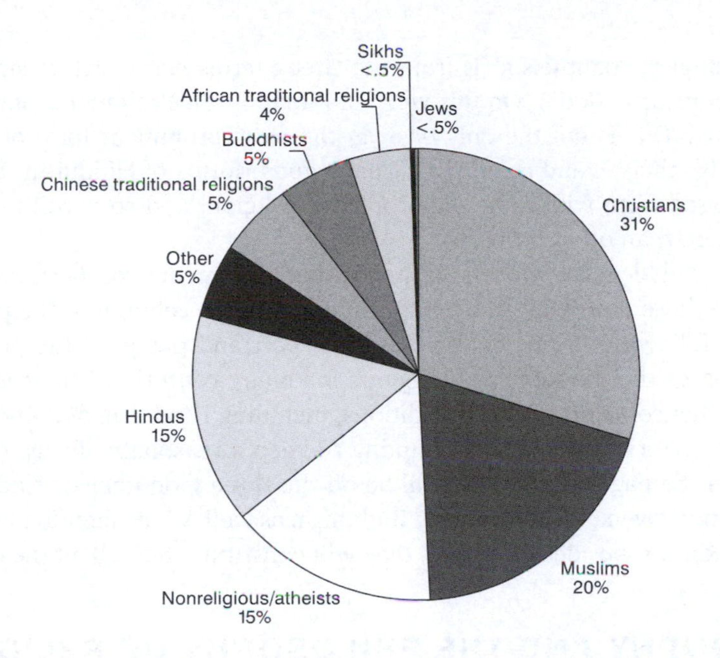

Figure 1.1 World religions

First, since I am writing from within the English-speaking world and am most familiar with the traditions predominant within it, it makes sense to emphasize them over others. For someone else with a different background and writing from a different place, other emphases would be appropriate. So, emphasis will be placed on the monotheistic religions of Judaism, Christianity, and Islam. Historically, the monotheistic traditions have included the belief that there is only one God – a personal God who is omniscient (all-knowing), omnipotent (all-powerful), and omnibenevolent (completely good in every way), and thus worthy of worship. This God is the creator and sustainer of the world. Furthermore, a distinction is often made among monotheists between *theists*, who believe that God is distinct from the world and yet actively involved in the world (guiding human history, for example, and offering divine revelation); *deists*, who believe that God is distinct from the world and not actively involved in the world; and *panentheists*, who believe that God permeates and is co-dependent with the world.

Second, besides the monotheistic traditions, Hinduism and Buddhism have also received more attention by philosophers of religion in the English-speaking world than other traditions have received. The school of thought within Hinduism which has received the most attention is Advaita Vedānta ("Advaita" is a Sanskrit term which means "non-dual," and "Vedānta" means pertaining to the Hindu scriptures called the Vedas). The view of God, or Brahman, for those affirming Advaita Vedānta is called *monistic pantheism* ("monism" is from the Greek term *monus* which means "one" or "single"; "pantheism" is from the Greek terms *pan* which means "all" and *theos* which means "God"). On this view, Brahman is all; Brahman is one; Brahman is everything. This is not the only or even the most prominent form of Hinduism; there are also theistic and *polytheistic* (many gods) forms of Hinduism. But it is the most discussed form within the philosophy of religion, and so it will receive more attention here than other forms.

Third, the dialectical process of presenting arguments for positions, offering rebuttals to those positions, and giving responses to the rebuttals – the process that we will be following in this book – has been part and parcel of the philosophical examination of the monotheistic religions for many centuries. This has also been the case within some of the other traditions, including Hinduism and Buddhism. So, given these factors, along with attempting to keep a reasonable focus, the primary emphasis in the pages that follow will be on the three monotheistic traditions with some attention given to Hinduism and Buddhism as well. While mention will be made of other traditions besides these five, they will constitute the bulk of the discussion.

PHILOSOPHY AND THE PHILOSOPHY OF RELIGION

Philosophy of religion is currently a major field of study, and the range of topics encompassed within it is considerable. Nevertheless, its scope is fairly narrow, for philosophy of religion is simply the philosophical reflection on religious ideas. The terms "philosophical reflection" and "religious ideas" need elucidation. "Philosophical reflection" in this context includes the careful analyses of words, reasons and evidences for claims, hypotheses, and arguments. These analyses themselves include fundamental issues about the nature of reality (metaphysics) and the way in which we come to know things (epistemology).

Regarding these fundamental issues, philosophy of religion and, indeed, philosophy itself have taken new directions in recent times. While philosophical reflection on religious ideas has been occurring for centuries, even millennia, it underwent a momentous setback in the early-to-mid twentieth century through the work of the logical positivists. Logical positivists held, among other things, that for a claim to be true and meaningful it must be empirically verifiable. As religious claims were for the most part taken to be empirically unverifiable, philosophical reflection on religious themes was widely considered to be a specious endeavor and religious ideas were often taken to be meaningless. However, due to the work of a number of leading philosophers who were responding to positivism and defending the philosophical viability of religious beliefs – philosophers such as John Hick and Alvin Plantinga – by the 1970s the field began to take a significant turn. Today, philosophy of religion is flourishing and it is not uncommon to see philosophy journals, anthologies, and monographs devoted exclusively to religious themes.[5]

Logical Positivism (later called "logical empiricism") is a philosophical position which grew out of philosophical discussions in the 1920s by a group of philosophers referred to as the Vienna Circle. The positivists maintained that all cognitively meaningful language is in principle either empirically or formally verifiable.

By the phrase "religious ideas" I mean the primary issues and concepts which have been discussed and debated within the religious traditions throughout the centuries, including for example the existence and nature of God or Ultimate Reality; conflicting truth claims among the different religious traditions; the relation between science and religion; creation; *nirvana*; and salvation, among other topics. It is important to note that these are not just abstract and ethereal concepts discussed and debated among ivory-tower theologians and philosophers. To the contrary, they are fundamental issues in the life and thought of those in living traditions – traditions which have deep, existential meaning and ongoing significance for much of contemporary humanity.

Philosophy of religion has a rich and diverse history. As the timeline (Table 1.1) demonstrates, the history of philosophy of religion has been a global enterprise which can be demarcated by four historical time periods: the ancient world, the medieval world, the modern world, and the contemporary world.

PHILOSOPHY OF RELIGION TIMELINE

Dates	*Events/Descriptions*	*Relevant People*
Ancient World		
c. 2600 BCE	Indus Valley civilization Religious Hindu images created	
c. 1500–1200 BCE	Development of Brahmanism Likely composition of Hindu Vedas	
c. 1300 BCE	Moses and the Ten Commandments	Moses
c. 1000 BCE	Kingdom of Israel begins	David/Solomon
c. 800–400 BCE	Likely composition of early Hindu Upanishads	
c. 800–200 BCE	Axial Period*	
c. 660–583 BCE	Founder of Zoroastrianism	Zoroaster
c. 640–546 BCE	Western philosophy begins	Thales
c. 599–527 BCE	Founder of Jainism	Mahavira Jeni
586–587 BCE	Fall of Jerusalem/Jews taken into captivity in Babylon	
c. 570–510 BCE	Founder of Taoism and author of early form of the Tao-Te-Ching	Lao Tzu
c. 570–495 BCE	Ionian (Greek) mathematician and philosopher and developed the Pythagorean theorem	Pythagoras
c. 551–479 BCE	Founder of Confucianism	Confucius
566–486 BCE	Founder of Buddhism	Sidhartha Guatama (Buddha)
c. 500–450 BCE	Greek philosopher, chief representative of the Eleatic school	Parmenides
c. 500 BCE	Founding of Shintoism (Japan)	
c. 469–399 BCE	Greek philosopher	Socrates
427–347 BCE	Greek philosopher	Plato
384–322 BCE	Greek philosopher	Aristotle
c. 372–289 BCE	Confucian philosopher	Mencius
341–270 BCE	Founder of Epicurean philosophy	Epicurus

*The phrase "Axial Period" was so dubbed by philosopher Karl Jaspers to denote the period from roughly 800 BCE to 200 BCE – a time of widespread revolution in religious and philosophical thought which occurred in both the East and the West. It includes such important figures as Homer, Socrates, Isaiah, Zoroaster, Siddhartha Gautama, Confucius, and the authors of the Hindu Vedas. During this time new "axes" were created which influenced philosophical and religious thought for the next two millennia.

Dates	Events/Descriptions	Relevant People
334–331 BCE	Alexander the Great spreads Greek culture, philosophy and religion throughout the Eastern Mediterranean	
c. 333–264 BCE	Founder of Stoic philosophy	Zeno the Stoic
c. 300 BCE	Likely final composition of Tao-Te-Ching	
c. 200 BCE	Early portion of Bhagavad Gita written (completed in 400 CE)	
200–100 CE	Buddhism divides into Theravada and Mahayana	
c. 4 BCE–c. 30 CE	Founder of Christianity	Jesus of Nazareth
c. 10–c. 68	New Testament apostle and author of many New Testament letters	St. Paul
c. 30	Crucifixion of Jesus of Nazareth	
50–100	Likely composition of Christian Scriptures	
70	Temple in Jerusalem is destroyed by the Romans	
c. 150–200	Founder of Madhyamika school of Buddhism (India)	Nagarjuna
205–270	Founder of Neoplatonism	Plotinus
c. 215–276	Founder of Manicheanism	Mani
325	Christian Council of Nicaea (focuses on Trinitarian doctrine)	
354–430	Last Christian Church Father	St. Augustine
410	Fall of Rome	
451	Christian Council of Chalcedon (focuses on Christocentric issues)	
c. 480–524	Christian Roman philosopher	Boethius
Medieval World		
570–632	Founder of Islam	Mohammed the Prophet
c. 788–820	Founder of Advaita Vedānta Hinduism	Adi Shankara
c. 800–866	Islamic philosopher	Al-Kindi
c. 870–950	Islamic philosopher	Al-Farabi
980–1037	Islamic philosopher	Ibn Sina (Avicenna)
1017–1137	Founder of Vishishtadvaita Vedānta Hinduism	Ramanuja
1033–1109	Christian monk; developed the ontological argument	St. Anselm of Canterbury
1058–1111	Islamic philosopher	Al-Ghazali

Dates	*Events/Descriptions*	*Relevant People*
1126–1198	Islamic philosopher	Ibn Rushd (Averroës)
1135–1204	Jewish philosopher/theologian	Moses Maimonides
1200–1253	Japanese Zen master (founder of Soto school)	Dogen Kigen
1225–1274	Christian philosopher/theologian	St. Thomas Aquinas
1266–1308	European philosopher, logician, and Franciscan theologian	John Duns Scotus
c. 1285–1349	English philosopher and Franciscan friar	William of Ockham
1400s	European Renaissance	
1473–1543	Polish astronomer who offered the first modern formulation of a heliocentric solar system	Nicholas Copernicus
1483–1546	Protestant Reformer	Martin Luther
1469–1539	Founder of Sikhism	Guru Nanak Dev
1496–1561	Founder of Anabaptist Protestant movement	Menno Simons
1500–1600	European Scientific Revolution	
1509–1564	French theologian, Protestant Reformer, and founder of Calvinism	John Calvin
1515–1582	Christian mystic	St. Teresa of Avila
1517	Protestant Reformation begins with Luther's "95 Theses"	
1542–1591	Spanish Carmelite friar	St. John of the Cross
1545–1564	Council of Trent	
1560–1609	Dutch theologian and founder of Arminianism—the anti-Calvinistic school in Reformed Protestant theology	Jacobus Arminius
1564–1642	Italian astronomer, physicist, and philosopher	Galileo Galilei
Modern World		
1596–1650	French rationalist philosopher (founder of modern Western philosophy)	René Descartes
1623–1662	French physicist, mathematician, and religious philosopher	Blaise Pascal
1632–1677	Jewish rationalist philosopher from Amsterdam	Benedict (Baruch) Spinoza
1643–1727	English physicist, astronomer, mathematician, and natural philosopher	Sir Isaac Newton
1646	Westminster Confession	

Dates	*Events/Descriptions*	*Relevant People*
1646–1716	German rationalist philosopher	Gottfried Wilhelm Leibniz
1685–1753	Irish bishop and empiricist philosopher	George Berkeley
1694–1778	French Enlightenment philosopher	Voltaire
1703–1758	American theologian and Congregational pastor	Jonathan Edwards
1711–1776	Scottish philosopher, historian, and economist	David Hume
1724–1804	German philosopher	Immanuel Kant
1743–1805	Christian philosopher and apologist	William Paley
1770–1831	German philosopher	Georg Wilhelm Friedrich Hegel
1809–1882	British naturalist who established evolution by common descent	Charles Darwin
1813–1855	Danish philosopher	Søren Kierkegaard
1817–1892	Founder of Baha'i	Baha'u'llah
1818–1883	German philosopher and political economist	Karl Marx
1844–1900	German philosopher	Friedrich Nietzsche
1893	World Parliament of Religions, Chicago, Illinois	
Contemporary World		
1842–1910	American pragmatist philosopher	William James
1804–1872	German philosopher	Ludwig Feuerbach
1856–1939	Austrian neurologist and founder of the psychoanalytic school of psychology	Sigmund Freud
1861–1947	British mathematician and philosopher	Alfred North Whitehead
1870–1945	Japanese philosopher who atempted to assimilate Western philosophy into the Oriental spiritual tradition	Kitaro Nishida
1870–1966	Japanese Zen Buddhist philosopher and author who was instrumental in bringing Zen to the West	Daisetz Teitaro (DT) Suzuki
1872–1970	British logician, mathematician, and philosopher	Bertrand Russell
1879–1955	German-born theoretical physicist and author of the general theory of relativity	Albert Einstein
1888–1975	Indian philosopher and second president of India	Sarvepalli Radhakrishnan
1889–1951	Austrian philosopher	Ludwig Wittgenstein

Dates	*Events/Descriptions*	*Relevant People*
1889–1976	German philosopher	Martin Heidegger
1898–1963	Cambridge Medievalist, novelist, and Christian apologist	C. S. Lewis
1905–1980	French existentialist philosopher, novelist, and dramatist	Jean-Paul Sartre
1886–1968	Reformed Christian theologian and a leader of the neo-orthodox movement	Karl Barth
1908–1986	French author and philosopher	Simone de Beauvoir
1919–2001	British analytic philosopher	Elizabeth (G.E.M.) Anscombe
1922–1996	American philosopher of science	Thomas Kuhn
1922-	Philosopher of religion and Christian theologian	John Hick
1923-	British philosopher and former atheist (now a deist)	Antony Flew
1926–1984	French post-structuralist philosopher	Michel Foucault
1929-	Scottish moral philosopher	Alasdair MacIntyre
1930–2004	French literary critic and deconstructionist philosopher	Jacques Derrida
1932-	American philosopher of religion	Alvin Plantinga
1934-	British philosopher of religion	Richard Swinburne
1935-	Supreme head of Tibetan Buddhism	Tenzin Gyatso, the 14th Dalai Lama
1959–	Feminist philosopher of religion	Pamela Sue Anderson
1963–1965	Second Vatican Council	Pope John XXIII

RELIGIOUS BELIEFS AND PRACTICES

There are a variety of beliefs held by the religions or by religious people. The monotheistic religions, for example, assert that a personal God exists and that God is good. Buddhists maintain that the Four Noble Truths provide a path to enlightenment. Many Hindus affirm that Brahman is the one reality. Taoists (also Daoists) affirm that the *dao* is the fundamental process of reality itself. And so on. Most religious adherents consider the central claims of their religion to be true. But an important philosophical question is whether these religious claims are true or false in the same way that other claims, such as scientific ones, are true or false. There are two very different positions taken by philosophers of religion with respect to the concept of truth in religious discourse: realism and non-realism.

Realism

Probably the vast majority of religious adherents are religious realists.[6] That is, most religious adherents hold that their beliefs are about what really exists independent of the human beings who are having those beliefs. Assertions about Allah, for example, or Brahman, or salvation, or *moksha*, or reincarnation are true if there are actual referents for them. Thus, for Muslims, the claim that Allah is the one true God is true if, in fact, there is a being who exists independently of human conceptual frameworks or thoughts and beliefs about (or practices related to) Allah and is identifiable as Allah, the one true God. The same holds for adherents of the other religions who are realists: they believe that the claims of their religion have actual referents beyond their own beliefs and practices.

Non-realism

Although they are in the minority, there are also religious non-realists. While there are different forms of religious non-realism, in general non-realists maintain that religious claims are not about realities which transcend human language, concepts, and social forms; religious claims are not about something "out there." The following words from a leading religious non-realist helpfully summarize the distinction between realism and non-realism:

> Today, a realist is the sort of person who, when his ship crosses the Equator, looks overboard, expecting to see a big black line across the ocean. Realism tries to turn cultural fictions into objective facts. A non-realist sees the whole system of lines of latitude and longitude as a framework, imposed upon the Earth by us, that helps us to define locations and to find our way around. For a realist Truth exists ready-made out there; for a non-realist we are the only makers of truth, and truth is only the current consensus amongst us. We cannot any longer suppose that our knowledge is validated by something wholly extra-human… .
>
> In religion, the move to non-realism implies the recognition that all religious and ethical ideas are human, with a human history. We give up the old metaphysical and cosmological way of understanding religious belief, and translate dogma into

Don Cupitt (1934–) is a Life Fellow and former Dean of Emmanuel College, Cambridge. He is one of the leading religious non-realists and is often described as a "radical theologian." He has written over forty books, including *Way to Happiness*, *Taking Leave of God* and *After God: The Future of Religion*.

Sigmund Freud (1856–1939) was an Austrian psychologist and medical doctor who founded the psychoanalytic school of psychology. Widely regarded as one of the most influential thinkers of the twentieth century, he wrote extensively about religion, describing it this way: "Religion is an illusion and it derives its strength from the fact that it falls in with our instinctual desires." Three of his most important books devoted to religion are *Totem and Taboo* (1913), *The Future of an Illusion* (1927), and *Civilization and Its Discontents* (1930).

> spirituality (a spirituality is a religious life-style). We understand all religious doctrines in practical terms, as guiding myths to live by, in the way that Kant, Kierkegaard and Bultmannn began to map out. We abandon ideas of objective and eternal truth, and instead see all truth as a human improvisation. We should give up all ideas of a heavenly or supernatural world-beyond. Yet, despite our seeming scepticism, we insist that non-realist religion can work very well as religion, and can deliver (a sort of) eternal happiness.[7]

Among non-realists there are those who are, as it were, favorable toward religion and those who are not. Consider the words of Sigmund Freud:

> These [religious ideas], which are given out as teachings, are not precipitates of experience or end-results of thinking: they are illusions, fulfillments of the oldest, strongest and most urgent wishes of mankind. The secret of their strength lies in the strength of those wishes.[8]

For Freud, there are no referents for religious beliefs about transcendent entities such as God, the *dao*, and so forth. Rather, religion is an illusion and religious beliefs are merely manifestations of this illusion. The belief in God, for example, is simply the projection of a Father image.[9]

More recently, Oxford geneticist Richard Dawkins (1941–) and philosopher Daniel Dennett (1942–) have advanced the notion that a Darwinian account of cultural evolution may explain religion and religious beliefs via the replication of something very much like genes. There are, they suggest, *cultural* replicators, what they refer to as *memes*, which are units of cultural transmission or imitation.[10] Says Dawkins:

> Just as genes propagate themselves in the gene pool by leaping from body to body via sperm or eggs, so memes propagate themselves in the meme pool by leaping from brain to brain by a process which, in the broad sense of the term, can be called imitation.[11]

He includes the following beliefs as religious memes:

- You will survive your own death.
- Belief in God is a supreme virtue.
- Faith is a virtue.
- There are some weird things (such as the Trinity, transubstantiation, incarnation) that we are not *meant* to understand.[12]

For Dawkins, the widespread belief in God is not due to there actually being such an entity, or because there are good reasons for believing there are. Rather, people believe because the "god-meme" has spread – in ways akin to a virus – throughout human populations. Religion turns about to be an "accidental by-product – a misfiring of something useful."[13] So too with all attending religious beliefs.[14]

Other non-realists are more favorable toward religion. Ludwig Wittgenstein (1889–1951) for example – one of the most influential philosophers of the twentieth century – took religion very seriously, even to the point of considering the priesthood.[15] Nevertheless, he was opposed to natural theology, the attempt to demonstrate the existence of God from evidence in the natural world, and to the development of religious doctrines. He was more interested in religious symbol and ritual.

In his later works Wittgenstein understood language to be not a fixed structure directly corresponding to the way things actually are, but rather to be a human activity susceptible to the vicissitudes of human life and practice. Language does not offer a picture of reality, he argued, but rather it is a set of activities which he described as "language games."[16] The concept of a language game was "to bring into prominence the fact that the speaking of language is part of an activity, or a form of life."[17] Wittgenstein uses the example of a builder to make the point:

> The language is meant to serve for communication between a builder A and an assistant B. A is building with building-stones: there are blocks, pillars, slabs and beams. B has to pass the stones, in the order in which A needs them. For this purpose they use a language consisting of the words "block," "pillar," "slab,"

Ludwig Wittgenstein (1889–1951) is considered by many to be one of the leading philosophers of the twentieth century. His two major works, *Tractatus Logico-Philosophicus and Philosophical Investigations* were fundamental in establishing first logical positivism and then ordinary language philosophy. His work on language and religion is much discussed and relevant to the realism/ non-realism debate.

> "beam." A calls them out; – B brings the stone which he has learnt to bring at such-and-such a call.[18]

In teaching language, one needs to be able to respond to words in certain contexts; speech and action work together. In many cases, then, the meaning of a word is its use in the language.[19] For Wittgenstein, this is true in religious discourse as it is elsewhere. Thus in speaking of God or Brahman or *nirvana* or the *dao*, the meanings of such words have more to do with their use than with their denotation.[20] The language games of the religions reflect the practices and forms of life of the various religious adherents, and so religious claims should not be taken as providing literal pictures of reality which somehow lie beyond these activities.[21]

Religious non-realists who are favorable toward religion also make note of the alleged failure of realism to provide evidences for the objective truth of any religion, or of religion in general. Whether referring to arguments for the existence of God, or evidences for divine inspiration of sacred scriptures, for example, non-realists maintain that such apologetic projects are abject failures. We will look at some of the evidences for faith in later chapters. But such non-realists are convinced that since there are no conclusive reasons to believe that a religion is true, a better way of approaching religious claims and beliefs is to view them through non-realist lenses.

Realists respond to this argument in various ways. For one, some agree that there are no solid reasons to believe any religion is true. Nevertheless, they claim that it does not require evidence. We will explore this position in Chapter 8. Other realists respond by claiming that there are good reasons and evidences for religious faith, and we will explore some of these reasons in Chapters 4, 5, 6, 9 and 10.

Another reason for holding to religious non-realism is the fact that religious claims, beliefs, and practices do in fact exist within a given social context and involve human language and concepts. Since religious claims and activities are always made within a particular human context, and since the mind structures all perception within that context, the meanings of these claims are determined and limited by that context. One need not – indeed, one legitimately cannot, it is argued – posit objective, transcendent realities beyond human language and cognition. To do so is to simply go too far.

Realists respond by noting that while much of what occurs in religious discourse (and practice) is of human origin, one need not take a reductionist stance in which all religious meanings and symbols are reducible to human language. As already noted, some realists argue that there are reasons for believing that a particular religion is true – that there are objective referents for their claims.[22]

I have given space here to non-realism – more so than for realism – both because it is an important development in contemporary philosophy of religion and because, in lieu of the predominant work in the field, the remainder of the book is oriented toward a realist perspective.

SUMMARY

Our world is in many ways a religious world, with roughly 85 percent of the populace affirming some form of religious belief. But religions and their attending beliefs are diverse. Some affirm a personal deity, some don't; some believe in many deities; some only one; some maintain that Ultimate Reality and the universe are one or co-dependent, others disagree. The differences are multifarious. But there are also similarities as all religions include beliefs, ideas, and practices centered around a transcendent Reality – a Reality which provides ultimate meaning and purpose to life.

The philosophical reflection on religious beliefs and ideas – an activity which has been ongoing for millennia – underwent a major challenge in the last century with the critiques of the logical positivists. However, with the demise of positivism in the 1970s, it re-emerged and is today a flourishing field of study.

In contemporary philosophy of religion discussions it is not only the different beliefs and practices of the various religions which are discussed and debated, but the more fundamental question of what religious beliefs and practices are about is of central concern. Religious realists maintain that religious beliefs are about transcendent realities which actually exist outside of human language and conceptual frameworks. Religious non-realists deny this. Some non-realists, such as Sigmund Freud and Richard Dawkins, maintain that religions are human constructions and religious beliefs are illusions or perhaps even delusions. Other non-realists, such as Don Cupitt and Ludwig Wittgenstein, agree that religions are about human practices, beliefs, and ideas. Nonetheless they maintain that religion is a meaningful human enterprise.

In the following chapters we will explore the rich diversity of religious beliefs and experiences, claims to religious truth, and other important areas of religious agreement and disagreement as we engage in the philosophy of religion.

QUESTIONS FOR REVIEW/DISCUSSION

1. How would you define "religion"? Does your definition include all and only what are generally taken to be the religions?
2. What are some similarities and differences between beliefs systems such as communism or secular humanism and religion?
3. The circular graph at the beginning of the chapter includes the current numbers of adherents among the world religions. Do the numbers affect your assessment of a religion's credibility? Should they? Explain.
4. Do you think it is possible to understand and assess a religion without actually being a believing member of the religion? Of any religion? What are some ways of attempting such understanding and assessment?
5. What are some areas of agreement and disagreement between religious realists and non-realists?
6. Do you consider yourself to be a religious realist or non-realist? What do you deem to be plausible reasons for affirming one or the other?
7. Do you believe that religion can and should be subject to rational or scientific investigation? Why or why not?
8. How might the positions of realism and non-realism affect the way one thinks about the following issues: human rights, religious tolerance, global responsibility?
9. Mohandas Gandhi stated that "A religion that takes no account of practical affairs and does not help to solve them is no religion." Do you agree? Is there a connection between religion and ethical action? Explain.
10. What are some possible areas of common ground between religious realists and non-realists? Can you think of ways for developing a rapprochement between them?

FURTHER READING

Byrne, Peter (2003) *God and Realism*. Burlington, VT: Ashgate. (A critical survey of issues relevant to the realist/non-realist debates.)

Cupitt, Don (1997) *After God: The Future of Religion*. New York: Basic Books. (A non-realist presentation in which God is viewed not as a transcendent reality but a reflection of the human self.)

Kant, Immanuel (1960) *Religion Within the Limits of Reason Alone*. Trans. Theodore M. Greene and Hoyt H. Hudson. New York: Harper & Brothers. (Interprets religious faith in ethical terms.)

Meister, Chad and Paul Copan, eds. (2007) *The Routledge Companion to Philosophy of Religion*. London: Routledge. (Includes many entries relevant to the material in this chapter with each offering further annotated bibliographies.)

Phillips, D. Z. (2001) *Religion and the Hermeneutics of Contemplation*. Cambridge: Cambridge University Press. (Working through central ideas of Hume, Feuerbach, Marx, Freud,

Durkheim, and others, he makes the case that religious thinkers should be focused on understanding religion rather than being for or against it.)

Purtill, Richard (1978) *Thinking about Religion: A Philosophical Introduction to Religion*. Upper Saddle River, NJ: Pearson/Prentice Hall. (A solid work introducing philosophical thinking about religion.)

Sarvepalli, Radhakrishnan and Charles A. Moore, eds. (1957) *A Sourcebook in Indian Philosophy*. Princeton, NJ: Princeton University Press. (Includes a large selection of texts which amount to a survey of the major philosophies of India spanning the last three millennia.)

Sharma, Arvind (1993) *Our Religions: The Seven World Religions Introduced by Preeminent Scholars from Each Tradition*. San Francisco, CA: HarperSanFrancisco. (An excellent general survey of seven world religions.)

Smart, Ninian (1999) *Worldviews: Crosscultural Explorations of Human Beliefs*. 3rd edn., Upper Saddle River, NJ: Prentice Hall. (Explores a number of religious traditions and worldviews and shows how they define human values and life forms.)

Smith, Wilfred Cantwell (1963) *The Meaning and End of Religion: A Revolutionary Approach to the Great Traditions*. Oxford: Oneworld. (Argues that religion, as now understood, is a fairly recent European construct.)

Taliaferro, Charles (1998) *Contemporary Philosophy of Religion*. Oxford: Blackwell. (One of the best introductions to thinking philosophically about religion.)

Ward, Keith (2008) *The Case For Religion*. Oxford: Oneworld. (Examines and replies to a wide range of arguments against religion.)

Wittgenstein, Ludwig (1953) *Philosophical Investigations*. Ed. G. E. M. Anscombe and R. Rhees. Trans. G. E. M. Anscombe. Oxford: Blackwell. (Wittgenstein's later work in which he discusses the influential notion of language games, forms of life, and family resemblance.)

WEBSITES

http://plato.stanford.edu/entries/philosophy-religion/
A concise entry from the *Stanford Encyclopedia of Philosophy* on philosophy of religion written by Charles Taliaferro.

http://www.religionfacts.com/
A helpful and well-documented site; contains a useful comparison chart of religions.

http://www.philosophyofreligion.info/
Introduces many of the major areas of philosophy of religion as well as major philosophers of religion.

http://www.aarweb.org/
A professional society of teachers and research scholars whose primary object of study is religion.

http://apa.udel.edu/apa/
The primary professional organization for American philosophers.

2 Religious diversity and pluralism

THE DIVERSITY OF RELIGIONS

There is an abounding plurality and rich diversity of religions in the contemporary world – both in terms of religious beliefs and practices – and globalization is creating a widespread awareness of this fact. Perhaps not surprisingly, along with the plethora of religious diversity, conflict in the name of religion is also pervasive and multifarious. From religious wars to individual acts of violence to verbal assault, discord among religions is an unfortunate reality of the past and present. In response, Tenzin Gyatso – the current Dalai Lama – has recently suggested that interreligious harmony can be achieved by developing understanding of other traditions and appreciating the value inherent within each of them.[1] I believe he is right about this.[2] In fact, it would behoove every educated person to have at least a basic understanding of the major religions, for ignorance in this domain tends to lead to suspicion, bigotry, and sometimes even violence, whereas understanding can lead to respect, empathy, and perhaps even trust.

In this chapter we will examine the issue of how one should understand and interpret the claims made by the various religions. And lest it be missed, religions do make claims – claims about reality and our place in it. As philosopher of religion Keith Yandell notes:

> *Of course* religions make claims – if they asserted nothing, there would be no religions… . It is in the very nature of a religion to offer an account of our situation, our problem, and its solution. Not every problem can arise in every situation; not every problem has the same solution. The account of our problem depends on the account of our situation; the account of our salvation depends on what we are and what we need to be saved from. To accept a religion is to embrace some particular and connected account of the situation and problem and solution.[3]

The Dalai Lama Tenzin Gyatso (1935–) – the fourteenth Dalai Lama – is the spiritual leader of the Tibetan people. Tibetan Buddhists believe the Dalai Lama is one of innumerable incarnations of the bodhisattva of compassion. Tenzin Gyatso has received international recognition, including the Nobel Peace Prize, for his assiduous efforts for human rights and world peace. He has written many important books, including *Ethics for the New Millennium*, *The Universe in a Single Atom: The Convergence of Science and Spirituality*, and *The Art of Happiness*.

Some of these claims offered by the various religions are similar, if not identical. Others, however, directly contradict one another. And it is generally the contradictions which cause the most difficulty and lead to conflict. Consider the following views from several major world religions regarding a fundamental concern of religion – the soteriological (salvation) goal as typically understood in the respective traditions:

- **Hinduism**: the ultimate soteriological goal is *moksha*, release from the cycle of death and rebirth (*samsara*), and absorption into Brahman. This can be accomplished by following one of the three paths (*margas*): (1) the path of knowledge (*jnanamarga*), (2) the path of devotion (*bhaktimarga*), or (3) the path of action (*karmamarga*).[4]
- **Buddhism**: the soteriological goal is *nirvana*, liberation from the wheel of *samsara* and extinction of all desires, cravings, and suffering. This is accomplished by understanding the four noble truths and practicing the final one: (1) all existence is suffering (*dukkha*), (2) all suffering is caused by craving (*trishna*), (3) all suffering can be ended (*nirvana*), and (4) the way to end suffering and achieve *nirvana* is by practicing the noble eightfold path (*astingika-marga*) of right views, right resolution or aspiration, right speech, right behavior, right livelihood, right effort, right thoughts, and right concentration.
- **Judaism**: the soteriological goal is blessedness with God – here and perhaps in the hereafter. This may be accomplished by fulfilling the divine commandments (*mitzvot*) which include engaging in the following practices (*sim chat Torah* – "the joy of the Torah"): (1) observance of the Sabbath, (2) regular attendance at synagogue, (3) celebration of the annual festivals, and (4) strict obedience to Jewish Law.[5]
- **Christianity**: the soteriological goal is spiritual transformation and spending eternity with God in the kingdom of heaven. This is accomplished by (1) God's grace (*charis*) manifested through Christ's atonement (*hilasterion*) for sin (*hamartion*), (2) receiving divine grace through faith (*pistis*) in Christ and the sacraments,[6] and (3) following the law (*nomos*) of God out of appreciation for the gift of grace.
- **Islam**: the soteriological goal is blessedness in paradise through submission to the laws of Allah and by His mercy. This may be accomplished by following the five pillars: (1) faith in Allah and his prophet Muhammad (*shahada*), (2) five daily prayers (*salah*), (3) almsgiving (*zakah*), (4) fasting (*sawm*), and (5) the pilgrimage to Mecca (*hajj*).

There are a number of philosophical approaches to religious diversity – specifically regarding the conflicting truth claims of the various religions. A helpful delineation can be gleaned from the works of Joseph Runzo and Harold Netland:[7]

PHILOSOPHICAL APPROACHES TO RELIGIOUS DIVERSITY

1 **Atheism**: all religions are false; there is no religion whose central claims are true.
2 **Agnosticism**: there is no way to determine which, if any, of the religions is most likely to be true, and thus the best response is to remain agnostic about the claims of any religion.
3 **Religious relativism**: while each religion can be regarded as "true" and "effective" for its adherents, there is no objective or tradition-transcending sense in which we can speak of religious truth.
4 **Religious pluralism**: ultimately all world religions are correct, each offering a different path and partial perspective *vis-à-vis* the one Ultimate Reality.
5 **Religious inclusivism**: only one world religion is fully correct, but other world religions participate in or partially reveal some of the truth of the one correct religion; it is possible, however, to obtain salvation (or *nirvana*, or *moksha*, etc.) through other religions.
6 **Religious exclusivism**: one world religion is correct and all others are mistaken; salvation (or *nirvana*, *moksha*, etc.) is found only through this one religion.

Analyses of and responses to (1) and (2) are offered in Chapters 4 through 6. Obviously, neither of these positions is held by religious believers. In this chapter we will focus on (3)–(6). (3) and (4) are newcomers to the religious landscape, and at this time relatively few religious adherents actually affirm them. (5) and (6), on the other hand, are widely held by religious believers today, and it is with these two most prominent approaches that we begin.

RELIGIOUS INCLUSIVISM AND EXCLUSIVISM

Religious inclusivists and exclusivists (as understood in this chapter) are in agreement on a number of issues related to religious diversity, including the belief that there is an objective reality to which religious truth claims point or correspond. They agree that one religion is, in some sense, closer to the truth about matters of God/Ultimate Reality and salvation/liberation[8] than the other religions. As noted above, most religious believers are inclusivists or exclusivists and thus hold that the central beliefs of their religion are truer, or closer approximations of the truth, than the central

Table 2.1 Some central elements of five world religions

	Hinduism	**Buddhism**	**Judaism**	**Christianity**	**Islam**
God/Ultimate Reality	Brahman (for some Hindus Brahman is the impersonal All)	*Nirvana* (Ultimate Reality – a state of perfection)	Yahweh (monotheism)	God (monotheistic trinitarianism)	Allah (monotheism)
The self	*atman* (for some Hindus, atman is Brahman)	*anatman* (non-self – the absence of a subsistent self or soul)	body/soul	body/soul	body/soul
Soteriological goal	*moksha* (liberation) from reincarnation	*nirvana* (liberation)	presence of Yahweh	eternity with God in heaven	eternity with Allah in paradise
Founder/ Messiah/ prophets/ founding priests	Brahmanic priests	Siddhartha Gautama – "The Buddha"	Abraham/ Moses	Jesus – "The Christ" (Abraham/ Moses/Paul)	Muhammad – "The Prophet" (Abraham/ Moses)

beliefs of the other religions. They emphasize the fact that the different religions contain within them seemingly incompatible truth-claims. For example, some of the essential beliefs of several of the major religions are captured in Table 2.1.[9]

While inclusivists and exclusivists agree that the different traditions contain incompatible truth-claims, they disagree about whether those religions outside their own also contain fundamental truths, and whether adherents of the other religions can obtain salvation/liberation. For exclusivists, fundamental truth is found in only one religion, and salvation/liberation is also exclusive to that one true religion. Inclusivists disagree. While they maintain that only one religion is privileged, they affirm that other religions also contain important truths. And they typically hold that true religious seekers – from whatever tradition – will, in the eschaton at least, find salvation/liberation. Theistic inclusivists affirm that God is present and working in and among all of the religions, even though God is most clearly manifested in one religion. They maintain that other theistic religions are right about there being a personal God (unlike Buddhists, say), but they disagree with other religions on different issues, such as the means for obtaining salvation/liberation. Non-theistic inclusivists affirm that Ultimate Reality is found by truth seekers from all of the world religions, but it is most clearly understood and articulated in the one privileged religion.[10]

Objection to inclusivism and exclusivism: the "myth of neutrality"

One prominent objection to religious exclusivism and inclusivism is sometimes dubbed the "myth of neutrality," and it has been expressed in many forms. The basic idea is that there are no religiously neutral or objective criteria by which to determine whether one religion or worldview is true and others false, or whether one has more truth or falsity than another. So to claim that one religion is true, or offers the only way of salvation, is inappropriate and perhaps even morally offensive.

In reply, some exclusivists and inclusivists have argued that it doesn't matter if there are no criteria for such assessment, for religious beliefs are not the kinds of things which should be subject to rational assessment and that doing so perhaps reflects a lack of faith. This view is known as *fideism*, and will be discussed in Chapter 8. Other exclusivists and inclusivists disagree; they maintain that they are justified in affirming that their beliefs are exclusively (or inclusively) true because they are *warranted* – either by evidences from natural theology or by their beliefs being properly basic (also to be discussed in Chapter 8).[11]

The justice objection

It is sometimes argued that exclusivists are committed to a position which is unjust. The problem is multifaceted, but one aspect of it is that there are billions of people, currently and historically, completely unaware of religions beyond their own. For the exclusivist, they are held morally and/or epistemically responsible for affirming religious truths of which they are not even aware. This objection is typically leveled against monotheistic religions which include a final judgment in the afterlife. How, for example, could the God of Christianity (if such a God exists) deny salvation to the countless people who have never even heard about the Christian faith? It seems unjust that God would condemn people to eternal perdition simply due to their lack of knowledge. And certainly there are good, sincere, devoted people in all of the major world religions. This is not so much a problem for inclusivists, for they do not agree that there is no salvation/liberation for those who haven't encountered the one true religion in this life. Some Christian inclusivists, for example, maintain that it is faith in God as God has revealed himself to the individual, as well as the atoning work of Christ, that brings salvation, and this could occur in this life or in the afterlife.[12]

Exclusivists have offered responses to the justice objection. For example, they sometimes draw upon the notion of God's middle knowledge and the counterfactuals of freedom to explain how a loving, omniscient, and omnipotent God could allow the "unreached" to miss the soteriological mark. As William Lane Craig argues, it is possible that there are no persons who have not heard the salvation message who would have responded in faith had they so heard that message.[13] Another response is that our human sense of justice may not be in harmony with God's sense of justice, for "God's ways are beyond our ways" (Isaiah 55:8–9). Yet another response exclusivists have offered is that because of sin, all people are deserving of divine judgment and wrath, and it is only by God's grace that any are saved. He chooses, then, for his own purposes, those who will and those who will not receive salvific grace.[14] This leads to the next objection.

Counterfactuals of freedom: counterfactual propositions (hypothetical statements in the subjunctive mood) which express the content of a free choice (e.g. "If you were to offer me a latte tomorrow at 5:30 p.m. while discussing religious pluralism, I would freely accept it.").

Middle knowledge: God's knowledge, logically prior to God's decree to create the world, of all true counterfactuals of creaturely freedom; that is, God's knowledge prior to creation of what every possible free creature would do under any possible set of circumstances.

> Religious Exclusivism is neither tolerable nor any longer intellectually honest in the context of our contemporary knowledge of other faiths.
>
> Joseph Runzo[15]

The "scandal of particularity"

The phrase "scandal of particularity" is generally applied to the Christian view that God became human uniquely in Jesus of Nazareth. This view is considered "scandalous" because it seems incredible and even troubling that one particular, isolated event roughly 2,000 years ago would be the way in which God revealed Himself to the world. As noted above, there are billions of religious devotees who are unaware of Christianity – or any other religion beyond their own, for that matter – and know nothing about the God of the Christians. And so it is with the other religions taken from an exclusive point of view. Are we to believe that only those within one religion got it right? Are we to believe that they, and they alone, have the absolute truth about God/Ultimate Reality and salvation/ liberation, while everyone else got things completely wrong? Furthermore, doesn't the view whereby only one religion offers the true soteriological goal seem arrogant, imperialistic, and perhaps even immoral and oppressive?

One response to this objection is that God, if God exists, could reveal himself in any way he so chooses.[16] There could well be legitimate reasons why God may reveal himself in this way or that. Furthermore, just because some people may be unaware of a fact does not make it false. There are many important matters about which lots of people know nothing. For example, many people still do not know that the AIDS virus is spread from an infected person to an uninfected person through unprotected sex. Such ignorance should cause those "in the know" to work all the harder at communicating the "truth." So too, argue exclusivists, should those "in the *spiritual* know" work hard at communicating religious truth to those unaware.

Yet another response to this objection is that just because one makes an exclusive claim does not entail that he or she is arrogant, imperialistic, immoral or oppressive.[17] In fact, one who argues that exclusivism is false is, in a fundamental way, doing just as the exclusivist does: making a claim such that the opposing view is held to be false. So it seems that one cannot consistently judge exclusivism on these grounds without being hypocritical.

RELIGIOUS PLURALISM

Given the above concerns as well as others, some have denied exclusivism and gone farther than inclusivism in affirming truth within the different religions. One way of accomplishing this is through religious pluralism, the two most prominent versions being the pluralistic hypothesis and aspectual pluralism. We will look at each of them in turn.

The pluralistic hypothesis

John Hick has developed one of the most impressive approaches to religious pluralism to date. He argues that there is a plurality of paths to salvation, and each of the great world religions offers such a path. He denies the view (widely held by atheists and others) that religion is only a human projection. However, utilizing Immanuel Kant's distinctions of noumena (things as they really are in themselves) and phenomena (things as they are experienced by us given the categories of our minds), Hick argues that one's experiences and descriptions *do* depend on the interpretive concepts through which one sees, structures, and understands them. So, while some experience and understand Ultimate Reality, or "the Real," in personal, theistic categories (e.g. as Allah or Yahweh), others do so in impersonal, pantheistic ways (e.g. as nirguna Brahman). Yet others experience and understand Ultimate Reality as completely non-personal (e.g. as *nirvana* or the *dao*). The Hindu parable of the blind men and the elephant poignantly reflects this point (see box below). For Hick, in our groping for the Real we are very much like the blind men – our viewpoints are constricted by our enculturated concepts.

In his monumental work, *An Interpretation of Religion*, Hick utilizes these distinctions and argues for the pluralistic hypothesis:

> that there is an ultimate reality, which I refer to as the Real ... which is in itself transcategorial (ineffable), beyond the range of our conceptual systems, but whose universal presence is humanly experienced in the various forms made possible by our conceptual-linguistic systems and spiritual practices.[18]

The Blind Men and the Elephant: God is like a large elephant surrounded by several blind men. One man touches the elephant's tail and thinks it is a rope. Another touches the trunk and thinks it is a snake. Another touches a leg and thinks it is a tree. Yet another touches the elephant's side and thinks it is a wall. They are all experiencing the same elephant but in very different ways. The same goes for God and the various religions.

John Hick (1922–) is Danforth Professor of the Philosophy of Religion, Emeritus, at Claremont Graduate University. He is one of the leading contemporary philosophers of religion and theologians, and the most prominent advocate of religious pluralism. He has published several widely influential books, including *An Interpretation of Religion*, *God Has Many Names*, and *The Myth of God Incarnate*.

Religious doctrines and dogmas are important for Hick, but what is fundamental in religion is the personal transformation that occurs within the religion. Thus, elsewhere, he adds that

> the great world faiths embody different perceptions and conceptions of, and correspondingly different responses to, the Real within the major variant ways of being human; and that within each of them the transformation of human existence from self-centeredness to Reality-centeredness – from non-saints to saints – is taking place.[19]

Hick uses several analogies to describe the pluralistic hypothesis with respect to different aspects of religion. One of the most interesting is the duck-rabbit picture which Ludwig Wittgenstein used in his influential work entitled the *Philosophical Investigations*[20] (see Figure 2.1[21]). A culture which has plenty of ducks but no familiarity with rabbits would see this ambiguous diagram as being a picture of a duck. Persons in this culture would not even be aware of the ambiguity. So too with the culture which has plenty of rabbits but no familiarity with ducks. Persons in this culture would see it as a picture of a rabbit. Hick's analogy is that the ineffable Real ("ineffable" means that its nature is beyond the scope of human concepts) is capable of being experienced – authentically experienced – in the different religions, *as* Yahweh, or *as* Allah, or *as* Vishnu, or *as* the *dao*, or *as* ... , depending on one's religious concepts through which the individual experiences occur.

A number of objections have been raised against the pluralistic hypothesis and Hick's view in general. We will focus on two.

Pluralism is logically contradictory

For Hick, no (major world) religion is superior to or truer than any other; they are on a par insofar as they produce saints (it could be argued that certain religions – Satanism, for example – do not produce saints). The great world religions, however, all include the notion that they are true; that they offer the right soteriological goal one should aim for and that they offer the best means for achieving that goal. So here's the problem. The pluralistic hypothesis seems to stand above the religions and

Figure 2.1 Duck/rabbit image used by Ludwig Wittgenstein in his influential *Philosophical Investigations*

make an exclusive (non-pluralistic!) claim about the Real and salvation/liberation; namely, that the Real is experienced equally validly among the various religions and that they each offer valid expressions of the soteriological goal. But this appears to be self-contradictory. For in asserting that no religious position in reference to the Real and the soteriological goal is superior to or truer than another, Hick has in fact done just that – he has asserted that his own view is truer than and superior to all others.

In response, one could argue that that the pluralistic hypothesis is a meta-theory – a higher order theory *about* the religions rather than simply one more religious position among many – and as such is not susceptible to the charge of logical inconsistency.

Pluralism leads to skepticism about the Real

The pluralistic view of the Real leads to another objection. The position that religious truth claims are entirely contextually bound and only about the phenomena (rather than the noumena) leads to a knowledge block (epistemic opacity) which arguably lands one in skepticism or agnosticism about the Real.[22] For if it is impossible to think or speak about the Real, and if attributes such as being good, loving, powerful, just (or impersonal, non-dual, etc.), don't actually apply to the Real since it is beyond our human conceptual field, how then can we be sure that the Real isn't merely a human psychological projection or wish fulfillment?

Hick's response, in good Kantian fashion, is that given the historically rich and broad religious experiences within the faith traditions, we must *posit* an objective Real to account for the rich experiences and transformations. However, the Real as construed by Hick is "beyond characterizations" and "neither personal nor nonpersonal." As such one wonders what it is that is posited and how such an "ineffable" posit can lead to the personal, moral transformation so integral to Hick's position.

Aspectual pluralism

A second version of religious pluralism attempts to avoid some of the philosophical and other pitfalls of the pluralistic hypothesis. For the aspectual pluralist, there is an *objective* Ultimate Reality, and this Reality is *knowable* to us. Thus, unlike the pluralistic hypothesis, and in very non-Kantian fashion, we can offer valid descriptions of the noumenal – we can "get at" the Real. In fact, as philosopher and theologian Peter Byrne maintains, each of the different religions is reflecting some aspect of the Real: "the different systems of religious discourse are descriptive of one and the same reality because that reality has multiple aspects ... [and] ... the one transcendent manifests itself in diverse ways."[23] Byrne uses the notion of natural kinds in order to clarify the position. Just as the natural kind *gold* has an unobservable essence as well as observable properties or qualities – being yellow, lustrous, and hard – so too the Real has an essence with different experienced manifestations. The Real manifests different aspects of itself in the different religions given their own unique conceptual schemes, religious structures, and practices.[24]

Aspectual pluralism leads to syncretism

One alleged problem with this view is that since each of the religions is capturing only an *aspect* of the Real, it seems that one would obtain a better grasp of the Real essence by creating a new syncretistic religion in order to glean more aspects of the Real.[25] Byrne grants that "the fact that pluralism sees the individual traditions as aspects of an overlapping encounter with the one reality does indeed imply that as traditions they may well profit from sharing insights, spiritualities, and the like."[26] But he doesn't believe this must lead to syncretism. It could be argued, for example, that each tradition captures an aspect of the Real via the enculturated concepts within the tradition, and this aspect would be lost in a new syncretistic religion. If this is the case, the religious traditions are each necessary *as they are believed and practiced* in order for religious adherents to best understand and experience the Real.

Natural kinds are often understood to be groupings which are natural groupings. For example, human beings, dogs, and gold are each examples of natural kinds. They are distinct from the *properties* (such as being yellow, for example, or being 6′3″) which are had by the individuals of the kind. Kinds cannot be reduced to the properties which are had by them.

Aspectual pluralism leads to skepticism

A related problem is that, on the aspectual view, since religious adherents are only glimpsing the Real through properties which are themselves enculterated within the various traditions, descriptions of the Real cannot be adequate *knowledge* claims about the Real. So, one is left with religious skepticism. Byrne clarifies the problem:

> If pluralism is true, then rich, living, doctrinally loaded accounts of the nature of transcendent reality and of salvation are both necessary and inevitably flawed … They are inevitably flawed, for from the nature of the case they cannot claim strict truth with any certainty. That is to say, taken literally and positively they cannot claim with certainty to correspond in detail with the reality they refer to. The pluralist does not know which of these detailed, first-order beliefs is false. Some may be true. He or she considers that they are all radically uncertain.[27]

Byrne's response is that this type of objection can be deflected, but only partly so. He grants that pluralists are "mitigated skeptics." One just cannot be certain that any of the religions has got it right, and so it's best to recognize this and be agnostic about the interpretations of the religions.[28] However, the fundamental doctrinal claims of the religions, such as "Jesus is *the* Son of God," do have a cognitive point (they will help fashion modes of religious practice and experience, for example), and they *might* even have referential success and metaphorical truth. But the pluralist cannot in good conscience affirm that doctrinal statements are unequivocally and objectively true.

RELIGIOUS RELATIVISM

A third way of responding to the conflicting truth claims of the different faith traditions is to remain committed to the truth of one's religious teachings while at the same time agreeing with some of the central concerns raised by pluralism. This can be accomplished by positing a view known as religious relativism. Joseph Runzo, perhaps its most prominent defender, has presented a version of religious relativism – what he calls "henofideism" – derived from the Greek term *heno* (one) and the Latin term *fide* (faith) – whereby the correctness of a religion is relative to the worldview of its community of adherents.[29]

Runzo grants that different religions are constituted by different experiences and mutually incompatible sets of truth claims, and that the different religions and experiences are themselves rooted in distinct worldviews which are incompatible with, if not contradictory to, the other religions and worldviews.[30] But he maintains that these differing experiences and incompatible worldviews emerge from the plurality of *phenomenal* divine realities experienced by the adherents of the religions.

On this view, it is understood that a person's worldview (that is, "the total cognitive web of our interrelated concepts, beliefs, and processes of rational thought"[31]) determines how one comprehends and experiences Ultimate Reality. Furthermore, "corresponding to differences of worldview, there are mutually incompatible, yet individually adequate, sets of conceptual-schema-relative truths."[32] In other words, the truth of a religion is determined by its adequacy to appropriately correspond to the worldview of which it is a part.

Runzo notes that religious relativism has several advantages over Hick's pluralistic hypothesis: (1) it offers a better account of the actual cognitive beliefs held by the adherents of the great world religions, for it affirms that each of the religions are making *true* fundamental claims, (2) it maintains the dignity of the various religions by accepting their differences as real and significant, and (3) it does not reduce the sense of the reality of the Real to a mere "image" as pluralism unintentionally does. Rather, it keeps the Real as the direct object of religious faith.

Furthermore, I would add that it has several advantages over aspectual pluralism: (1) it offers a better account of the actual cognitive beliefs held by the adherents of the great world religions, (2) it isn't offering only a partial (aspectual) view, but rather a full and (arguably) conceptually adequate description of the Real as professed within the different religions, and (3) it doesn't demand a new, syncretistic religion in order to better grasp Ultimate Reality.

Despite these advantages over pluralism, however, there are also significant objections to this version of religious relativism.

An inadequate description of actual religious beliefs

While relativism seems to offer a *better* account than pluralism of the actual cognitive beliefs of the adherents of the religions, it nevertheless falls short of their *actual* beliefs. For example, Muslim adherents haven't historically held, nor do their scholars and teachers (imams) typically hold, that Allah is the *true* God *only with respect to the worldview of Islam*. To the contrary, for Muslims the truth of Allah as described in the Qur'an is taken to be unequivocally and objectively true. For the Islamic believer, Allah is the one and only true God for everyone regardless of what one's worldview happens to be. So too among the other faith traditions; their beliefs are typically understood to be true in an objective and absolute sense. In effect, adherents of the religions have historically been exclusivists rather than relativists.

Nonetheless, one could reply that simply because religious adherents typically are and have been exclusivists has no bearing on whether they (and we) should remain so. Up until the last century, most people held to some form of Euclidean space as reflecting the true nature of the world, but that does not mean we should do so today.

Relativism is incoherent

Another objection is that religious relativism is logically incoherent since it cannot be consistently maintained that truth is individualistic – a position entailed by relativism. However, it can be argued that while this is perhaps a fair assessment of what's referred to as "subjectivism" (a position in which truth is relative to each person's idiosyncratic worldview), this does not apply to henofideism, for on the henofideists' account, truth is relativized to the worldview of a culture rather than relativized individually.

EVALUATING RELIGIOUS SYSTEMS

As noted at the beginning of the chapter, religions make claims – truth-claims – and they make such claims about fundamental matters of human existence, Ultimate Reality, life after death, and so on. As we also saw above, there are different approaches to understanding the truth-claims made by the religions: some maintain that religious truth-claims are all false (atheists) or that there is no way to know if religious claims are true or false (agnostics); others maintain that each religion has its own truth, but that there is no objective or universal truth regarding religious claims (relativism); still others maintain that all the world religious truth-claims are true in the sense that adherents are understanding and experiencing Ultimate Reality through their own enculturated concepts (pluralism); and yet others maintain that there is only one true religion by which a person can be saved and that the truth-claims of the other religions are false (exclusivism) or that while one religion is privileged in some sense, yet all religions contain important elements of truth (inclusivism).

If one agrees with most of the religious adherents that the religions are, in fact, making claims which are true, then it may well be that there are certain objective criteria which can be utilized in evaluating them. One manner of doing so entails evaluating religious *systems*; that is, religions taken as reasonable systems of thought. Of course the prospect of evaluating religious systems is controversial, but nothing of much significance in religious discourse is not so! Below, I have included five criteria for evaluation which have been utilized by philosophers of religion and which are, arguably, objective, and religiously neutral.[33]

We will briefly examine each of the five.

Logical consistency

One criterion for assessment that seems to transcend religious systems is logical consistency, and one of the basic laws of classical logic is the law of non-contradiction: a statement cannot be both true and false. While the rational undeniability of this

CRITERIA FOR EVALUATING RELIGIOUS SYSTEMS

1 **Logical consistency**: the fundamental, defining propositions of the religious system must be logically consistent with one another and not self-defeating.
2 **Coherence of overall system**: the fundamental, defining propositions of the religious system must be related to one another such that they offer a unified understanding of the world and one's place in it.
3 **Consistency with knowledge in other fields**: the fundamental, defining propositions of the religious system should not contradict well-established knowledge in other fields, such as science, history, psychology, and archaeology.
4 **Reasonable answers to fundamental human questions**: the religious system should be able to account for and explain fundamental human questions.
5 **Existential plausibility**: the religious system must be livable based on its own fundamental beliefs and should not require borrowing such beliefs from another religious system which contradict it.

law has been expressed for millennia,[34] various attempts to deny its role in religion have appeared from time to time. For example, Gavin D' Costa notes that Zen and Madhyamika ("Middle School") Buddhism – especially in the writings of Nagarjuna (c. 150–250 CE) – are examples of religions which hold that logical consistency doesn't apply to religious truth-claims. Nagarjuna, for example, utilized the rules of logic only to demonstrate why no logical system can ultimately be rationally affirmed. And Zen Buddhists also accept certain rules of logic to demonstrate that *satori* (enlightenment) transcends logical conceptions.[35]

However, it is not clear what is meant by the statement that reality transcends logical conception, or that logic does not apply to religious truth-claims. One must use logical concepts and rational principles of thought to even comprehend these statements themselves. Furthermore, it seems that whatever religious system one adheres to (be it the Madhyamika school or otherwise), he or she utilizes reason and logic in virtually every other area of life. Denying them in religion seems unwarranted, if not incoherent. This is especially significant regarding the fundamental, defining propositional claims of the religious systems. There could certainly be disagreement about what the fundamental claims are of any given system. But as we saw earlier, each of the major religious systems is attempting to provide propositional claims about the nature of the Real, the nature of the self, the soteriological goal, and the means for obtaining that goal. Since each of these claims is generally taken to be a non-negotiable of the system, if they contradict one another, they cannot be true.

Similarly, logic applies to each of the individual claims within a religious system. If a claim is self-defeating, then it cannot be true. For example, if a fundamental claim of a religious system is that all viewpoints are ultimately false, then that is a self-refuting claim (for it too must be false!). Some have argued that the Madhyamika school of Buddhism affirms such a view. If so, then it would be self-defeating, and thus false.

Coherence of overall system

Not only should each of the fundamental claims of the religious system be logically consistent with the other fundamental claims and not self-defeating, but the overall system should be coherent as well. "Coherence" in this context is the idea that the fundamental claims should have an interconnectedness and systematization that is both clear and appropriate. In this vein, philosopher of religion William Wainwright notes that the claims ought to "hang together" appropriately. He uses monotheism and polytheism to make the point: "Monotheism ... seems more coherent than polytheisms that posit a number of gods but don't clearly explain the connections among them."[36]

Consistency with knowledge in other fields

Another significant criterion for assessing a religious system is its consistency with various fields of knowledge. Several important fields are history, psychology, and the hard sciences (physical sciences, life sciences, and earth sciences). If a well-established claim from one of these domains contradicts a fundamental religious belief, this should at least be cause for considering the rejection of the belief. This could also provide a defeater for the system as a whole.

For example, if a religious system claims that God created the world in a perfect state several thousand years ago, and that therefore dinosaurs could not have really existed in history, the solid evidence from archaeology should be cause for rejecting that belief. If rejection of the belief is not possible without rejection of the system as a whole, then so much the worse for the system. Of course adherents of a given religious system may find reason for holding firm to the belief despite other evidence to the contrary. The difficult task, then, is to determine whether the reason (or reasons) for maintaining the belief are more justified than the evidence to the contrary.

Reasonable answers to fundamental human questions

A religious system should provide reasonable and adequate answers to fundamental religious questions. Such questions include: Who am I? Why am I here? What is the nature of the Real? What is the solution to the human condition? What happens after death? And so on. If the system either lacks answers to such questions or the answers are unreasonable or inadequate, this should be cause for concern. No doubt, determining whether such answers are reasonable or not is no easy task. But the process of inquiry here may be fruitful nonetheless. For example, if the answer to the question Who am I? turns out to be that I am not a substantial individual self but rather a bundle of experiences, this raises an important question of reasonableness and adequacy.[37]

Existential plausibility

Another seemingly non-arbitrary criterion for assessing religious systems is whether the system can be lived out on its own terms or whether it must borrow ideas from another system. If one must borrow, say, *core* beliefs from another system in order to live a meaningful life, then one's own system (or the one under analysis) is probably inadequate if not false. For example, if one holds to the belief (widely held by adherents of certain pantheistic traditions) that physical pain and suffering are mere illusions, then he or she should live consistently with that belief. The scriptures of the Christian Science religion, for example, affirm that "evil is but an illusion, and it has no real basis. Evil is a false belief."[38] Adherents of Christian Science are taught not to seek medical help for this very reason – pain and evil do not exist. But one could ask whether such a view is existentially plausible. If an adherent of this religious system could not take the existential pressure to ignore medical care, for example, it may be cause for him or her to reject the system. Similarly, if persons within the system are "cheating," as it were, by secretly seeking medical care for illness, perhaps that would be reason for one analyzing the belief to reject it, if not to reject the system as a whole.

Another example is moral claims. If a religious system includes a moral position which is not existentially sustainable in one's life, it should probably be rejected. For example, if a religious system includes the claim that right and wrong are mere illusions, but then one feels the existential need to live in accordance with certain moral values, then the religious claim, if not the system as a whole, should probably be rejected.

Religions are complex systems of human thought and practice, and the "great world religions" have been lived and expressed over many centuries and millennia. The complexity of the religions makes their evaluation a difficult task indeed. But given that these religions do express themselves in propositional and meaningful form, this allows for their reasonable assessment as *systems* of thought and practice. Given their significance in the way one thinks about oneself, the nature of Ultimate Reality, and salvation/liberation, their evaluation is perhaps one of the most important human endeavors imaginable.

However, the evaluation of a religious system raises another important issue worthy of careful reflection: religious tolerance.

RELIGIOUS TOLERANCE

As we have seen, the world in which we live is flourishing with diverse perspectives about fundamental religious questions. As the world becomes more globalized, we will continue to grow in awareness of the richness and wide diversity of religious traditions (many of which are radically different from our own). If we do hold the view that religions can be evaluated – and even most pluralists would agree that some religions are worse than others (think of the American UFO religion Heaven's Gate, for example) – must religious *intolerance* follow? The answer to this question partly depends on what we mean by "tolerance" and "intolerance." If by "tolerance" we mean affirming that all traditions are equally true and "intolerance" denying that they are all equally true, then of course any evaluation would be an intolerant endeavor. However, if by "tolerance" we mean recognizing and respecting the beliefs and practices of others, then evaluation and tolerance need not be at odds.

As encounters with religious "others" become commonplace, conflicts concerning doctrinal, cultural, and practical differences will also increase. In response to this conflict, as noted at the beginning of the chapter, the Dalai Lama proposes an interreligious harmony that appreciates the value of other faith traditions. He notes that an important first step in accomplishing this harmony is developing an understanding of other faith traditions and appreciating the value inherent within each of them. In the coming decades and centuries, if we are going to flourish together as human beings, and as *religious* human beings, we must take seriously this proposal. We must advance in tolerance, and this will involve learning about religious others – what they believe and why, and how they practice their beliefs – and striving to understand. This need not entail a capitulation to an "everyone's right" attitude, but it could be argued that it should become an "everyone's significant" attitude. After all, whatever our religious convictions, we are all *homo sapiens* – all part of the great community we call "humanity."

SUMMARY

Much territory has been covered in this chapter. We began with an overview of the growing diversity of the global religious landscape. We saw that the great religions all make claims about fundamental matters of human life and thought – claims about the self, Ultimate Reality, and the meaning and means of salvation/liberation, among others. A number of these fundamental claims contradict one another, and this raises the question of how we should philosophically approach such disagreements. We then examined six basic approaches in response to the conflicting truth-claims of the religions: atheism, agnosticism, relativism, pluralism, inclusivism, and exclusivism. As the first two approaches are dealt with in other chapters, we analyzed the latter four, looking at pros and cons of each of them.

We then considered the task of evaluating religious systems. We examined five criteria for such evaluation: logical consistency, coherence of the overall system, consistency with knowledge in other fields, reasonable answers to fundamental human questions, and existential plausibility. It can be argued that these criteria are religiously neutral and objective means for making such evaluations.

The task of evaluating religious systems raises the important issue of religious tolerance, for evaluation – which involves the possible conclusion that one belief or system of beliefs is true and another false – can lead to an attitude of arrogance or superiority. This need not be so. Truth and tolerance are distinct concepts, and one could be an intolerant relativist or pluralist just as one could be a tolerant exclusivist or inclusivist. With the growing awareness of religious others and the rise in co-mingling of people from various traditions, it has become increasingly more important for us to be religious learners, respecting the beliefs and practices of others who hold views very different from our own.

That is the religious challenge of the twenty-first century.

QUESTIONS FOR REVIEW/DISCUSSION

1. Is religious truth different from scientific truth? Does it matter? Explain your answer.
2. Is it reasonable to believe that one's own religion is true in its core beliefs and other religious are false in their core beliefs while also being tolerant of those religions? Why or why not?
3. How would you describe Professor Hick's pluralistic hypothesis? Is it plausible? Do you believe it? Why?
4. Explain aspectual pluralism. What are some benefits of this view? What are some concerns about it?
5. How does religious relativism differ from religious pluralism? What are some similarities?
6. Which of the six approaches to religious diversity do you find most persuasive? Why?
7. Do you believe it is possible to compare rival religious systems in such a way that one can objectively assess their plausibility? Explain your answer.
8. The Dalai Lama has said the following: "It is unhelpful to try to argue on the basis of philosophy or metaphysics that one religion is *better* than another. The important thing is surely its *effectiveness* in individual cases" (emphasis mine). Comment on this claim.
9. If a fundamental claim of a religious system is that God created the world, including flora and fauna (plants and animals), does this contradict biological evolution in such a way that the system should be rejected? Explain your answer.
10. Can one hold to exclusivism or inclusivism and also be religiously tolerant? What would tolerance mean in these cases?

FURTHER READING

Basinger, David (2002) *Religious Diversity: A Philosophical Assessment*. Aldershot: Ashgate. (Offers a study of the major epistemic issues concerning religious diversity.)

Byrne, Peter (1995) *Prolegomena to Religious Pluralism: Reference and Realism in Religion*. New York: St. Martin's Press. (A clear analysis of philosophical consequences of religious pluralism.)

Eck, Diana L. (2002) *A New Religious America*. New York: HarperSanFrancisco. (Drawing on her work with the Pluralism Project, she notes and reflects on the explosive growth of religious traditions in America.)

Griffiths, Paul J. (2001) *Problems of Religious Diversity*. Oxford: Blackwell. (Analyzes a number of philosophical questions raised by religious diversity.)

Gyatso, Tenzin, the Dalai Lama (2001) *Ancient Wisdom, Modern World: Ethics for a New Millennium*. London: Abacus. (An important work on ethics and tolerance from a significant religious leader.)

Hick, John (2004) *An Interpretation of Religion*. 2nd ed. New Haven, CT: Yale University Press. (A classic on religious pluralism.)

Hick, John (2007) "Religious Pluralism" in Chad Meister and Paul Copan, eds., *The Routledge Companion to Philosophy of Religion*. London: Routledge. (A concise presentation of pluralism by its most ardent defender.)

Knitter, Paul, ed. (2005) *The Myth of Religious Superiority: A Multifaith Exploration*. New York: Orbis. (Essays by Christian, Jewish, Muslim, Hindu, and Buddhist pluralists.)

McKim, Robert (2001) *Religious Ambiguity and Religious Diversity*. Oxford: Oxford University Press. (Focuses on themes related to divine hiddenness and religious diversity and their implications for religious belief.)

Meister, Chad and Paul Copan (2007) *The Routledge Companion to Philosophy of Religion*. London: Routledge. (A collection of newly commissioned essays by leading philosophers of religion on a host of significant topics.)

Netland, Harold (1991) *Dissonant Voices*. Grand Rapids, MI: Eerdmans. (An analysis of truth in religion and a defense of religious exclusivism.)

Plantinga, Alvin (2007) "A Defense of Religious Exclusivism" in Chad Meister, ed., *The Philosophy of Religion Reader*. London: Routledge. (A rigorous defense of religious exclusivism.)

Quinn, Philip L. and Kevin Meeker, eds. (2000) *The Philosophical Challenge of Religious Diversity*. New York: Oxford University Press. (A philosophical engagement in a variety of issues relevant to religious diversity.)

Runzo, Joseph (2001) *Global Philosophy of Religion: A Short Introduction*. Oxford: Oneworld. (An exceptionally clear and insightful textbook on global philosophy of religion; Chapter 2 includes Professor Runzo's reflection on religious relativism/henofideism and pluralism.)

Smith, Huston (1991) *The World's Religions*. San Francisco, CA: Harper. (A classic overview of the major world religions.)

Ward, Keith (2007) "Truth and the Diversity of Religions" in Chad Meister, ed., *The Philosophy of Religion Reader*. London: Routledge. (A response to Hick's pluralism.)

Zagorin, Perez (2005) *How the Idea of Religious Toleration Came to the West*. Princeton, NJ: Princeton University Press. (A scholarly but readable and engaging presentation of the origins of religious toleration in the West since the Enlightenment.)

WEBSITES

http://www.pluralism.org

The Pluralism Project at Harvard University. Headed up by Diana Eck – Professor of Comparative Religion and Indian Studies at Harvard – the goal of the Pluralism Project is "to help Americans engage with the realities of religious diversity through research, outreach, and the active dissemination of resources."

http://www.science.uva.nl/~seop/entries/religious-pluralism/

A helpful and concise entry from the *Stanford Encyclopedia of Philosophy* on pluralism and religious diversity written by philosopher of religion David Basinger.

http://www.religionfacts.com

Religion facts. A helpful and well-documented site; contains a useful comparison chart of religions.

http://www.le.ac.uk/pluralism/centre_publications.html

Centre for the History of Religious and Political Pluralism. The aims of the Centre include facilitating the study of the history of pluralism/diversity through active research and publications and promoting understanding of pluralism/diversity.

http://www.religioustolerance.org

Ontario Consultants on Religious Tolerance. This informative site promotes religious freedom and diversity as positive cultural values.

http://www.un.org/Overview/rights.html

The Universal Declaration of Human Rights adopted by the General Assembly of the United Nations.

3 Conceptions of ultimate reality

Within every major religion is a belief about a transcendent reality underlying the natural, physical world. From its beginnings, the philosophy of religion has been concerned with reflecting on, as far as possible, how religions might understand what it calls "Ultimate Reality". How the various religions conceptualize that reality differs, especially between Eastern and Western religions. In Western religion,[1] by which I am referring primarily to the three religions of Abrahamic descent, namely Judaism, Christianity, and Islam, Ultimate Reality is conceived of in terms of a personal God. God is not only personal, but the creator of all, and perfect in every respect. Many other properties are attributed to God as well, including omniscience, omnipotence, and immutability.

In Eastern religion – and here I am referring primarily to Buddhism, Taoism, and the Advaita Vedānta school of Hinduism – Ultimate Reality is understood quite differently. It is not a personal creator God, for example, but an absolute state of being. It cannot be described by a set of attributes (such as omniscience or omnipotence) for it is undifferentiated, Absolute Reality. Taoists refer to it as the *dao*; Hindus refer to it as Brahman; for Buddhists, the name varies – *sunyata* for example, or *nirvana*. These different conceptions of Ultimate Reality bring with them distinct understandings of other significant issues as well, such as salvation/liberation, life after death, and evil and suffering, among others.

In this chapter we will focus specifically on the two different conceptions of Ultimate Reality, beginning with Eastern religion.

ULTIMATE REALITY: THE ABSOLUTE AND THE VOID

Hindu Absolutism

Dating back more than five thousand years, Hinduism is one of the oldest religions of recorded history. Unlike most other religions, Hinduism embraces many distinct belief systems and worldviews. There are theistic, polytheistic, pantheistic, and even atheistic forms of Hinduism. Because of this diversity, it is impossible to accurately summarize Hindu thought on any particular matter. For our purposes, however, we will home in on one school of Hinduism that is frequently discussed in the philosophy of religion literature: Advaita Vedānta. This school of Hinduism includes the belief that Ultimate Reality, indeed all reality, is Brahman and Brahman alone. A key figure espousing Advaita Vedānta was the eighth century Indian philosopher Shankara. As he explains it, only Brahman is real, and Brahman is devoid of all distinctions. He describes it this way:[2]

> Brahman is the reality – the one existence, absolutely independent of human thought or idea. Because of the ignorance of our human minds, the universe seems to be composed of diverse forms. It is Brahman alone.[3]

This is a form of Hindu Absolutism – the view that Ultimate Reality is the undifferentiated Absolute. It is also a form of *monism* in which there is only one reality; this reality – Brahman – includes no attributes, and all apparent distinctive characteristics within Brahman and between Brahman and the world are ultimately illusory. For the Advaitin, this is true of all distinctions, between all (apparent) things, even between one's self (*Atman*) and Brahman.

> Just as, my dear, the bees prepare honey by collecting the essences of different trees and reducing them into one essence, and as these (juices) possess no discrimination (so that they might say) "I am the essence of this tree, I am the essence of that tree," even so, indeed, my dear, all these creatures though they reach Being do not know that they have reached the Being. Whatever they are in this world, tiger or lion or wolf or boar or worm or fly or gnat or mosquito, that they become. That which is the subtle essence, this whole world has for its self. That is the true. That is the self. That are thou…[4]

It is sometimes difficult for Western minds to conceive of the absence of all distinctions, especially between oneself and all other (apparent) things. Our experiences imply that we are unique individuals, separate identities from other people, things, and God.

A question which naturally arises is why are we not experiencing this undifferentiated unity with Brahman? Why do we believe that we are separate, unique, individual entities and that distinctions are real? The Advaitin answer is that we begin in an unenlightened state because of the deleterious effects of *maya*, which ultimately infect us because of *karma*. In Hindu mythology, *maya* (also

Shankara and Advaita Vedānta. Shankara (c. 788–820 CE) is the most renowned Indian philosopher to develop the doctrine of Advaita Vedānta Hinduism. He wrote a number of works, including commentaries on the Vedas (sacred Hindu texts). There are various schools of Vedānta, and the one he expounded and defended is the non-dualistic system in which reality is one (*advaita* means "non-dual" and Vedānta means "end of the Vedas"). On this view, Ultimate Reality (Brahman) is undifferentiated unity, and the multifaceted phenomenal world is an illusion (*maya*).

Maya) is depicted as a divine goddess, Mahamaya, who deludes us. Hindu Advaitin philosophers typically interpret *maya* as the great veiling of the true, Unitary Self.

A second question, then, is how do we overcome this illusion? The Advaitin answer is that we need to advance to an enlightened state in order to overcome the veil of cosmic ignorance. We do this by moving beyond the rational mind, and we do it most effectively through various paths or Yogas.[5] By engaging in the right physical and mental practices we can escape the illusory power of *maya* and finally experience *moksha* – the enlightened realization that reality is one, multiplicity is illusion, and only the undifferentiated Absolute is real. While *moksha* is the goal, it is recognized in Advaita Vedānta that true enlightenment may not be achieved in this life. It may, indeed, take many reincarnations before the power of *maya*, and the negative influences of karma, are expunged (more will be said about karma in Chapter 10).

While Absolutism is a very ancient tradition within Hinduism, it has modern adherents as well, and one of its most prominent expounders in recent times was Bhagavan Sri Ramana Maharshi (1879–1950). Sri Ramana, as he is sometimes called, maintained that escaping the veiling power of *maya* is best accomplished by searching deeply within ourselves, a method of self-inquiry he referred to as "I-thought." By constantly focusing on the questions Who am I? and Where does this "I" come from? – keeping an inner attention on the "I" and excluding all other thoughts – one can eventually attain the Self-realization that the individual self is nothing other than *Atman* (Self), and that *Atman* is Brahman.[6]

While it is estimated that three-fourths of Hindu intellectuals affirm an Absolutist view of Ultimate Reality, it has never been widely popular among the general population of Hindus.[7] Nevertheless, it has been very influential in the history of Hindu thought.

Buddhist metaphysics

Buddhism emerged from within the Hindu tradition in India in roughly the fifth century BCE, and with respect to Ultimate Reality it is arguably most closely aligned with the Advaita Vedānta school of Hindu thought. However, Ultimate Reality in Buddhism, at least in one major school called Madhyamika (the school of the "Middle Way") as developed by Nagarjuna, is neither the Absolute of Hinduism nor the personal God of the theistic religions. Rather, it is *sunyata*, which is translated as "Emptiness" or "The Void."

At first glance it may seem that emptiness and Ultimate Realty are contradictory notions. How can something real be empty? But Buddhists of this school understand "being real" as "being independent of other things." Buddhist scholar Masao Abe clarifies:

> The Buddhists believe that to be called "substantial or real" a thing must be able to exist on its own. However, if we look at the universe, we find that everything in it exists only in relation to something else. A son is a son only in relation to his father; and a father similarly in relation to his son. Fatherhood does not exist on its own but only in relation to something else. The Buddhists use the word svabhāva to denote existence on its own, that is, nondependent existence, which alone, according to them, qualifies as true or genuine existence. But if everything in the world depends on something else for being what it is, then nothing in the universe can be said to possess svabhāva or genuine existence; hence it is empty.[8]

On the Buddhist metaphysic, there is no "thing" which has independent existence. Fundamental reality is in fact emptiness. There is neither *Atman* nor Brahman, there is no self but *Anatman*, or no-self (more about this in Chapter 10). All things – whether galaxies, mountains, trees, animals, or people (including you and me) – are in fact abstractions of events or processes, events or processes which are dependent on other events or processes. Even though things appear to be static or stable, this is due to abstracting from the various experiences one has and then positing a substantial self or static entity. But again, these are processes; in reality, all is in flux. One Buddhist text puts it this way:

> Whether Buddhas arise, O priests, or whether Buddhas do not arise, it remains a fact and the fixed and necessary constitution of being that all its constituents are transitory. This fact a Buddha discovers and masters, and when he has discovered and mastered it, he announces, teaches, publishes, proclaims, discloses, minutely explains, and makes clear that all the constituents of being are transitory.[9]

Nagarjuna (c. 150–250 CE) was an Indian Buddhist philosopher and perhaps the most influential Buddhist thinker besides Siddhartha Gautama – the Buddha (c. 563–483 BCE). He is primarily known for developing a view called *sunyata*, or emptiness, which unifies two other central Buddhist doctrines: no-self and interdependent arising. His writings formed the basis of the Madhyamika (Middle Way) school of Buddhism. He wrote many works, including *Fundamental Verses on the Middle Way* (*Mulamadhyamakakarika*), the *Seventy Verses on Emptiness* (*Sunyatasaptati*), and the *Sixty Verses on Reasoning* (*Yuktisastika*).

THE FOUR NOBLE TRUTHS AND THE NOBLE EIGHTFOLD PATH

The Four Noble Truths

1 The existence of suffering (*dukkha*) – life is suffering.
2 The arising of suffering (*samudaya*) – the cause of suffering is attachment and selfish desire.
3 The cessation of suffering (*nirodha*) – the path out of suffering is the cessation of attachment and selfish desire.
4 The way of cessation (*marga*) – the path for achieving the cessation of attachment and selfish desire is the Noble Eightfold Path.

The Noble Eightfold Path

1 Right views – understanding Buddhist doctrines such as *Anatman*, interdependent arising, and the Four Noble Truths.
2 Right resolve – resolving to renounce the world and to act with charity toward all.
3 Right speech – speaking the truth with kindness and respect.
4 Right conduct – acting according to moral principles.
5 Right livelihood – living in a way that does no harm to anyone or anything.
6 Right effort – attempting to live a noble life and to avoid an ignoble life.
7 Right mindfulness – attending to wholesome thoughts; compassion.
8 Right meditation – focused concentration on the Eightfold Path and the unity of all life.

Thus all that exists does so only in relation to other things. Furthermore, all things originate out of a self-sustaining causal nexus in which each link arises from another. This is the Buddhist doctrine of interdependent arising (*pratitya-sumutpada*), and it is an important element of Buddhist metaphysics. Everything is dependent on and connected to other things. Nothing in the nexus is independent; everything arises from something else.

Buddhists also hold to the idea of karma, the notion that actions – past, present, and future – have effects on the actor. This is one of the causes in the nexus of interdependent arising. Because of ignorance (*avidya*), we continue to experience the effects of karma, which keeps us within the cycle of cause and effect, death and reincarnation. The way to escape the illusory world of permanence is explained by Nagarjuna as recognizing *sunyata*, by becoming aware of Emptiness, or the Void, by seeing that there are no finite or infinite substances – no individual or permanent selves or beings – and ultimately breaking through the illusion of the phenomenal world, escaping the cycle of rebirth and experiencing *nirvana*, the final extinction of ego and personal desire.

Just as with the Advaita Vedānta claim that "*Atman* (Self) is Brahman and Brahman is undifferentiated Ultimate Realty" is not readily apparent and even contrary to typical human experience, so too with the Buddhist doctrines of *sunyata* and *Anatman*. Thus, a question which naturally arises is why are we not experiencing emptiness, no-self, and the interconnectedness of all things? Why do we tend to believe that we are substantial selves and that we are separate from ultimate reality? The Madhyamika Buddhist answer is that we need to be enlightened in order to rightly apprehend these fundamental truths. The path to enlightenment, or *nirvana* (which is an indescribable state of ultimate bliss; the extinction of the self), is the discovery, understanding, and practice of the Four Noble Truths and the Noble Eightfold Path.

ULTIMATE REALITY: A PERSONAL GOD

While Eastern thinkers, such as those above, maintain that Ultimate Reality is the undifferentiated, impersonal Absolute and deny the existence of a substantial divine being, philosophical reflection about the nature of a *personal God* – what is sometimes dubbed "philosophical theology" – has been part and parcel of the Western philosophical enterprise since its inception more than two millennia ago. Many of the early Greek philosophers, for example, reflected on and wrote about the divine. In later centuries, thinkers from the Western religions utilized the work of these "pagan" philosophers in their attempt to comprehend and articulate the nature and attributes of God from within their own religious traditions.

But what is meant by the term "God" from the perspective of Western religion? For the Abrahamic faiths (Judaism, Christianity, and Islam), God is a personal, perfect being who created the world and who has certain divine properties, or attributes, which set God apart from all other beings. This is called "theism," and it is the view of God traditionally held not only by adherents of the three great monotheistic

Ramanuja (c. 1017–1137) was the chief proponent of a qualified non-dualist form of Vedānta Hinduism called *Vishishtadvaita* which includes a view of Brahman more akin to monotheism than to pantheism. He was also one of the main Hindu philosophers to systematically interpret the Vedas, or Hindu scriptures, from a theistic perspective, and he argued for the soteriological (salvific) importance of *bhakti*, or devotion to God.

religions, but also by those within a longstanding Hindu tradition who, unlike the Advaita Vedāntins, affirm certain attributes of Ultimate Reality. One such depiction of God, or Brahman, as he is called, from within this tradition was offered by the Hindu philosopher Ramanuja (c. 1017–1137 – yes, it seems he lived quite a long life!):

> By the word "Brahman" is denoted the Supreme Person, who is by inherent nature free from all imperfections and possesses hosts of auspicious qualities which are countless and of matchless excellence. In all contexts the term "Brahman" is applied to whatever possesses the quality of greatness, but its primary and most significant meaning is that Being whose greatness is of matchless excellence, both in His essential nature and in His other qualities. It is only the Lord of all who is such a Being. Therefore the word "Brahman" is primarily used only to signify Him. . . . [10]

Similarly Anselm (1033–1109), a Christian philosopher, theologian, and monk, described God this way:

> God is whatever it is better to be than not to be; and he, as the only self-existent being, creates all things from nothing.
>
> What art thou, then, Lord God, than whom nothing greater can be conceived? But what art thou, except that which, as the highest of all beings, alone exists through itself, and creates all other things from nothing? For, whatever is not this is less than a thing which can be conceived of. But this cannot be conceived of thee. What good, therefore, does the supreme Good lack, through which every good is? Therefore, thou art just, truthful, blessed, and whatever it is better to be than not to be. For it is better to be just than not just; better to be blessed than not blessed.[11]

We find parallel depictions in the other theistic traditions as well.

Philosophical reflection about God has moved in new directions in recent times, and a central discussion these days has to do with the coherence of theism. Some philosophers argue that the traditional concept of God is plausible; that the divine attributes, as historically held, can be reasonably articulated and affirmed. Others argue that theism is internally inconsistent in a way that God turns out to be a logically impossible being. Others argue that the traditional concept of God must be significantly modified in order for it to be logically coherent. Still other philosophers argue that overall the concept of God is coherent, but some of the classic attributes are in need of modification. In recent discussions on the coherence of theism, two concerns have been central: the logical coherence of each of the divine attributes considered individually, and the logical compatibility of the divine attributes taken together. Below we will focus our attention on the first of these concerns.

The traditional theistic concept of God includes a cluster of properties attributed to God, including the following five:

THE COSMOLOGICAL ARGUMENT FOR ATHEISM

1 The big bang singularity (the beginning point of the universe where the curvature of space becomes, theoretically at least, infinite) is the earliest state of the universe.
2 The earliest state of the universe is inanimate (2 follows from 1 since the singularity involves the life-hostile conditions of infinite temperature, infinite curvature, and infinite density).
3 No law governs the big bang singularity and consequently there is no guarantee that it will emit a configuration of particles that will evolve into an animate universe (based on Stephen Hawking's *principle of ignorance* in which the singularity is inherently chaotic and unpredictable).
4 The earliest state of the universe is not guaranteed to evolve into an animate state of the universe (entailed by premises 1–3).
5 Premise 4 is inconsistent with the hypothesis that God – the classical Judeo–Christian–Islamic view of God as creator of the universe – created the earliest state of the universe since it is true that if God created the earliest state of the universe, then God would have ensured that the earliest state of the universe evolved into an animate state of the universe.
6 Therefore, the classical Judeo–Christian–Islamic God does not exist (entailed by premises 4–5).

time-reversed contracting universe vanishes into non-being. There was no first instant of the universe juxtaposed to the singularity. The temporal series is like a series of fractions converging toward 0 as its limit: ½, ¼, ⅛,..., 0. Just as there is no first fraction, so there is no first state of the universe. The singularity is thus ontologically equivalent to nothing.[33]

Craig argues further that a good reason for interpreting the singularity as unreal is that it is described as having no spatial dimensions and no temporal duration. As he puts it:

"The singularity has zero dimensionality and exists for no length of time; it is in fact a mathematical point."[34] To hold that such a point is real is to reify a mere mathematical construct.

Smith counters this objection by arguing that there is no reason for rejecting the reality of the singularity; to the contrary, he argues that in standard big bang cosmology the singularity is the *real* terminus of the converging past-directed space–time paths. The debate, then, centers on the metaphysics of time, space, and mathematics.

Big bang singularity: a hypothesized point in space–time where the laws of physics break down and the density of the universe and the curvature of space–time becomes infinite. On most big bang models of the universe, this is the point where time itself began.

Objection 2: God is not bound by laws or a lack of them for accomplishing God's purposes

According to this objection, premise 3 is false for at least two reasons. First, it could be the case that God's plan was to intervene in the early stages of the universe in order to ensure that living organisms, including human beings, would eventually evolve. It is not, necessarily, a sign of poor or irrational planning on God's part to do so. It could be that, unlike the clockmaker universe posited by the deists, God is creatively involved in the universe at different stages of its development. While this may not be the most efficient way to create a universe, argue objectors, the God of the theistic religions is not primarily concerned with efficiency. Such a God is not worried about running out of power.

Second, it could be that, contrary to Smith (and Hawking), the singularity is not a "violent, terrifying caldron of lawlessness."[35] Perhaps there are laws governing the singularity that have yet to be discovered – laws which will demonstrate that the principle of ignorance is false.

Another related response is to deny premise 5 that God would have ensured an animate state of the universe. There doesn't seem to be any logical or metaphysical necessity in God's creating this universe over and above some non-animated one, or for not creating any universe at all, for that matter. However, theists admit that there does seem to be some existential force to, and possibly religious support for, the belief that the God of the major theistic religions would create living organisms (especially rational, moral ones). But perhaps such feelings are wishful anthropocentrisms.

Objection 3: the theistic hypothesis of creation is simpler, and thus more likely to be true, than the atheistic hypothesis

This objection, raised by philosopher Richard Swinburne (1934–) is that a divine creation is simpler than the atheistic view, and as such it is more likely to be true.[36] Swinburne is operating on the scientific principle that the simpler an explanation for a thing, the more likely it is to be true. This principle, along with supposition (1) that the physical universe is a rather complex thing, and supposition (2) that God is a simple being (simple in that a being with infinite power, knowledge, and goodness is simpler than a being, or object, with finite values), leads to the conclusion that a theistic explanation for the universe is more likely to be true than an atheistic one.

The atheist can respond in a least two ways. First, he could grant the simplicity principle and supposition (2) but deny supposition (1). This is precisely what Smith does. He grants the principle but denies supposition (1) for the following reason: since the singularity has zero spatial volume, zero temporal duration, and does not have particular finite values for its density, "It seems reasonable to suppose…[that] this instantaneous point is the simplest possible physical object."[37] Granting that this simple object is at least as simple as the theistic hypothesis, it is simpler to suppose that the universe began from the same basic kind of stuff (i.e. material stuff) than to posit some additional kind of stuff (i.e, immaterial "God-stuff").

A second response an atheist can offer is to deny the principle of simplicity (probably not a good move, given the way science is actually practiced) or to deny supposition (2).

SUMMARY

In this chapter, four cosmological arguments were presented: three supporting theism and one supporting atheism. The first argument – the argument from contingency – concluded that God, a necessary being, must exist in order to cause the contingent things in the universe to exist. Five major objections were raised against it. The second argument – the argument from sufficient reason – concluded that there must be an explanation outside of the universe, one that is sufficient unto itself (a necessary being), since everything which exists in the world needs an explanation for its existence, and nothing in the world provides an explanation for itself. Four objections were raised against it, each one focusing on some enigmatic aspect of the notion of a sufficient reason or explanation. The third argument – the kalam argument – concluded that there must be a personal cause for the universe. It utilized one philosophical argument and two scientific evidences to support the premise that the universe began to exist, and also included a philosophical argument that this beginning must be personal. Four objections were raised, two for the first philosophical argument and one for each of the alleged scientific evidences. Objections against a personal beginning were also noted. The fourth argument – the cosmological argument for atheism – concluded that God must not exist, for God's existence is incompatible with the unpredictable and chaotic state of the big bang singularity. Three objections were raised against this argument.

Various versions of the cosmological argument have been debated for centuries, and with recent advances in astronomy, cosmology, and astrophysics, there continues to emerge new material for rich and fruitful dialogue.

QUESTIONS FOR REVIEW/DISCUSSION

1. Is it reasonable to be a theist without evidence? Is it reasonable to be an atheist without evidence? What kind of evidence should count in such discussion (e.g. philosophical, scientific, experiential, etc.)?
2. Five objections were offered to the argument from contingency. What are your thoughts on these objections and the responses and counter-responses to them? Can you think of other objections?
3. How does the argument from contingency differ from the argument from sufficient reason? Do you find either of them persuasive? Why or why not?
4. What do you make of the parable of the translucent sphere? Who do you believe is being more reasonable in this case – the theist or the atheist? Why?
5. What does the universe having a beginning have to do with the existence of God?
6. How would you explain, in your own words, the two scientific evidences for the beginning of the universe? What about the objections to them?
7. The crossing the infinite argument for the beginning of the universe is somewhat abstract. Do you understand it? If so, how would you explain it to someone who is not familiar with it? Is it plausible?
8. Explain the argument that the beginning of the universe is personal. Is it more or less plausible than an impersonal explanation?
9. The cosmological argument for atheism is logically valid. What do you make of the objections raised in order to disprove one or more of its premises?
10. Are you persuaded by either of the three cosmological arguments for God's existence described in this chapter? Are they more persuasive taken together?

FURTHER READING

Aquinas, Thomas (1948) *Summa Theologica*. Trans. Fathers of the English Dominican Province. Notre Dame, IN: Ave Maria Press. (Contains the classic presentation of several versions of the cosmological argument.)

Craig, William Lane (1980) *The Cosmological Argument from Plato to Leibniz*. London: Macmillan. (An excellent overview of the history of the cosmological argument; it's especially helpful in delineating the arguments of the medieval Arabic and Jewish thinkers.)

Craig, William Lane and Quentin Smith (1993) *Theism, Atheism, and Big Bang Cosmology*. New York: Oxford University Press. (Craig, a Christian theist, and Smith, an atheist, go head to head – chapter by chapter – defending their views; technical, but an outstanding work.)

Everitt, Nicholas (2004) *The Nonexistence of God*. New York: Routledge. (Chapter 4 focuses on cosmological arguments; highly readable.)

Geisler, Norman and Winfried Corduan (1988) *Philosophy of Religion*. 2nd ed. Grand Rapids, MI: Baker Books. (Chapter 8 contains a helpful list of many different kinds of cosmological arguments and objections.)

Kant, Immanuel (1929) *Critique of Pure Reason*. Trans. and ed. N. Kemp Smith. London: Macmillan. (This classic work contains influential criticisms of the cosmological argument and other arguments as well.)

Leibniz, G. W. (1898) "Monadology," in *The Monadology and other Philosophical Writings*. Trans. R. Latta. Oxford: Oxford University Press. (This work contains Leibniz's cosmological argument from sufficient reason.)

Le Poidevin, Robin (1996) *Arguing for Atheism: An Introduction to the Philosophy of Religion*. New York: Routledge. (An erudite but readable presentation by a leading philosopher; note especially Chapters 1 and 3.)

Mackie, J. L. (1982) *The Miracle of Theism: Arguments for and against the Existence of God*. Oxford: Clarendon Press. (Mackie was a well-known and well-respected atheist philosopher; Chapter 5 argues against cosmological arguments.)

Plato ([c.360–347 BCE] 1980) *Laws*. Trans. Thomas L. Pangle. Chicago, IL: University of Chicago Press. (This work offers one of the earliest forms of the cosmological argument.)

Rowe, William (1998) *The Cosmological Argument*. New York: Fordham University Press. (A careful examination of different versions of the cosmological argument.)

Silk, Joseph (2001) *The Big Bang*. 3rd ed. New York: Henry Holt and Company. (Silk is the Head of Astrophysics at Oxford University, and in this work he draws upon the latest theories and empirical evidences in describing big bang cosmology from the first microseconds of the universe through its evolution to the present and on into the future.)

WEBSITES

http://www.science.uva.nl/~seop/entries/cosmological-argument/
A helpful and concise entry from the *Stanford Encyclopedia of Philosophy* on the cosmological argument by philosopher Bruce Reichenbach.

http://groups.yahoo.com/group/reformed-epistemology
A discussion group focused on questions in religious epistemology – most especially the work of twentieth-century philosophers who maintain that religious belief can be rational and justified.

http://www.infidels.org
A website operated by the Internet Infidels, an organization dedicated to defending and promoting a naturalistic worldview; contains a number of articles on the cosmological argument.

http://www.ditext.com/russell/debate.html
An online transcript of the Copleston/Russell debate on the argument from contingency.

http://www.leaderu.com
Leadership University is a web-based organization that contains a number of articles in support of the theistic worldview, including articles on the cosmological argument by William Lane Craig and other scholars.

http://map.gsfc.nasa.gov/universe/
A NASA-based web page on cosmology; it also contains links to big bang theory and related topics, including significant images.

5 Teleological arguments for God's existence

Teleological argument: derived from the Greek terms *telos* (end or goal) and *logos* (reason or rational account). The teleological argument, first developed by ancient Greek and Indian philosophers, takes a variety of forms. The common theme among them all is that the means/ends order which exists in the natural world is best explained by purposive design.

As we saw in the last chapter, cosmological arguments begin with the fact that there are contingently existing things in the world and conclude with the existence of a *non-contingent creator* to account for the *existence* of those things. Teleological arguments (or *arguments from, or to, design*), on the other hand, are quite different, for they begin with certain properties in the world and conclude with the existence of a *grand designer* of the world – a designer with certain mental properties such as intention, knowledge, and purpose.

The beginnings of the teleological argument go back to ancient thinkers in the East and the West. In India, for example, the argument was propounded by the Nyāya school (100–1000 CE), which argued for the existence of God based on the order of the world – order they compared to artifacts and the human body.[1] In the West, the argument can be traced back to Heraclitus (fl. 500 BCE), Plato, Aristotle, and the Stoics. While the argument continued to be utilized from time to time throughout history, its rebirth occurred in the early nineteenth century with perhaps its most ardent defender: William Paley (1743–1805).

PALEY'S DESIGN ARGUMENT

William Paley's book, *Natural Theology* (1802), is a sustained defense and explication of the design argument. It begins with these words:

> In crossing a heath, suppose I pitched my foot against a *stone*, and were asked how the stone came to be there; I might possibly answer, that, for any thing I knew to the contrary, it had lain there for ever: nor would it perhaps be very easy to show the absurdity of this answer. But suppose I had found a *watch* upon the ground, and it should be inquired how the watch happened to be in that place; I should hardly think of the answer which I had before given, that, for any thing I knew, the watch might have always been there. Yet why should not this answer serve for the watch as well as for the stone? Why is it not as admissible in the second case, as in the first? For this reason, and for no other, viz. that, when we come to inspect the watch, we perceive (what we could not discover in the stone) that its several parts are framed and put together for a

William Paley (1743–1805) was an English theologian, philosopher, and Christian apologist. He became a fellow at Christ College, Cambridge, in 1766. He wrote a number of books including *The Principles of Moral and Political Philosophy* which became the ethical textbook at the University of Cambridge. His most famous work is *Natural History: Or Evidences of the Existence and Attributes of the Deity, Collected from the Appearances of Nature* (1802) – the book in which he presents his watchmaker analogy.

purpose, *e. g.* that they are so formed and adjusted as to produce motion, and that motion so regulated as to point out the hour of the day; that, if the different parts had been differently shaped from what they are, of a different size from what they are, or placed after any other manner, or in any other order, than that in which they are placed, either no motion at all would have been carried on in the machine, or none which would have answered the use that is now served by it… . This mechanism being observed (it requires indeed an examination of the instrument, and perhaps some previous knowledge of the subject, to perceive and understand it; but being once, as we have said, observed and understood), the inference, we think, is inevitable, that the watch must have had a maker: that there must have existed, at some time, and at some place or other, an artificer or artificers who formed it for the purpose which we find it actually to answer; who comprehended its construction, and designed its use… .

… [E]very indication of contrivance, every manifestation of design, which existed in the watch, exists in the works of nature; with the difference, on the side of nature, of being greater and more, and that in a degree which exceeds all computation.[2]

Paley is using an argument from analogy: since we infer a designer of an artifact such as a watch, given its evident purpose and ordered structure, so too we should infer a grand designer of the works of nature, since they are even greater in terms of their order and complexity – what he later describes as "means ordered to ends." Paley's argument can be sketched in the manner of the "Paley's design argument" box.

Paley's argument has not, of course, gone unchallenged. Some of the most ardent objections arise from the works of David Hume and Charles Darwin.

Objections 1–3: Hume's rebuttals

Perhaps the most familiar objections to Paley's design argument are those rebuttals offered by skeptic philosopher David Hume in his book, *Dialogues Concerning Natural*

PALEY'S DESIGN ARGUMENT

1 Artifacts (such as a watch), with their means to ends configurations, are the products of (human) design.
2 The works of nature, such as the human hand, resemble artifacts.
3 Thus the works of nature are probably the products of design.
4 Furthermore, the works of nature are much more in number and far greater in complexity.
5 Therefore, the works of nature were probably the products of a grand designer – one much more powerful and intelligent than a human designer.

Religion (1779).[3] One important Humean rebuttal is that the analogy between the works of nature and human artifacts is not particularly strong.[4] There are various reasons why the analogy is weak, including: (1) unlike watches, there is only one universe, and thus we have no other universes to compare it to or judge it by, and (2) in many ways the world (i.e. the accumulation of the works of nature) is not like a human artifact or machine and could just as easily be conceived of as a great animal or vegetable. As such, it begs the question to suppose that it was designed.

Another rebuttal is that even if we could infer a grand designer of the universe, this designer turns out to be something less than the God of the theistic religions. Since "like effects arise from like causes," from a finite world we cannot infer an infinite designer. Furthermore, there are gross imperfections and considerable evils in the world. So, if the world is designed, it is reasonable to conclude that the designer (or designers, since there is no reason to presume only one), must have these corresponding defects as well.

A third rebuttal is that just because a universe has the appearance of design, it does not follow that it is in fact designed.[5] Hume cites as one alternative the hypothesis of Epicurus who proposed that the universe consists of a finite number of particles moving in random motion. Eventually these particles will end up in a stable state, and

David Hume (1711–1776), Scottish philosopher and historian, is widely recognized to be the most important philosopher to write in English and one of the most significant thinkers in the history of Western philosophy. Among his most significant philosophical works are *A Treatise of Human Nature* (1739–1740), *Enquiries Concerning Human Understanding* (1748), and his most controversial work, *Dialogues Concerning Natural Religion* (published posthumously in 1779) in which he attacks the design argument.

this state would have the appearance of design without actually being so. In other words, the apparently designed universe may turn out to be the result of mere chance.

What might be said in response to these rebuttals? First, contrary to Hume's claim, it can be argued that while the world is unique, it does not follow that an argument from analogy cannot apply. If analogies could not be applied to unique events, absurd conclusions would follow. For example, one could never come to the conclusion about a unique artifact (discovered from an ancient time period, say) that it was designed. But such conclusions are frequently reached by archaeologists. Second, while the watch/world analogy may not be perfect, it nonetheless captures the central point: where purpose, order, and intention are evident, it is reasonable to posit a designer. And the works of nature do seem to reflect purpose, order, and intention. More will be said about this below.

Regarding the second rebuttal, several replies can be offered. First, Hume is right to note that the argument does not prove that the God of the religions exists. Nonetheless, it does arguably provide evidence that there is likely a grand designer of the world (that is, a designer of the works of nature of which the world is composed). Other arguments could be used to buttress this one in an attempt to demonstrate the existence of the God of the religions. Second, regarding the evil and imperfections in the world, it can be replied that this argument is not addressing the issue of divine omnibenevolence but rather purpose, intention, and design. God may not be able to create a world with free creatures who never commit evil acts, even if God is an omnibenevolent and omnipotent being.[6]

Hume's third rebuttal, that the world could have arisen from mere chance, leads us to a fourth objection to Paley's argument, and to Charles Darwin.

Objection 4: a Darwinian view of biological organisms

Perhaps the most influential thinker of the nineteenth century was Charles Darwin (1809–1882). In his book *Origin of Species* (1859), Darwin proposed what became one of the most significant theories in the history of human thought: that living organisms developed from simpler to more complex forms gradually over time and through the purely natural and non-purposive processes of random variation, natural selection and survival of the fittest.[7] This is, of course, Darwin's theory of evolution.

At first glance the theory of evolution appears to sound the death knell for Paley's design argument, for here we have chance and the laws of nature, rather than intention, purpose, and design, accounting for the works of nature. So there is no need to posit a grand designer of the world. The following is a common view of Darwin's apparent destruction of the design argument:

> It has been generally agreed (then and since) that Darwin's doctrine of natural selection effectively demolished William Paley's classical design argument for

> the existence of God. By showing how blind and gradual adaptation could counterfeit the apparently purposeful design that Paley… and others had seen in the contrivances of nature, Darwin deprived their argument of the analogical inference that the evident purpose to be seen in the contrivances by which means and ends were related in nature was necessarily a function of the mind.[8]

While Darwin's theory has clearly provided a significant alternative to a grand creation story about the works of nature, at least two responses can be offered to its apparent destructive force to the design argument. First, as we will see below, not everyone is convinced that a purely naturalistic, non-purposive account provides a complete explanation of all the flora and fauna which exist in the natural world. Second, even given a full-blown Darwinian view of things, the defender of the design argument could maintain that this evolutionary process is the very method by which the designer is bringing about his intentions and purposes for the world.[9]

In fact, Darwin himself may have held this view, at least at one point in his career. The year after he published the *Origin of Species*, he said the following in a letter to Harvard biologist Asa Gray:

> I am inclined to look at everything as resulting from designed laws, with the details, whether good or bad, left to the working out of what we may call chance… . I cannot think that the world as we see it is the result of chance; yet I cannot look at each separate thing as the result of Design."[10]

Nevertheless, Hume's rebuttals, combined with Darwin's evolutionary account of living organisms, all but sunk the design argument in the nineteenth and early-to-mid twentieth centuries. However, it was resurrected toward the latter half of the twentieth century in a variety of forms and even now is probably the most widely discussed and influential argument for the existence of God. Two of the most important recent versions are the fine-tuning and intelligent design arguments. We will first take a look at fine-tuning.

Charles Darwin (1809–1882) was an English naturalist who is considered to be one of the most influential thinkers in the history of Western civilization. His observations made during his five-year voyage on the *Beagle* were instrumental in developing his theory of natural selection. His book, *On the Origin of Species* (1859), established evolution by common descent as the central scientific explanation for the development and diversification of biological organisms. In *The Descent of Man* (1871) he applied his theory directly to human beings.

A FINE-TUNING ARGUMENT

A number of scholars who believe that the seemingly purposive, means-to-ends structures in the realm of biology can be fully explained by natural evolutionary processes also maintain that certain non-biological or inorganic aspects of the universe are best explained by means of an intelligent designer. Some have argued that the fundamental laws and parameters of physics and the initial conditions of the universe are extraordinarily balanced – or "finely tuned" – with just the right conditions for life to occur and flourish. Robin Collins for example, one of the foremost defenders of the fine-tuning teleological argument, asserts that "the initial conditions of the universe are balanced on a 'razor's edge'" for the existence of life.[11] Dozens of such parameters and conditions have been proposed, including the following described by Collins:[12]

1. If the initial explosion of the big bang had differed in strength by as little as one part in 10^{60}, the universe would have either quickly collapsed back on itself, or expanded too rapidly for stars to form. In either case, life would be impossible. (As John Jefferson Davis points out, an accuracy of one part in 10^{60} can be compared to firing a bullet at a one-inch target on the other side of the observable universe, twenty billion light years away, and hitting the target.)[13]
2. Calculations indicate that if the strong nuclear force, the force that binds protons and neutrons together in an atom, had been stronger or weaker by as little as five percent, life would be impossible.[14]
3. Calculations by Brandon Carter show that if gravity had been stronger or weaker by one part in 10^{40}, then life-sustaining stars like the sun could not exist. This would most likely make life impossible.[15]
4. If the neutron were not about 1.001 times the mass of the proton, all protons would have decayed into neutrons or all neutrons would have decayed into protons, and thus life would not be possible.[16]
5. If the electromagnetic force were slightly stronger or weaker, life would be impossible, for a variety of different reasons.[17]

Many of the parameters and conditions are apparently unrelated and, if so, this lowers the probability even further of their occurring by chance. The explanatory options are basically limited to three: the fine-tuning of the parameters and conditions happened by chance, by necessity, or by intelligent design.

Thus, we can sketch a fine-tuning teleological argument in the way shown in the box overleaf.

A FINE-TUNING TELEOLOGICAL ARGUMENT

1. The fine-tuning of the universe either happened by chance, necessity, or intelligent design.
2. The fine-tuning of the universe did not happen by chance or necessity.
3. Therefore, the fine-tuning of the universe happened by intelligent design.

Responses to the fine-tuning argument

Not surprisingly, a number of scholars disagree that intelligent design must be conjectured in order to account for the existence of the "finely tuned" parameters and initial conditions of the universe. The premise of the argument that is primarily challenged is 2: *The fine-tuning of the universe did not happen by chance or necessity*. We will consider three prominent responses.

The many-universes hypothesis

One way of explaining our finely tuned universe without positing an intelligent designer is to suggest that there are a very large number of universes – perhaps an infinite number of them. Given this large number, it is not surprising that at least one of them (ours in this case) include life-permitting initial conditions and parameters. While it is more probable that a universe arising from chance would include life-*prohibiting* parameters, if the number of universes is large enough, certainly some of them would have just the right parameters for life. Fortunately for us, our universe happens to be one of them. While science fiction writers have enjoyed much success in creating such scenarios, recent advances in string theory and inflationary cosmology have also led scholars to take seriously the notion of multiple universes.

Critics, however, note that there is currently no *experimental* evidence in support of the many-universes hypotheses. While there is some support in physics for string theory and inflationary cosmology, they are currently provisional and highly speculative.[18] Furthermore, as philosopher Robin Collins has argued, even if there are an infinite number of universes, it seems that they must be produced by some kind of a "many-universe generator." Such a device, however, would itself need to be finely tuned, and is thus in need of an intelligent designer explanation.[19] For, he argues, even a simple mechanism like a bread maker needs to be well designed to produce loaves of bread. How much more so a universe maker that produces finely tuned universes like our own.[20]

The anthropic principle

There are different versions of the anthropic principle ("anthropic" meaning related to human beings). The most widely held version of it is what physicists John Barrow and Frank Tipler call the Weak Anthropic Principle, or WAP. Here is the definition they offer:

> Weak Anthropic Principle (WAP): The observed values of all physical and cosmological quantities are not equally probable, but they take on values restricted by the requirement that there exist sites where carbon-based life can evolve and by the requirement that the Universe be old enough for it to already have done so.[21]

They also note a central feature that emerges from this principle:

> The basic features of the Universe, including such properties as its shape, size, age, and laws of change, must be *observed* to be of a type that allows the evolution of observers, for if intelligent life did not evolve in an otherwise possible universe, it is obvious that no one would be asking the reason for the observed size, shape, age, and so forth of the Universe.[22]

In other words, if the physical laws and constants of the universe were not just as they are – finely tuned for life – we would not be here to realize that fact. There would be no observers in a universe which lacked the conditions necessary for life. Thus, since we are here to observe them, we should not be surprised that the conditions are just right for life even if we live in a purely naturalistic universe. Therefore, there is no need to conjecture an intelligent designer of the universe.

In response, it can be argued that our being here to recognize the fine-tuning neither negates the amazement of the conditions nor eliminates the need for an intelligent design explanation. Richard Swinburne uses the following analogy to demonstrate this point.

> Suppose that a madman kidnaps a victim and shuts him in a room with a card shuffling machine. The machine shuffles ten packs of cards simultaneously and then draws a card from each pack and exhibits simultaneously the ten cards. The kidnapper tells the victim that he will shortly set the machine to work and it will exhibit the first draw, but that unless the draw consists of an ace of hearts from each pack, the machine will simultaneously set off an explosion which will kill the victim, in consequence of which we will not see which cards the machine drew. The machine is then set to work, and to the amazement and relief of the victim the machine exhibits an ace of hearts drawn from each pack. The victim thinks

> that this extraordinary fact needs an explanation in terms of the machine having been rigged in some way. But the kidnapper, who now appears, casts doubt on this suggestion. "It is hardly surprising," he says, "that the machine drew only aces of hearts. You could not possibly see anything else. For you would not be here to see anything at all, if any other cards had been drawn." But of course the victim is right and the kidnapper is wrong. There is something extraordinarily in need of explanation in ten aces being drawn. The fact that this particular order is a necessary condition of the draw being perceived at all makes what is perceived no less extraordinary and in need of explanation.[23]

The debate thus turns on whether such "anthropic coincidences" are more reasonably taken to be accidental or intentional.

Who designed the designer?

A third response to the fine-tuning argument is that putting forward an intelligent designer as an explanation for the finely tuned universe simply moves the debate back one step, for we can then ask the question, "Who designed the Designer?" In his familiar dialogue on religion, David Hume raises this objection:

> How shall we satisfy ourselves concerning the cause of that Being whom you suppose the Author of Nature ... the Ideal World into which you trace the material? Have we not the same reason to trace that ideal world into another ideal world or new intelligent principle? But if we stop and go no farther, why go so far? Why not stop at the material world? How can we satisfy ourselves without going on *in infinitum*? And, after all, what satisfaction is there in that infinite progression? Let us remember the story of the Indian philosopher and his elephant. [The Indian philosopher said that the world was resting on the back of an elephant, and the elephant was resting on the back of a great tortoise, and the tortoise on the back of he knew not what.] It was never more applicable than to the present subject. If the present world rests upon some ideal world, this ideal world must rest upon some other, and so on without end. It were better, therefore, never to look beyond the present material world. By supposing it to contain the principle of its order within itself, we really assert it to be God; and the sooner we arrive at the Divine Being, so much the better. When you get one step beyond the mundane system, you only excite an inquisitive humor which it is impossible ever to satisfy.[24]

In other words, even if we can explain the apparent fine-tuning of the world as being the product of an intelligent designer, that designer must have a mind that is just as "finely-tuned" as the natural world. So the designer, too, is in need of an explanation, as is the designer of the designer, and so on. If we enter the fray of needing an explanation for apparent design, this process goes on indefinitely. But why add hypotheses unnecessarily? Why not simply stop with the physical world?[25]

AN INTELLIGENT DESIGN ARGUMENT

Another recent form of the teleological argument is often referred to as the *intelligent design argument*. This argument is rooted in the work being done by a group of philosophers, scientists, and others who are a part of the Intelligent Design Movement. What the members of this group have in common is the belief that certain probabilistic methods can be utilized in determining whether a given biological system has been designed. William Dembski, a leader in the movement, argues that "[d]emonstrating transcendent design in the universe is a scientific inference, not a philosophical pipedream."[26] He has developed what he calls an *Explanatory Filter* for detecting design. In simplified form, the filter asks three questions in the following order:

1 Does a law explain it?
2 Does chance explain it?
3 Does design explain it?

First, one sets about determining whether law (i.e. regularity/necessity) best explains an event, object, or structure. If an event (I'll use "event" here to mean an event, object, or structure) has a fairly high probability of occurring, then it is explainable by law. For example, the rising of the Atlantic tide twice daily is a regular event – one best explainable by the laws of nature. If law does not explain an event, however, then we turn to chance. For example, if I spin a roulette wheel, I use chance to account for why the wheel stopped where it did.[27] In order to then eliminate chance

Intelligent Design Movement: the intelligent design movement, first begun in the 1980s, includes philosophers, scientists, and other scholars who regard the Darwinian vision that undirected natural causes could produce the full diversity and complexity of life as inadequate, and who propose a research program wherein intelligent causes become the key for understanding this diversity and complexity. Leading figures in the movement include Phillip Johnson, Michael Behe, William Dembski, Paul Nelson, and Stephen Meyer.

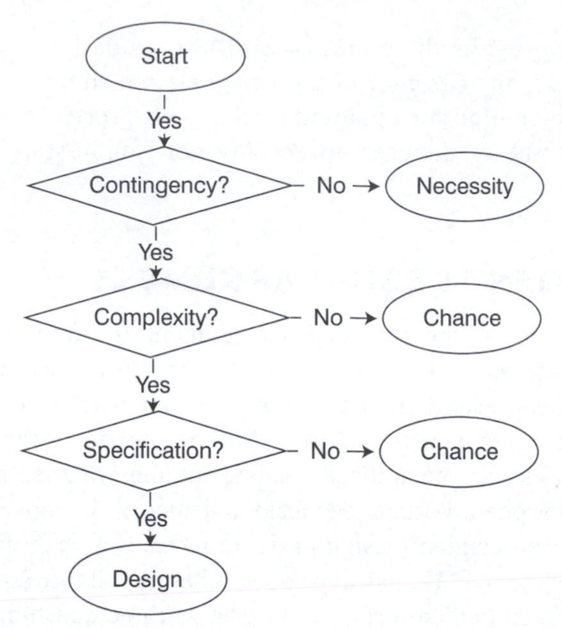

Figure 5.1 Explanatory filter algorithm

and conclude with design as the best explanation of an event, Dembski applies what he calls *specified complexity*, for which he offers the following description:

> A single letter of the alphabet is specified without being complex (i.e. it conforms to an independently given pattern but is simple). A long sequence of random letters is complex without being specified (i.e. it requires a complicated instruction-set to characterize but conforms to no independently given pattern). A Shakespearean sonnet is both complex and specified.[28]

The explanatory filter algorithm is diagrammed in Figure 5.1

Thus, if there are events, objects or structures in the natural world which are both complex and specified, Dembski concludes that design best explains them.

One example that intelligent design proponents often use as a case of specified complexity in nature is "irreducibly complex" systems. The person who coined the term is biochemist Michael Behe. Behe defines it this way:

> By *irreducibly complex* I mean a single system composed of several well-matched, interacting parts that contribute to the basic function, wherein the removal of any one of the parts causes the system to effectively cease functioning. An irreducibly complex system cannot be produced directly (that is, by continuously improving the initial function, which continues to work by the same mechanism) by slight,

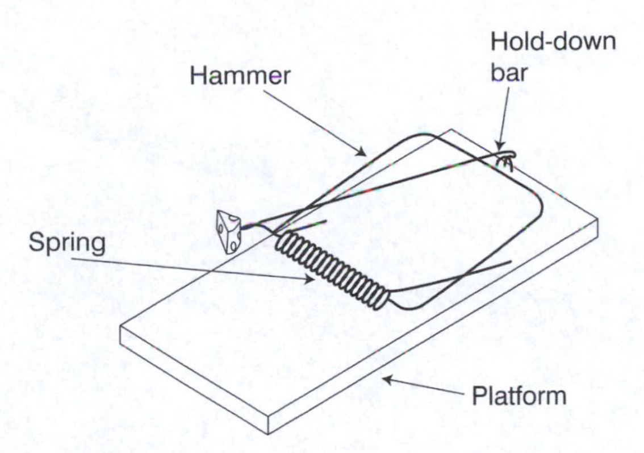

Figure 5.2 Standard mousetrap

> successive modifications of a precursor system, because any precursor to an irreducibly complex system that is missing a part is by definition nonfunctional.[29]

Behe uses the simple analogy of a mousetrap to demonstrate his point.

A typical mousetrap consists of a hammer, spring, holding bar, and a platform or base to which all the other parts are connected. Each of these parts is a *necessary* component for catching the mouse, and taken together the parts constitute a *sufficient* condition for catching a mouse. If any of the parts that make up the trap were missing, it wouldn't work as a mouse-catching device. It is thus an irreducibly complex mechanism in that it cannot be reduced in terms of components and still function as a mousetrap.

Behe's point, then, is that the biochemical world has a number of systems which consist of finely calibrated, interdependent parts which would not function without each of their components operating together. These systems, being irreducibly complex, cannot therefore be explained by the gradualism and natural selection of evolutionary theory. Positing a designer for them is a much better hypothesis.

A primary example Behe uses of an irreducibly complex biochemical system is the bacterial flagellum ("flagellum" is derived from Latin and means a whip or shoot). In the early 1970s, certain bacteria were seen to move about by rotating their flagella, or whip-like tail, which whirls about at high rates of speed – some of them hundreds of revolutions per second. The structure of these bacteria includes what is likened to an outboard motor. As Figure 5.3 indicates, there are a number of different components (about forty in all) which work together in the movement of the bacteria, including a hook, filament, stator, and rotor.[30]

What is of interest here is that the forty parts of which this flagellar motor consists apparently must be arranged just so. If any one of them is misplaced or absent, the "motor" will not function at all. It is thus an irreducibly complex mechanism. Defenders of the intelligent design argument maintain that it is more reasonable

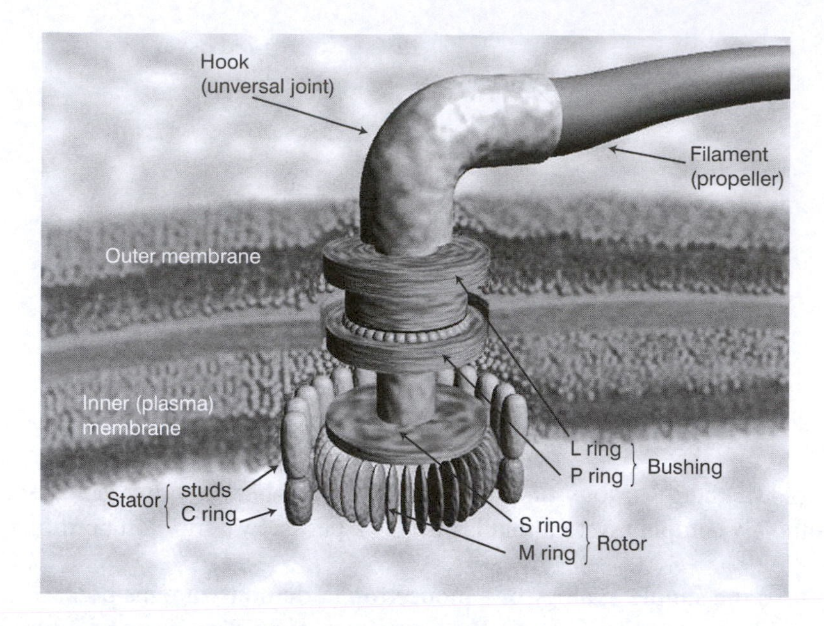

Figure 5.3 Flagellar motor, an example of an "irreducibly complex" mechanism (figure courtesy the Access Research Network)

to believe that an intelligent designer was involved in creating such a system than that the system developed gradually through naturalistic Darwinian processes. For unless the mechanism is fully functional, natural selection would have no reason to preserve it.[31]

An intelligent design argument can thus be put in the form stated in the 'Intelligent design argument' box below.

AN INTELLIGENT DESIGN ARGUMENT

1 If there are events, objects or structures in the natural world which are both complex and specified, then it is reasonable to conclude that they are the result of design.
2 There are events, objects or structures in the natural world, such as irreducibly complex molecular systems, which are both complex and specified.
3 Therefore, it is reasonable to conclude that they are the result of design.

Objections to an intelligent design argument

There are numerous objections to the intelligent design argument. Below are two significant ones – the first focused on premise 1 and the second focused on premise 2.

Objection 1: the intelligent design argument rests on contentious philosophical assumptions rather than on scientific inference

One objection to Dembski's explanatory filter is that it presupposes that if there is not a known scientific process by which to account for the phenomenon in question, then that is reason enough to conclude that there is no such process. However, it is quite a contentious claim that simply because an event is unexplainable given currently known natural laws and processes, it is therefore best explainable by intelligent design. This raises a variety of epistemic concerns, not the least of which is that it seems to violate the very nature of the scientific method of discovery; namely, searching for explanations of contingent natural phenomenon in terms of physical principles, laws, and processes. As one scholar puts it, "[I]t turns out that decisively identifying an instance of [specified complexity] requires commitment to philosophical assumptions that are not themselves concomitant with the practice of science."[32]

In response, it could be argued that the design filter is providing the best process of discovery given the available scientific evidence and the most reasonable method for explaining events. If further evidence leads one to a non-intentional, non-purposive, naturalistic explanation of the event, then the design explanation can be revoked. Of course, it could be maintained that all biological explanations should include non-intentional, non-purposive, naturalistic explanations. But to make this an a priori, metaphysical assumption before examining the evidence may well be unwarranted bias against the very possibility of intelligent design.

Objection 2: challenges to alleged examples of irreducible complexity

A second type of objection focuses on the examples offered as being irreducibly complex. One leading challenger of Behe's examples of irreducible complexity is professor of biology Kenneth Miller. Miller offers the following criticism of the bacterial flagellum as evidence of irreducible complexity:

> Evolution produces complex biochemical machines by copying, modifying, and combining proteins previously used for other functions. Looking for examples? The system in Behe's essay will do just fine. He writes that in the absence of "almost any" of its parts, the bacterial flagellum "does not work." But guess

> what? A small group of proteins from the flagellum *does* work without the rest of the machine – it's used by many bacteria as a device for injecting poisons into other cells. Although the function performed by this small part when working alone is different, it nonetheless can be favored by natural selection.[33]

The objection is straightforward. The flagellum is a case of *reducible* complexity, not *irreducible* complexity, since at least some of its components have a function without the flagellum taken as a whole. Natural selection could then have favored these individual components in the evolutionary development of the flagellum; no intelligent design hypothesis is required, and thus the mousetrap analogy is flawed. He continues:

> Ironically, Behe's own example, the mousetrap, shows what's wrong with the idea. Take away two parts (the catch and the metal bar), and you may not have a mousetrap but you do have a three-part machine that makes a fully functional tie clip or paper clip. Take away the spring, and you have a two-part key chain. The catch of some mousetraps could be used as a fishhook, and the wooden base as a paperweight… . The point, which science has long understood, is that bits and pieces of supposedly irreducibly complex machines may have different – but still useful – functions.[34]

One rebuttal to Miller's objection is that that while there are specific functions of individual proteins before they form together to make up a bacterial flagellum – just as there could be individual functions of some of the parts of a mousetrap – there is yet the difficulty of explaining how all the individual parts formed together into the complex, machine-like flagellum. Paperclips, fishhooks, and key chains don't conjoin into mousetraps without a design plan and yet, it is claimed, the interrelations of the elementary proteins that make up the flagellar motor have surfaces which are much less suitably matched, if *randomly* integrated, than the parts of mousetrap. Furthermore, at this time only ten percent of the flagellum's forty motor parts are found in other structures of the cell, and so the other parts of the system lack a Darwinian explanation.[35]

Of course, one could respond by noting that just because there is no current naturalistic explanation for the interrelations of the proteins, or for the other parts of the system, or for their joining together, that does not imply that there is no such explanation. And this leads us right back to Objection 1, that the intelligent design argument rests on certain philosophical assumptions rather than on scientific inference.

SUMMARY

The design argument has had a checkered history. It began with the ancient Greeks and Indus Valley peoples of India roughly 2,000 years ago, but it reached its peak in the nineteenth century with William Paley. Paley's version of the argument – and his clever watch analogy – caught widespread attention. However, through the writings of David Hume and Charles Darwin's revolutionary theory of evolution, the design argument stalled in the West for roughly a century.

In recent decades, however, the design argument has experienced somewhat of a renaissance. There are now a variety of design arguments which are discussed in monographs, companions, and academic journals. One type is the fine-tuning argument. Utilizing discoveries in physics and cosmology, defenders of this argument maintain that the fundamental laws and parameters of physics and the initial conditions of the universe are finely tuned for life in our universe. They claim that given the narrow limits of dozens of laws and physical constants, a grand designer better explains them than does chance or necessity. However, a variety of alternative explanations have been offered for the appearance of design. These explanations include the many universes hypothesis and the anthropic principle. It is also argued that the design argument begs the question of who designed the designer, and the designer's designer, and so on. Why not just stop with the universe itself?

Another type of teleological argument in recent times is the "intelligent design" argument. Its leading proponents include William Dembski and Michael Behe. They are proposing a research program in which intelligent causes are included as a component for understanding the diversity and complexity of life. Objections to this movement are multifaceted and include both challenges to its theoretical underpinnings as well as to the alleged scientific evidence in support of it.

There is currently much scholarly activity occurring concerning design arguments. Some are convinced that one or more of the arguments point to a grand designer of the cosmos; others are convinced that they do not; and still others are undecided. In any event, Paley and Hume would perhaps be delighted to know that their legacies on this topic continue to our own day … with no end in sight.

QUESTIONS FOR REVIEW/DISCUSSION

1. Create your own argument from analogy. What are its strengths? What are some weaknesses? Do these strengths or weaknesses apply to the design argument from analogy?
2. Which of Hume's rebuttals to Paley's design argument do you find most persuasive? Why?
3. Does it make sense to affirm the existence of a grand intelligent designer of the universe given that much of what we find on planet Earth, for example, does not seem to reflect "optimal design"? Explain your answer.
4. Are evolution and creation compatible? Explain your answer.
5. Does Swinburne's card-shuffling analogy rebut the anthropic argument response to the fine-tuning argument? Why or why not?
6. In response to the "who designed the designer" objection to the fine-tuning teleological argument, consider the following example. Suppose that during a deep-sea expedition, divers came upon what appeared to be an underwater city. It was like nothing they'd ever seen before, but there were structures apparently designed to sustain oxygen-breathing creatures, including large rooms from which water could be pumped out, long tubes which could be used to pump in oxygen from above water, and inlets and outlets which could be used for various transportation purposes.

   In such a scenario, it could be argued that it would be more reasonable to believe that intelligent design was involved in creating such a place than it would be to suppose that it came into existence through underwater evolutionary erosion and/or other chance naturalistic processes, and that we would not claim that there is no need to suggest intelligent design for the city since such intelligence itself may be in need of further explanation. So too, goes the argument, with the world and a grand designer.

   What do you make of this analogy?
7. What are some differences between Paley's design argument and the intelligent design argument? What are some similarities?
8. How would you respond to the following claim? "Natural science must presuppose a purely naturalistic or materialistic methodology; to do otherwise is to bring into science an *unwarranted philosophical presupposition* of religion and the supernatural."
9. Do you find any of the three teleological arguments presented in this chapter persuasive? If so, which one(s), and why? If not, what is your best reason for rejecting one or more of them?
10. What evidence do you have to support your belief in, or disbelief in, God?

FURTHER READING

Behe, Michael (1996) *Darwin's Black Box*. New York: Free Press. (Offers Behe's argument for irreducible complexity.)

Dawkins, Richard (1987) *The Blind Watchmaker.* New York: Norton. (Perhaps the most influential book defending naturalistic evolution and challenging the intelligent design of living organisms.)

Dembski, William (1998) *The Design Inference.* Cambridge: Cambridge University Press. (Presents Dembski's method for detecting intelligent causes.)

Dembski, William and Michael Ruse (2004) *Debating Design: From Darwin to DNA*. Cambridge: Cambridge University Press. (A collection of essays, pro and con, on intelligent design by some of the leaders on both sides of the debate.)

Everitt, Nicholas (2004) *The Nonexistence of God*. New York: Routledge. (Chapter 5 focuses on teleological arguments.)

Hacking, Ian (1987) "Inverse Gambler's Fallacy: The Argument from Design." *Mind* 96, 331–40. (Spells out the gambler's fallacy of concluding that, on the basis of an unlikely outcome of a random event, the event is likely to have occurred a number of times before.)

Hume, David ([1779] 1998) *Dialogues Concerning Natural Religion.* Ed. Richard Popkin. Indianapolis, IN: Hackett. (A classic critique of the design argument.)

Johnson, Phillip (1991) *Darwin on Trial.* Downers Grove, IL: InterVarsity. (The book which put the intelligent design movement on the map.)

Le Poidevin, Robin (1996) *Arguing for Atheism: An Introduction to the Philosophy of Religion*. New York: Routledge. (An erudite but readable presentation by a leading philosopher; Chapters 4 and 5 deal with design issues.)

Leslie, John (1989) *Universes*. London and New York: Routledge. (An important work on the anthropic principle.)

Mackie, J. L. (1982) *The Miracle of Theism: Arguments For and Against the Existence of God*. Oxford: Clarendon Press. (Mackie was a well-known and well-respected atheist in the twentieth century, and Chapter 8 includes his rebuttal to the design argument.)

Manson, Neil, ed. (2003) *God and Design: The Teleological Argument and Modern Science.* New York: Routledge. (Includes arguments, pro and con, on the design argument.)

Meister, Chad, ed. (2007) *The Philosophy of Religion Reader*. London: Routledge. (Contains several classic and contemporary essays on the design argument.)

Moreland, J. P. (2007) "The Argument from Consciousness," in Chad Meister and Paul Copan, eds. *The Routledge Companion to Philosophy of Religion*. London: Routledge, 373–84. (A design argument for the existence of God based on the mind and consciousness.)

Paley, William ([1802] 1963) *Natural Theology.* Indianapolis, IN: Bobbs-Merrill. (The classic defense of the design argument, including the watch analogy.)

Ruse, Michael (1982) *Darwinism Defended*. Reading, MA: Addison-Wesley. (A solid defense of Darwinism by a leading philosopher of biology.)

Swinburne, Richard (1991) *The Existence of God.* New York: Clarendon. (A very cogent defense of theism; Chapter 8 focuses on teleological arguments.)

WEBSITES

http://plato.stanford.edu/entries/teleological-arguments/

A helpful and concise entry from the *Stanford Encyclopedia of Philosophy* on teleological arguments by philosopher of science Del Ratzsch.

http://www.arn.org
A website devoted to providing accessible information on science, technology and society from an intelligent design perspective.

http://home.messiah.edu/~rcollins/ft.htm
Robin Collins' fine-tuning website; maintained by philosopher Robin Collins (Messiah College).

http://www.anthropic-principle.com/
A site devoted to the anthropic principle; maintained by Nick Bostrom (Oxford University).

http://www.infidels.org/library/modern/theism/design.html
An infidels.org site which includes a good number of articles on the design argument and related topics.

6 Ontological arguments for God's existence

Ontological argument: derived from the Greek terms *ontos* (being), and *logos* (rational account). The ontological argument, first developed by Saint Anselm of Canterbury, takes a variety of forms. The common theme among them is that they begin a priori – proceeding from the mere concept of God – and conclude that God must exist.

In the last two chapters we examined cosmological and teleological arguments, both of which focused on some feature of the universe and concluded either that God must be posited to account for it (cosmological argument) or that it pointed to a designer of the universe (teleological argument). These arguments are a posteriori, for they are based on premises that can be known only by experience of the world. Another kind of argument attempts to demonstrate that God's non-existence is impossible – this is the ontological argument. It is unique among the traditional arguments for God's existence in that it is an a priori argument, for it is based on premises that can allegedly be known independently of experience of the world.

The ontological argument has bedeviled philosophers – atheists and non-theists alike – for centuries. There are different versions of the argument, and I am including here what are perhaps two of its strongest formulations: Anslem's classic argument and Plantinga's contemporary argument.[1]

ANSELM'S ONTOLOGICAL ARGUMENT

One of the most creative thinkers of the Middle Ages was Saint Anselm of Canterbury (1033–1109). He was both a devoted monk and an apologist of Christian orthodoxy, and all of his writings are centered on Christian theology – either explaining it or defending it. Two of his books, the *Monologion* and *Proslogion*, include arguments for the existence of God. In the former work, Anselm's arguments are complex and probably not too effective at convincing others of their conclusions. In the *Proslogion* he seeks

> a single argument which would require no other for its proof than itself alone; and alone would suffice to demonstrate that God truly exists, and that there is a supreme good requiring nothing else, which all other things require for their existence and well-being ..."[2]

Anselm desired an argument which would not fail in convincing others of its truth, and he believed that he had done so with the ontological argument. This argument was first developed by Anselm in Book II of his *Proslogion*, and some have argued

Saint Anselm of Canterbury (1033–1109) was a leading Christian thinker of the eleventh century. He was the Archbishop of Canterbury and opposed the Crusades while holding this office. He is best known today for his ontological argument, but his work in natural theology and philosophical theology goes well beyond it. He also developed other arguments for God's existence and wrote on such matters as the nature of God, the incarnation, free will, sin and redemption. His works include the *Monologion*, *Proslogion*, and *Cur Deus Homo* (*Why Did God Become Man?*).

that he presents different versions of it in Books II and III. For our purposes we will focus on the argument as presented in Book II, a reflective commentary on a passage in the Old Testament book of Psalms which reads "... the fool hath said in his heart, there is no God." (Psalm 14:1)

> And so, Lord, do thou, who dost give understanding to faith, give me, so far as thou knowest it to be profitable, to understand that thou art as we believe; and that thou art that which we believe. And, indeed, we believe that thou art a being than which nothing greater can be conceived. Or is there no such nature, since the fool hath said in his heart, there is no God? ... But, at any rate, this very fool, when he hears of this being of which I speak – a being than which nothing greater can be conceived – understands what he hears, and what he understands is in his understanding; although he does not understand it to exist.
>
> For, it is one thing for an object to be in the understanding, and another to understand that the object exists. When a painter first conceives of what he will afterwards perform, he has it in his understanding, but he does not yet understand it to be, because he has not yet performed it. But after he has made the painting, he both has it in his understanding, and he understands that it exists, because he has made it.
>
> Hence, even the fool is convinced that something exists in the understanding, at least, than which nothing greater can be conceived. For, when he hears of this, he understands it. And whatever is understood, exists in the understanding. And assuredly that, than which nothing greater can be conceived, cannot exist in the understanding alone. For, suppose it exists in the understanding alone: then it can be conceived to exist in reality; which is greater.
>
> Therefore, if that, than which nothing greater can be conceived, exists in the understanding alone, the very being, than which nothing greater can be conceived, is one, than which a greater can be conceived. But obviously this is impossible. Hence, there is no doubt that there exists a being, than which nothing greater can be conceived, and it exists both in the understanding and in reality.[3]

The writing here is somewhat elusive and thus lends itself to different interpretations.[4] Here is one way of explicating the argument:

1 Everyone (even the atheist) is able to understand by the term "God" a being than which none greater can be conceived.
2 So, a being than which none greater can be conceived exists in the mind (i.e. the understanding) when one hears about such a being.
3 We can conceive of a being than which none greater can be conceived which exists both in the mind and in reality.
4 To exist in reality is greater than to exist in the mind alone.
5 If, therefore, a being than which none greater can be conceived exists in the mind alone and not in reality, it is not a being than which none greater can be conceived.
6 Therefore, a being than which none greater can be conceived exists in reality.

Let us unpack the argument. First, premise 1 is fairly straightforward. It is not making any claims about whether God exists or not; it is simply claiming that any rational person should be able to understand what one means when they define God as a being than which none greater can be conceived (i.e. the greatest imaginable being). To deny that God exists is to deny that a being than which none greater can be conceived exists. It seems that even an atheist could at least grant Anselm this definition.

The second premise is making the point that in some sense a being than which none greater can be conceived exists in the mind of the one who understands the concept. In order to affirm or deny the existence of a being than which none greater can be conceived, one must understand what it is that is being affirmed or denied. So a being than which none greater can be conceived exists at least as a mental entity, or concept, if it is affirmed or denied. It's important here to note that there are several ways things can exist (or, several modes of existence):

a) in the mind but not in reality (examples include centaurs, unicorns, Santa Claus);
b) in reality but not in the mind (such as an undiscovered star);
c) both in the mind and in reality (such as Tony Blair);
d) neither in the mind nor in reality (such as the internet in 500 BCE).

The claim in premise 2 is simply that a being than which none greater can be conceived exists in the mind (and so exists either as *a* or *c*).

In premise 3 the claim is that we can understand the notion of a being than which none greater can be conceived as existing both mentally and in reality (as in *c*). Tony Blair currently exists both in reality and as a concept or idea in the mind. So, too, we can at least conceive of God as existing in the mind and in reality (but whether God actually exists in reality is a different matter at this point). Premise 4 makes the point

> I remember the precise moment, one day in 1894, as I was walking along Trinity Lane, when I saw in a flash (or thought I saw) that the ontological argument is valid. I had gone out to buy a tin of tobacco; on my way back, I suddenly threw it up in the air, and exclaimed as I caught it: "Great Scott, the ontological argument is sound!"
>
> Bertrand Russell[5]

that it is *greater* to exist in reality than in the mind alone. This is clearly a debatable premise, and for many the soundness of the argument hinges on it. We will explore it further below when we examine Kant's objection.

The fifth premise simply follows from the previous one. If it is true that it is greater to exist in reality than in the mind, then a being which exists only in the mind would not be the greatest conceivable being; to affirm otherwise is to contradict yourself, for you would be affirming that the greatest possible being (one which exists in reality) is not the greatest possible being. Therefore, we are led logically to conclude that God (a being than which none greater can be conceived) exists in reality.

Criticisms of Anselm's argument

Criticisms have been raised against Anselm's ontological argument from its very inception, even among devoted religious believers. We will focus here on two of the more influential ones.

The greatest possible island

One of the earliest objections to the ontological argument was offered by one of Anselm's fellow monks, Gaunilo of Marmoutiers (c. 11th century). Gaunilo offered several objections to the argument, but perhaps the most well-known is an objection based on the analogy of the greatest possible island. Consider the idea of a perfect island – an island which exists but was lost to humanity. Following the same structure as Anselm's argument described above, we could construct the following:

1 Everyone is able to understand by the term "Perfect Island" an island than which none greater can be conceived.
2 So, an island than which none greater can be conceived exists in the mind (i.e. the understanding) when one hears about such an island.
3 We can conceive of an island than which none greater can be conceived which exists both in the mind and in reality.

4 To exist in reality is greater than to exist in the mind alone.
5 If, therefore, an island than which none greater can be conceived exists in the mind alone and not in reality, it is not an island than which none greater can be conceived.
6 Therefore, an island than which none greater can be conceived exists in reality.

This strategy of Gaunilo's lost island is called a *reductio ad absurdum* argument. It is an argument form in which you (1) assume a position for the sake of argument, (2) follow the argument structure and derive an absurd or ridiculous outcome, and (3) then conclude that the original argument structure must have been wrong as it led to an absurd conclusion. Gaunilo concludes his rebuttal this way:

> If a man should try to prove to me by such reasoning that this island truly exists, and that its existence should no longer be doubted, either I should believe that he was jesting, or I know not which I ought to regard as the greater fool: myself, supposing that I should allow this proof; or him, if he should suppose that he had established with any certainty the existence of this island.[6]

His point, of course, is that the perfect island argument does not really prove that such an island exists – it would be absurd to believe that there is a perfect island – so this argument must be flawed. And, since Anselm's ontological argument follows the same basic structure, it too must be flawed.

Anselm offers his own reply to Gaunilo:

> Now I promise confidently that if any man shall devise anything existing either in reality or in concept alone (except that than which a greater cannot be conceived) to which he can adapt the sequence of my reasoning, I will discover that thing, and will give him his lost island, not to be lost again.
>
> But it now appears that this being than which a greater is inconceivable cannot be conceived not to be, because it exists on so assured a ground of truth; for otherwise it would not exist at all.[7]

Anselm's point is that, unlike with a being than which none greater can be conceived, the greatest possible island is not something that one can "discover" in following his line of reasoning. Anselm seems to imply here that he can conceive of such an island's not existing. With God – that than which none greater can be conceived – it is impossible to conceive of such a being as not existing. But not so with the perfect island.

Assessing Anselm's reply is difficult. For one, it's not clear exactly what he means in this concise, perhaps glib, response. Furthermore, if he means that it is possible to conceive of a perfect island's not existing, it's not clear what he means by "conceivable" in this context. In any case, in evaluating the soundness of the

Gaunilo's rebuttal, much hinges on the meaning of the term *conceivable*, and there is lively, ongoing debate about it.[8]

Existence is not a predicate

Perhaps the most serious objection to Anselm's ontological argument (at least the version presented in *Proslogion* II) was raised by Immanuel Kant (1724–1804). He claimed that existence is not a real predicate.[9] The objection is raised against premise 4 (together with premise 3) in the argument above and can be spelled out this way: existence is not a predicate such that it is a property which can be affirmed of a thing. Existence does not add to the concept of a thing; rather, existence is the instantiation of a thing.[10]

Consider this example. Suppose you see a cat walk in front of you, and the cat happens to be black. When you make the claim that the cat is black, you are adding a property (blackness) to the concept of a cat. There are other cats which are not black; it is not essential to the concept of a cat that it be black. When you claim that the cat exists, however, you are not adding anything to the concept of a cat; you are only saying that the concept of a cat is exemplified or instantiated. In Anselm's argument he is implying that existence is a predicate which adds to the concept of a being than which none greater can be conceived (it is greater to have the property of existing than to not have it). But, argues Kant, asserting that something exists doesn't add anything to the concept of such a being (or to any concept, for that matter); it is just affirming that the concept is instantiated. So Anselm's argument is flawed.

In reply, the following point could be made. I can conceive of a particular cat in my mind – consider, once again, my friend's cat Jack – and I can think about this cat. I can look forward to taking care of it, to petting it, to feeding it (all of which I have actually done), and so on. But I can also think of another cat, a cat identical to Jack in every respect except this one: this cat exists only in my mind, not in reality; it is an imaginary cat. I can never actually take care of, pet, or feed this cat, for it exists only in my mind. It does indeed seem that there is something *greater* about the first cat – it really exists!

Immanuel Kant (1724–1804) was a German philosopher who is widely regarded as one of the most significant thinkers in the history of Western philosophy. His work in epistemology, metaphysics, ethics, and aesthetics has influenced much of the work in philosophy after him. His primary books include *Critique of Pure Reason*, *Religion within the Limits of Religion Alone*, and *Critique of Practical Reason*.

A rebuttal is that Jack's existence has not added anything new to the concept of Jack; there is no difference of properties between the concepts of the existing Jack and the non-existing Jack, only the different ways they are related to our experiences. I can actually feed and pet the existing Jack, not the imaginary Jack. But that does not involve a new property. And if existence is not a property, it cannot be a *greater* one. Thus, the fourth premise of Anselm's argument is false, and so the argument fails.[11]

PLANTINGA'S MODAL ONTOLOGICAL ARGUMENT

Recently Alvin Plantinga (1932–) devised a version of the ontological argument which utilizes the semantics of modal logic: possibility, necessity, and possible worlds.[12] A *possible world* is a world that is logically possible (unlike, say, a world that contains contradictions such as that John and Mary are shorter than each other simultaneously, or that there are round squares, or that $2 + 2 = 5$).[13] Keeping in mind that a *maximally excellent being* is one that is omniscient, omnipotent, and morally perfect in *every possible world*, his argument can be simplified and stated this way:[14]

1 It is possible that a being exists which is maximally great (a being that we can call God).
2 So there is a possible world in which a maximally great being exists.
3 A maximally great being is necessarily maximally excellent in every possible world (by definition).
4 Since a maximally great being is necessarily maximally excellent in every possible world, that being is necessarily maximally excellent in the actual world.
5 Therefore, a maximally great being (i.e. God) exists in the actual world.

This argument is formally valid (again, this means that if its premises are true, its conclusion must also be true). But is it sound? That is, are its premises true as well?

Plantinga himself does not believe that the argument provides conclusive proof that God exists, for some may deny the first premise. Nonetheless, he maintains, "there is nothing *contrary to reason* or *irrational*" in accepting it.[15] So, while it does not establish the truth that God exists, he believes it does at least establish its "rational acceptability."

Let us take the premises one at a time. The first premise states that it is possible that God – a maximally great being – exists. Whether it is possible that such a being exists is crucial to the argument, and we will examine that more closely below in the first objection.

Premise 2 brings into the argument the notion of possible worlds. This, too, is a crucial premise, and one for which there is widespread disagreement. On one description of possible worlds semantics (*semantics* has to do with the meanings of

Modal logic (from "modes" of the verb "to be") is a system of logic which utilizes such modal expressions as "*possibly*" and "*necessarily.*" Propositions are either true or false. Sometimes, however, a proposition is not just true but necessarily true. Other propositions are false but possibly true, and still others are false and necessarily false. Utilizing these notions of necessity and possibility, the basic principles of modal logic include such claims as "if something is impossible then it is necessarily false" and "that which is necessary is both truly actual and possible." Modal logic has become a frequently utilized tool in the formal analysis of philosophical arguments, especially in metaphysics, epistemology, and philosophy of religion.

terms and symbols), such worlds are not realities which actually or literally exist independent of our thinking about them; they are constructs which help us think through and understand a number of difficult concepts, such as counterfactuals, propositions, and properties. We could think of possible worlds as a very large conjunction: *a* & *b* & *c* & *d* … (the individual conjuncts each represent a proposition or claim).[16] A possible world then is not another universe, as real as the universe of which we are a part. Rather, it is a complete description of reality – a complete set of propositions – and there are countless descriptions of reality. For example, there is a possible world *a* & *b* & *c* & *d* … as noted above. But there is also a possible world –*a* & *b* & *c* & *d* … ("–*a*" means "not *a*"), and another *a* & –*b* & *c* & *d* …, and yet another –*a* & –*b* & *c* & –*d* …, and so on. One and only one of the descriptions of possible worlds will include only true conjuncts and thus will depict the world as it truly is; that is the actual world.

There is no possible world which contains contradictions or which is metaphysically inconceivable. For example, there is no possible world where everything in that world is both circular and rectangular at the same time, for to be so would be a contradiction. Nor is there a possible world in which George Bush is a color, for individual human beings cannot conceivably be identical to colors (of course, George Bush has a particular color, and the name "George Bush" could be assigned to any particular color, but these facts miss the point). To claim, then, that there is a possible world in which a maximally great being exists is not to claim that there is some "flesh and blood" universe where God is, but that the proposition *a maximally great being exists* consists in some maximal description of reality.

With the third premise there is simply the point that the definition of a maximally great being is necessarily omniscient, omnipotent, and morally perfect in every possible world. To describe a maximally great being as being less than omniscient, omnipotent, and morally perfect is to misconstrue the meaning of such a being as defined in this case.

Premise 4 is also rooted in the semantics of possible worlds. One of the possible worlds (i.e. one of the complete descriptions of reality) is the actual world. So, if a maximally great being is necessarily maximally excellent in every possible world, that being is necessarily maximally excellent in the actual world.

Finally, the conclusion follows logically from the previous ones: a maximally great being exists in the actual world.

Objections to Plantinga's modal argument

A number of objections have been raised against modal versions of the ontological argument. We will look briefly at three of them.

Objection 1: God's existence is a logical or metaphysical impossibility

Regarding premise 1, is it *possible* that a maximally great being exists? Some believe that it is not – that it is impossible for there to be a maximally great or excellent being. For example, as we will see in the next chapter, it can be argued that the presence of evil and suffering in the world disproves, or at least counts strongly against, the existence of a being which is omniscient, omnipotent, and morally perfect. It has even been argued that the two propositions, God exists and evil exists, are logical contradictions. If this is true, and if evil exists, then there is no possible world in which God exists.[17]

Other reasons have also been given to demonstrate that it is just not possible for a maximally great being to posses the properties traditionally attributed to God, including that such properties are internally contradictory.[18] For example, it has been argued that divine omniscience contradicts divine perfection (omniscience and perfection are two attributes commonly attributed to God). The argument can be put this way:[19]

1 A perfect being is not subject to change.
2 A perfect being knows everything.
3 A being that knows everything always knows what time it is.
4 A being that always knows what time it is is subject to change.
5 A perfect being is therefore subject to change.
6 A perfect being is therefore not a perfect being.
7 Ergo, there is no perfect being.

Replies can be offered, such as that premise 1 is false. But this objection to divine coherence as well as others are offered in the literature in an attempt to demonstrate the impossibility of God's existence.[20]

Objection 2: a problem with possible worlds semantics

An important question with respect to modal arguments such as this one is whether the modal logic utilized is the appropriate kind of logic for metaphysical possibilities. Some argue that it is not.[21] Another point to consider is that, while we can agree that the actual world exists, there is no universal agreement about the ontological or functional role possible worlds should play in metaphysical discussions. Consider this example. Jane Austen could have written a book about slavery in England in the eighteenth century. Or she could have written a book about the Trojan War. But does the fact that she could have written these books entail that they really exist in a possible world? What would it mean to say that they do? You cannot touch these books; you cannot read these books; you cannot even see these books. There is nothing you can do with these books because they are not real; they do not exist. So it seems odd to say that they *exist* in a possible world.

If one of the reasons that novels by Jane Austen on slavery and the Trojan War do not exist is because *nothing exists* in a possible world, then it would be false to assert that *God* (i.e. a maximally great being) exists in a possible world. And if God does not exist in a possible world, then premise 2 of Plantinga's argument is false, and the argument is unsound.[22]

Objection 3: the problem of fairies, ghosts, gremlins, and unicorns

Lastly, Michael Martin (1932–) has argued that Plantinga's modal argument can be parodied in such a way that if you affirm it you end up also affirming the existence of mythical creatures. He begins by defining the property of being a special fairy as being a tiny woodland creature with magical powers in every possible world. Modifying his argument to match Plantinga's ontological argument as described above, it runs this way:

1′ It is possible that a special fairy exists.
2′ So there is a possible world in which a special fairy exists.
3′ A special fairy is necessarily a tiny woodland creature with magical powers in every possible world (by definition).
4′ Since a special fairy is necessarily a tiny woodland creature with magical powers in every possible world, that fairy is necessarily a tiny woodland creature with magical powers in the actual world.
5′ Therefore, a special fairy exists in the actual world.

Martin's point is that premise 1′ is no more contrary to reason than premise 1, so if we affirm 1 and conclude that 5 is rationally acceptable, we must also affirm 1′ and conclude that 5′ is rationally acceptable. Following the same line of argument,

Michael Martin (1932–) is an analytic philosopher, atheist, and Professor Emeritus at Boston University. His work has focused primarily on philosophy of religion, and he has published numerous articles and books defending atheism and replying to arguments for the existence of God. He has written *Atheism: A Philosophical Justification*, *God, Morality and Meaning*, and *The Big Domino in The Sky and Other Atheistic Tales*.

we must also conclude that special ghosts, gremlins, unicorns and countless other mythical creatures exist as well.

In reply, one could argue that premise 1 is clearly contrary to reason whereas premise 1′ is not, for it is not possible that a special fairy exists since fairies are presumably physical objects (or essentially connected to physical objects). But no physical object can be a necessary being since it is possible that there are no physical objects whatsoever. Since Plantinga's maximally excellent being is not necessarily a physical object, Martin's objection does not apply to Plantinga's argument.[23] It is interesting to note that this rebuttal is similar, in important respects, to Anselm's rebuttal of Gaunilo. History does indeed repeat itself.

SUMMARY

In this chapter we have examined two versions of the ontological argument. First, we looked at Anselm's argument in which one begins with the premise that everyone, even the atheist, is able to understand by the term "God" a being than which none greater can be conceived. And everyone, even the atheist, can conceive of such a being as existing both mentally and in reality. Furthermore, to exist in reality is *greater* than mere mental existence. Since it would be a contradiction to affirm that the greatest possible being does not exist in reality but only in the mind (because existing in reality is greater than existing in the mind), he concludes that God must exist.

This is an intriguing argument. Many of the leading philosophers throughout the centuries have interacted with it, and some have attempted to refute it. We looked at two prominent objections. The first one was based on the analogy of the greatest possible island and was developed by Anselm's fellow monk, Gaunilo. Utilizing a *reductio ad absurdum* argument style, he argued that if we affirm Anselm's ontological argument, we must also affirm that the greatest possible island exists. Since that conclusion is absurd, so too is Anselm's conclusion. A second objection to Anselm's argument was offered by Immanuel Kant; namely, that existence is not a real predicate. Since existence does not add to the concept of a thing, and in Anselm's argument existence is treated as a real predicate, his argument is flawed.

The second form of the ontological argument we examined was Plantinga's modal argument. He provides a valid form of the ontological argument using the modal notions of possibility and possible worlds. Simply put, if it is possible that there exists a maximally great being (one that is maximally excellent in all possible worlds), then there actually exists a maximally excellent being (one that is omnipotent, omniscient, and morally perfect). However, the soundness of the argument has been challenged on multiple fronts.

One objection is that God's existence is logically or metaphysically impossible. There are various ways of arguing for God's impossibility, including that the properties attributed to a maximally great being are either internally contradictory or contradict other propositions which we know to be true. Second, since there is no universal agreement about the role modal logic should play in metaphysical discussions such as this one, concluding that the argument is sound is too hasty. Finally, the argument can be parodied such that if you affirm it you must also affirm the existence of mythical creatures such as fairies, ghosts, and gremlins.

Of the various arguments for the existence of God which have been proposed historically, ontological arguments have perhaps been the least effective at convincing unbelievers that theism is true. Nevertheless, more than a few of the leading minds in history have been convinced by at least one version of it – either its soundness or its rational acceptability. Moreover, since the ontological argument is deductive rather than inductive, if it is sound, it accomplishes more with a few simple premises than the other arguments accomplish with an accumulation of evidences and scientific considerations. Thus, though controversial, it has quite a powerful punch for those who are convinced of its soundness.

QUESTIONS FOR REVIEW/DISCUSSION

1. Describe one version of the ontological argument (either Anselm's version or Plantinga's modal version) in your own words. Is it sound? Defend your answer.
2. If the ontological argument proves that God exists (and, of course, this is hotly contested), does it prove that a particular deity exists (e.g. the Christian, Islamic, Jewish, or Hindu God)? Explain.
3. Is it greater to exist than to not exist, as Anselm claimed? Explain your answer. How does your answer affect the ontological argument?
4. Can you conceive of God's non-existence? If so, what follows from this regarding the ontological argument?
5. Explain Gaunilo's lost island rebuttal. Is it sound? Does it refute Anselm's ontological argument? Why or why not?
6. In your own words, explain Kant's objection that existence is not a predicate. Do you agree? Does it refute Anselm's argument? Defend your answers.
7. Does Plantinga's argument succeed in avoiding Kant's criticism? If so, how so? If not, why not?
8. Do research on reasons why some philosophers believe that God's existence is a logical or metaphysical impossibility (the footnotes and Further reading section offer helpful resources for this project). Explicate some of these reasons. Do you agree with them? Why or why not?
9. If it can be demonstrated that God exists because the concept of a necessary being entails God's existence, then does the concept of a perfect fairy prove that it exists, to? Explain the difference, if there is one.
10. How does the ontological argument differ from other classic arguments for the existence of God?

FURTHER READING

Anselm ([1077–8] 1962) *Proslogion*, in *St. Anselm: Basic Writings*. LaSalle, IL: Open Court Publishing. (Contains the original statement of the ontological argument.)

Davis, Stephen (2003) "The Ontological Argument," in Paul Copan and Paul K. Moser, eds. *The Rationality of Theism*. London: Routledge. (A supportive overview and analysis of two versions of the ontological argument.)

Everitt, Nicholas (2004) *The Non-existence of God*. London: Routledge. (Chapter 3 contains an overview and critique of ontological arguments.)

Gaunilo ([1078] 1962) *On Behalf of the Fool*, in *St. Anselm: Basic Writings*. LaSalle, IL: Open Court Publishing. (Contains criticisms of Anselm's ontological argument.)

Hartshorne, Charles (1965) *Anselm's Discovery: A Re-examination of the Ontological Proof for God's Existence*. (Includes an analysis of Anselm's argument as well as a history of replies.)

Kant, Immanuel (1963) *Critique of Pure Reason*. Trans. Norman Kemp Smith. New York: St. Martin's Press. (Kant's critique of the ontological argument is found in Book II, Chapter 3.)

Leftow, Brian (2005) "The Ontological Argument," in William J. Wainwright, ed. *The Oxford Handbook of Religious Diversity*. Oxford: Oxford University Press, 80–115. (Synopses and analyses of several versions of the ontological argument.)

Lowe, E. J. (2007) "The Ontological Argument," in Chad Meister and Paul Copan., eds. *The Routledge Companion to Philosophy of Religion*. London: Routledge. (A clear, concise and supportive overview of the argument.)

Martin, Michael (1990) *Atheism: A Philosophical Justification*. Philadelphia, PA: Temple University Press. (A magisterial critique of theism; Chapter 3 includes responses to different versions of the ontological argument.)

Oppy, Graham (1995) *Ontological Arguments and Belief in God*. Cambridge: Cambridge University Press. (Contains detailed reconstructions of historical forms of the ontological argument along with objections.)

Oppy, Graham (2008) "The Ontological Argument," in Paul Copan and Chad Meister, eds. *Philosophy of Religion: Classic and Contemporary Issues.* Oxford: Blackwell. (A valuable and terse overview and analysis of several different versions of the argument by a leading philosopher of religion.)

Plantinga, Alvin, ed. (1965) *The Ontological Argument*. Garden City, NY: Doubleday. (A collection of important works on ontological arguments.)

Plantinga, Alvin (1974) *The Nature of Necessity*. Oxford: Clarendon Press. (Includes a version of the ontological argument developed utilizing modal logic.)

WEBSITES

http://www.wakeup.org/anadolu/08/2/ontological.html

Website of the "Ontological Argument Revisited by Two Ottoman Muslim Scholars," Prepared by Ümit Dericioglu.

http://www.fordham.edu/halsall/basis/anselm-critics.html

"Philosophers' Criticisms of Anselm's Ontological Argument for the Being of God." Part of the *Internet Medieval Source Book* – a collection of public domain and copy-permitted texts related to medieval and Byzantine history.

http://plato.stanford.edu/entries/ontological-arguments/

Encyclopedia article on the ontological argument by Graham Oppy; *Stanford Encyclopedia of Philosophy*.

http://www.infidels.org/library/modern/theism/ontological.html

Infidels.org website which contains a number of essays and links offering rebuttals to versions of the ontological argument.

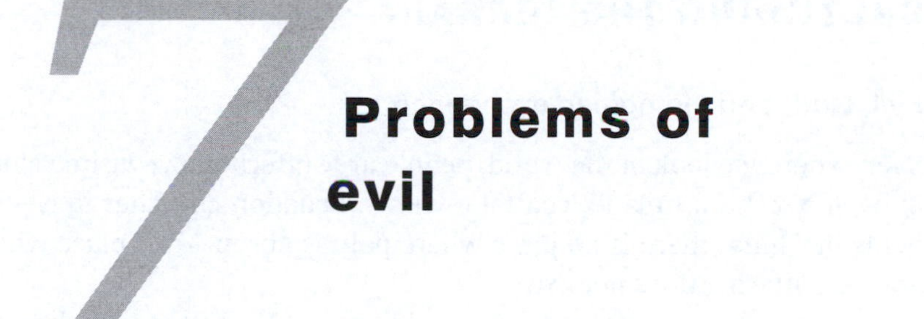

7 Problems of evil

SKETCHING THE TERRAIN

Evil, God, and the human experience

Everywhere we look in the world, people are suffering. I've visited slums in Calcutta, pubs in Northern Ireland, coastal towns in Ecuador, churches in New York City, rice fields in China; there is no place where pain is absent – no place where human and animal suffering does not exist.

In some ways it seems that our world has gotten better over the eons since *Homo sapiens* first emerged on planet Earth. Indeed, there has been solid progress, especially in harnessing nature. And much of the barbarism of ancient times seems to have waned overall. But the world is certainly no utopia…not yet, anyway. The twentieth century experienced terrible human atrocities. In that century, for example, close to half a billion people died from smallpox; over 200 million lives were spent in war and *democide* (the murder of people by a government);[1] and roughly twelve million died from AIDS – most of them in the last fifteen years of the century.[2]

There is always the hope that a new century will bring peace, prosperity, and the eradication of persisting evils. But the reality is that it may well be a hope unfulfilled. Most of us have the *desire*, but if only we had the *ability* to remove the turmoil in the world, we would do so in a heartbeat. If only we had the power, evil and misery would be gone in a flash.

But wait! Many believe that there is someone who has not only the desire but the knowledge and the power to forever remove the evil and suffering which exist in the world. For most theists, there is a God who exists as an all-powerful, all-knowing, and wholly good being. Certainly if this kind of being exists, he/she would destroy evil and suffering. So why does it persist? Philosophical skeptic David Hume recognized this problem and expressed it concisely:

> Is [God] willing to prevent evil, but not able? Then he is impotent. Is he able, but not willing? Then he is malevolent. Is he both able and willing? Whence then is evil?[3]

This is one important version of the problem of evil. The roots of this argument go as far back as the ancient Greek philosopher Epicurus (341–270 BCE), and the problem has taken on many forms throughout the centuries.

In this chapter we will examine the problem of evil in some of its most important manifestations – both the problem itself and various responses and solutions which have been offered historically and in recent times. Before moving on to the arguments themselves, however, let's first sketch some of the central issues relevant to the debate.

Classifying evil

Some familiar terms are fairly easy to understand but almost impossible to define. Take the word "game," for example. As Ludwig Wittgenstein pointed out, it is virtually impossible to define this word, even though we usually have no problem picking out a game from some other activity or event.[4] (If you doubt the difficulty of defining "game," just try to offer a definition that includes only games and excludes everything else.) Many other words are like this, including the term "evil." While a number of definitions of "evil" have been offered over the centuries, debates about how it should be defined are endless. So, rather than attempting to offer a formal definition, we will use familiar examples of what are commonly taken to be evils as our standard and guide. Here, then, are some common examples of evil: natural catastrophes such as earthquakes, hurricanes, and forest fires in which innocent life is killed; intense suffering and pain such as a child being beaten to death by a barbaric tribal enemy, or a pregnant woman dying from cancer, or a zebra being eaten alive by a lion; physical, mental, or emotional impairments such as being born with a cleft pallet, or having borderline personality disorder, or experiencing weakness of will at a crucial moment, and so on. Evil comes in all variety of shapes and sizes. Given this fact, philosophers have classified evil in various ways, and one of the most common classifications is distinguishing between natural evil and moral evil.

Natural and moral evil

John Hick offers a very concise description of this distinction when he writes: "Moral evil is what we human beings originate: cruel, unjust, vicious, and pervasive thoughts and deeds. Natural evil is the evil that originates independently of human actions: in disease…earthquakes, storms, droughts, tornadoes, etc."[5] Moral evil is the kind of evil for which a moral agent is morally responsible, including both actions (such as lying, raping, murdering, etc.) and character traits (such as maliciousness, greed, envy, and so on). Natural evil includes those events for which moral agents are not responsible.

Natural evil: evil which results from natural phenomena and is not brought about by the free will of a moral agent. It includes natural disasters and certain human illnesses.

Moral Evil: evil which results from a moral agent misusing his or her free will such that the agent is blameworthy for it. It includes human actions as well as character traits.

Horrendous and gratuitous evil

As I'm writing this chapter, I discovered that a dear colleague was diagnosed with stage three breast cancer. She has a husband and two small children and, given the odds, she doesn't stand a great chance of living more than five more years or so. Why did this happen? Why her? Why now? What can be gained from her going through several years of chemotherapy, pain, and the terrible thought of leaving her husband and children without a wife and mother?

I also just read in the local newspaper that a mother of several children was backing out of her driveway, unaware that her three-year-old daughter went out of the house and walked behind her vehicle. The mother inadvertently backed over the little girl, killing her in the process. Don't these events sound rather pointless? And if God – an omnipotent (all-powerful), omniscient (all-knowing), and omnibenevolent (wholly-good) being – exists, why would he let them happen? What's the point? These are examples of gratuitous evil, and they are innumerable.

There are also examples of evil of a different sort – what are referred to as horrendous evil. These are horrific evils which, when experienced by a person, give her reason to doubt that her life as experienced could be taken to be a great

The Bambi case (gratuitous evil): suppose in some distant forest lightning strikes a dead tree, resulting in a forest fire. In the fire a fawn is trapped, horribly burned, and lies in terrible agony for several days before death relieves its suffering. So far as we can see, the fawn's intense suffering is pointless. For there does not appear to be any greater good such that the prevention of the fawn's suffering would require either the loss of that good or the occurrence of an evil equally bad or worse. Nor does there seem to be any equally bad or worse evil so connected to the fawn's suffering that it would have had to occur had the fawn's suffering been prevented. Could an omnipotent, omniscient being have prevented the fawn's apparently pointless suffering? The answer is obvious, as even the theist will insist. An omnipotent, omniscient being could have easily prevented the fawn from being horribly burned, or, given the burning, could have spared the fawn the intense suffering by quickly ending its life, rather than allowing the fawn to lie in terrible agony for several days. Since the fawn's intense suffering was preventable and, so far as we can see, pointless, doesn't it appear that...there do exist instances of intense suffering which an omnipotent, omniscient being could have prevented without thereby losing some greater good or permitting some evil equally bad or worse[?]

good to her on the whole. Philosopher Marilyn McCord Adams offers examples of horrendous evils, including the rape of a woman and axing off of her arms, slow death by starvation, and having to choose which of one's children shall live and which will be killed by terrorists.[6] Two illustrious examples are commonly used to exemplify gratuitous and horrendous evil – examples referred to as the Bambi and Sue cases. The Bambi case was offered by William Rowe[7] and the Sue case by Bruce Russell[8] (see boxes). The Bambi case appears to be gratuitous (there seems to be no point to its occurrence), and the Sue case appears to be horrendous (you would be hard pressed to find a more grisly example of horrific violence in which the victim could legitimately question whether, given this evil, her short life could be taken overall to be a great good to her).

There are different ways of expressing the problems which exist, given evils like these and the alleged existence of an omnipotent, omniscient, and omnibenevolent

The Sue case (horrendous evil): in the early hours of New Year's Day, 1986, a little girl was brutally beaten, raped, and then strangled in Flint, Michigan. The girl's mother was living with her boyfriend, another man who was unemployed, and her three children including a nine-month-old infant fathered by her boyfriend.

On New Year's Eve, all three adults went drinking at a bar near the woman's home. The boyfriend, who had been taking drugs and drinking heavily, was asked to leave the bar at 8:00 p.m. After several reappearances he finally left for good at about 9:30 p.m. The woman and the unemployed man remained at the bar until 2:00 a.m. at which time the woman went home and the man went to a party at a neighbor's home. Perhaps out of jealousy, the boyfriend attacked the woman when she entered the house. Her brother intervened, hitting the boyfriend and leaving him passed out and slumped over a table. The brother left. Later, the boyfriend attacked the woman again and this time she knocked him unconscious. After checking on the children, she went to bed.

Later, the woman's five-year-old daughter went downstairs to go to the bathroom. The unemployed man testified that when he returned from the party at 3:45 a.m. he found the five-year-old dead. At his trial, the boyfriend was acquitted of the crime because his lawyer cast doubt on the innocence of the unemployed man. But the little girl was raped, severely beaten over most of her body, and strangled by one of those men that night.

God. We will next explore two different types of problem – theoretical and existential – followed up by various objections and responses to them.

THEORETICAL PROBLEMS OF EVIL

The logical problem of evil

As the title of the chapter indicates, there isn't simply one problem of evil; the problems are many and multifarious. Most of the problems stem from the following two beliefs: (1) God – an omnipotent, omniscient, and omnibenevolent being – exists and (2) evil – in its many manifestations – exists.

In one way or another, there seems to be an inconsistency with affirming both of these beliefs. One form of the problem claims that propositions 1 and 2 in the "Logical problem of evil" box are logically inconsistent. This claim itself has taken a variety of forms, but the general structure of the argument can be put as follows:

In response, theists have generally attempted to demonstrate that either premise 2, 4, or 5 is not necessarily true. For conclusion 7 to follow logically from premises 1–6, each one of them would need to be true. If one or more of them is false, however, or if there is good reason to doubt the truth of one or more of them, this causes the entire argument to be suspect.

Reply 1: the "impossible to prove otherwise" argument

One reply is that the logical problem of evil doesn't work because, in order for it to succeed, it must be demonstrated that God has no morally good reason to allow any particular evil to exist. But establishing that the existence of a particular evil and the

THE LOGICAL PROBLEM OF EVIL

1 If God exists, then God is omnipotent (all-powerful), omniscient (all-knowing), and omnibenevolent (wholly-good).
2 An omnipotent being would have the power to eliminate evil.
3 An omniscient being would have the knowledge to eliminate evil.
4 An omnibenevolent being would have the desire to eliminate evil.
5 An omnipotent, omniscient, and omnibenevolent being would eliminate evil.
6 Evil exists.
7 Therefore, God (an omnipotent, omniscient, and omnibenevolent being) does not exist.

existence of God are incompatible cannot be accomplished. Consider these words by Paul Draper (a proponent of the problem of evil and no adherent of theism):

> To understand why this is so, it is crucial to understand that the inability to produce things like round circles that are logically impossible to produce or to know statements like 2 + 3 = 10 that are logically impossible to know does not count as a *lack* of power or a *lack* of knowledge. In other words, not even an all-powerful and all-knowing being can have more power or more knowledge than it is logically possible for a being to have. Suppose, then, that some good, G, that is worth my suffering…logically implies that I suffer (or that God permits me to suffer). This certainly seems possible (epistemically).... Such goods would be known to an all-knowing being even if they are beyond our ken. Further, if there are such goods, then not even an all-powerful and all-knowing being could produce them without allowing me to suffer and hence even an all-powerful and all-knowing being could have a good moral reason to permit my suffering.[9]

We can even imagine cases where some evil may be necessary for good to result. For example, showing forgiveness to one who has evilly harmed you and is repentant, or showing courage in the face of torture, both logically require that I was harmed and tortured. Whether or not these are good examples is beside the point; it is logically possible that certain goods justify certain evils, and it is impossible to prove otherwise.

Reply 2: The free will defense

In the literature on God and evil, a distinction is often made between a defense and a theodicy. A *defense* is a response to antitheistic arguments from evil, and its aim is to demonstrate that such arguments fail. A *theodicy* is an attempt to account for why God is justified in allowing suffering and evil. Defenses are offered in response to a variety of arguments from evil, but they are typically coupled with logical arguments. We will first examine a prominent defense and then later explore several theodicies.

One important version of the free will defense is offered by Alvin Plantinga, and in truncated form it goes something like this:[10] It is possible that God, even being omnipotent, could not create a world with free creatures who never choose evil. Furthermore, it is possible that God, even being omnibenevolent, would desire to create a world which contains evil if moral goodness requires free moral creatures. Here is how Plantinga expresses the response in preliminary form:[11]

> A world containing creatures who are significantly free (and freely perform more good than evil actions) is more valuable, all else being equal, than a world containing no free creatures at all. Now God can create free creatures, but He can't *cause* or *determine* them to do only what is right. For if He does so, then they

> aren't significantly free after all; they do not do what is right *freely*. To create creatures capable of *moral good*, therefore, He must create creatures capable of moral evil; and He can't give these creatures the freedom to perform evil and at the same time prevent them from doing so. As it turned out, sadly enough, some of the free creatures God created went wrong in the exercise of their freedom; this is the source of moral evil. The fact that free creatures sometimes go wrong, however, counts neither against God's omnipotence nor against His goodness; for He could have forestalled the occurrence of moral evil only by removing the possibility of moral good.

So the logical argument from evil is unsuccessful because it is at least logically possible that God (an omnipotent and omnibenevolent being) could have created a world with free creatures and yet be unable to ensure that this world would have no evil in it. Thus premises 2 and 5 may be false, and so the conclusion does not necessarily follow; the argument is flawed.[12]

Critics of Plantinga's argument, such as atheist philosopher J. L. Mackie, have responded by maintaining that it presupposes an incompatibilist view of free will (whereby free will is incompatible with determinism – human or divine), and that a compatibilist view is much more plausible. Given a compatibilist notion of free will, God could create "free" creatures who do no evil, for he could *determine* every one of their actions. Currently, however, most philosophers have agreed that the free will defense has defeated the logical problem of evil. For even if one grants that compatibilism is true, Plantinga offers the argument as a *logical possibility* only. As long as it is logically possible that incompatibilism is true, then the necessary conclusion of the logical problem of evil is undercut.

Another point in support of the logical problem of evil is that while Plantinga's argument may succeed in undercutting the point that *moral* evil is inconsistent with the existence of God, it does not address the problem of *natural* evil, for the evils of nature are not brought about by free creaturely choices. Plantinga's response is to suggest that it is at least logically possible (although he isn't affirming or denying the truth of the matter) that perhaps free, nonhuman persons are responsible for natural evils (e.g. rebellious spirits or fallen angels). As long as this is a logical possibility, the claim that the existence of God and natural evils are inconsistent is rebutted.

Because of these and other replies, it is now widely accepted that the logical problem of evil has been sufficiently rebutted.

The evidential problem of evil

While the logical problem of evil has, many now believe, for all intents and purposes been rebutted, this has not left the atheist empty-handed in terms of an argument against belief in God given the facts of evil. One further type of argument attempts to demonstrate that the existence of evil counts against rational belief in God, even though the existence of the two is not logically inconsistent. This argument, also dubbed the "probabilistic problem of evil,"[13] comes in many forms, but the essence of it is that if the God of theism exists, he would probably not create a world like ours – a world filled with all of the horrendous and gratuitous evil we find in it. Since our world exists, such a God probably doesn't.

The probabilistic problem

The general structure of the argument can be put as in the box below.[14]

Unlike the conclusion of the logical problem of evil, this argument concludes by claiming that it is *improbable* that God exists rather than that it is *necessarily true* that God doesn't exist. This argument takes on special force when reflecting on the depths of evil which exist, such as the apparently gratuitous and horrendous evils mentioned at the beginning of this chapter. Isn't it more likely that God doesn't exist given the existence of these kinds of evils?

REPLY 1: LEIBNIZ'S LAPSE

Plantinga has responded to this argument by claiming that it is unsound, for it incorporates what he calls "Leibniz's Lapse."[15] The objection here is that premise 2 is possibly false. Contrary to the notion of Gottfried Leibniz that our world is the best of all (logically) possible worlds, it could be that God, although omnipotent, is

THE PROBABILISTIC PROBLEM

1 If God exists, then God is omnipotent, omniscient, and omnibenevolent.
2 An omnipotent, omniscient, and omnibenevolent being could create any logically possible world.
3 If an omnipotent, omniscient, and omnibenevolent being were to create a world, such a being would create the best of all possible worlds.
4 An omnipotent, omniscient, and omnibenevolent being would have the power, knowledge, and desire to prevent evil and suffering in the best of all possible worlds.
5 It is improbable that the world which exists (i.e. our world), which is filled with large amounts of horrendous and gratuitous evil, is the best of all possible worlds.
6 Therefore, it is improbable that God, an omnipotent, omniscient, and omnibenevolent being, exists.

not able to bring about just *any* logically possible world. If persons have libertarian free will, as described above, then there are certain worlds that even an all-powerful being could not create.[16]

Consider the following example. Suppose that the CEO of a large utility firm, we'll call him "Bob," is presented by his accountants with the fact that the company is in serious financial trouble. Suppose further that in discussions with Dave, his top accountant, Bob realizes that by shredding some documents, and making up a few white lies, he can bluff his way out of the situation and convince his stockholders that the company is doing exceptionally well. After a few years of this, he supposes, all will be well.

Now consider these two scenarios: (1) if Ron had been offered the chance by his accountant to shred documents and cover up the debt, he would have accepted the offer, and (2) if Ron had been offered the chance by his accountant to shred documents and cover up the debt, he would have rejected the offer.

Now, consider two possible worlds, *W* and *W**, which have Ron in them and are identical up to the point where Ron is offered the chance to shred documents and cover up the debt. Suppose that in *W* he accepts the offer and in *W** he does not accept it. Plantinga's point then is that whether *W* or *W** become actual is partly up to God and partly up to Ron. Given Ron's free will, if Ron accepts the offer to do wrong, then God could not have brought it about that Ron rejects the offer – God could not have brought about *W**.

Of course, much depends here on whether one accepts or rejects the libertarian view of free will. But if libertarianism is even *possible*, then premise 2 loses its force, and so too does the conclusion.[17]

REPLY 2: THERE IS NO BEST OF ALL POSSIBLE WORLDS

A second reply to the probabilistic problem of evil is that it presupposes that there is, in fact, a best of all possible worlds. However, according to a number of philosophers, there cannot be a best of all possible worlds. Consider this: for any best of all possible worlds imaginable, one could always imagine just one more good thing in that world (one more good apple, for example, or more "deliriously happy sentient creatures"[18]). If this is the case, then there could be a better world than the alleged best of all possible worlds, which is impossible.

One response to this objection is that while it may be the case that one could conceive of such a scenario, it does not follow that it could (metaphysically) happen. There could be reasons why adding one more good thing would not make a particular world better than it is.

ROWE'S EVIDENTIAL ARGUMENT FROM EVIL

1 Large amounts of horrendous and gratuitous evil exist which an omnipotent, omniscient, and omnibenevolent being *could* have prevented without losing some greater good or permitting some equally bad or worse evil.
2 An omnipotent, omniscient, and omnibenevolent being *would* have prevented the horrendous and gratuitous evils which exist, unless that being could not do so without losing some greater good or permitting some equally bad or worse evil.
3 Therefore, an omnipotent, omniscient, and omnibenevolent being does not exist.

Rowe's evidential argument

Another type of evidential/probability argument which attempts to avoid the criticisms of the probabilistic argument presented above has been offered by philosopher William Rowe. Here is his argument, offered in slightly modified form, is shown in the box above.

At first glance it appears that the theist would agree with both premises. However, since this argument is in a valid form, if one agrees with the two premises, then the conclusion necessarily follows – an omnipotent, omniscient, and omnibenevolent being does not exist. What is the theist to do?

OBJECTION 1: COGNITIVE EPISTEMIC LIMITATIONS

One objection to Rowe's argument is that since we are finite, limited human beings, we are simply not in an appropriate epistemic position to make a legitimate assessment about what an omniscient, omnipotent, and omnibenevolent being could or would do in any given situation, including situations where evil exists. Given our obvious temporal and spatial limitations, that is, we simply cannot justifiably make moral judgments about God.[19]

OBJECTION 2: GOD CAN USE EVIL AND SUFFERING FOR OUR GREATER GOOD

A second objection is that there may well be neither gratuitous nor horrendous evil as defined above. For example, after describing his personal journey through what seemed to him at first as gratuitous evil in his life and that of his family, philosopher John Feinberg offers ten "uses of suffering" in which a *Christian* theist might take comfort. We cannot delineate them here, but they include God's allowing pain in order to provide an opportunity to demonstrate true or genuine faith and to promote maturity in life.[20], [21]

OBJECTION 3: GRATUITOUS EVIL IS CONSISTENT WITH THEISM

A third objection has been proposed recently by adherents of open theism (discussed in Chapter 3). On this view, the existence of gratuitous (and perhaps horrendous) evil is not incompatible with theism. Open theists maintain (as do a number of traditional theists) that free will must be of an incompatibilist sort in order to be morally significant, and so it was good for God to create human beings with free will. But this freedom entails the possibility of free agents choosing both goods and evils. Neither God's omnipotence nor omniscience could preclude the existence of evil – even gratuitous evil – since real contingency turns out to be a part of the universe.[22]

THE EXISTENTIAL PROBLEM OF EVIL

The existential problem of evil (which is called by different names, including the "religious problem," "moral problem," "pastoral problem," "psychological problem," and "emotional problem"), is not easy to define or delineate. Simply put, it is the notion that the existential feel of certain kinds of evil leads to disbelief in God or religious belief in general. An example may clarify the meaning and power of the problem.

Some time ago I was with a group of friends waiting in line at a restaurant. We were engaged in a fairly sophisticated theological discussion (granted, I have unusual friends!) when a young woman standing ahead of us asked if we were talking about God. "Yes, we are," I said. "We're actually discussing the nature and attributes of God." "Well," she said, "I quit believing in God two years ago. While my dad was suffering and dying of cancer, I decided that I could no longer believe in God." As she said these words, she became emotional. I could almost feel her pain as tears began to stream down her face in her agony over her lost father and the pain he must have went through. This, no doubt, is a clear case of the existential problem of evil.

Furthermore, when considering the horrendous and gratuitous evils noted at the beginning of this chapter (especially if one has personally gone through such experiences), it is no surprise that people claim to be unable to view the world theistically – to be unable to believe in, let alone adore and worship, a personal God.

Reply

A common reply to the experiential problem of evil is that the "problem" here is not really an *argument* at all, and thus is not in need of a logical, rational response.

When an individual is personally confronted with significant evil and suffering, that is to say, the main thing she needs is not a logical or theoretical response, but rather care, sympathy, and friendship. As Plantinga puts it, in those moments of pain a person needs not "philosophical enlightenment," but "pastoral care."[23] Philosopher and theologian John Feinberg clarifies:

> Think of a young child who goes out to play on a playground. Sometime during her play, she falls and skins her knee. She runs to her mother for comfort. Now, her mother can do any number of things. She can tell her daughter that this has happened because she was running too fast and not watching where she was going. She must be more careful next time. The mother, if she knew them, might even explain the laws of physics and causation that were operating to make her child's scrape just the size and shape it is. The mother might even expound for a few moments on the lessons *God* is trying to teach her child from this experience.

If she then pauses and asks her daughter, "Do you understand, Sweetheart?" don't be surprised if the little girl replies, "Yes, Mommy, but it still hurts!" All the explanation at that moment doesn't stop her pain. The child doesn't need a discourse; she needs her mother's hugs and kisses. There will be a time for the discourse later; now she needs comfort.[24]

THREE THEODICIES

While pastoral care may well be an important element in responding to those experiencing pain and suffering, it does nothing to address the lingering theoretical problems noted above. Are there ways of actually explaining why God would permit evil in the world? There are, indeed. There have been a number of attempts to justify God and God's ways given the reality of evil. Such responses are called theodicies, and next we will examine three important ones.

Augustine's free will theodicy

As noted earlier, a theodicy is different from a defense in that the aim of a theodicy is to justify God and God's ways given the existence of evil in a world created by God, whereas a defense is an attempt to demonstrate that the antitheistic arguments from evil are unsuccessful. There are different types of theodicies, and one of the most historically significant is that offered by the great theologian and Church Father, St. Augustine. It's referred to as the *free will theodicy*, and one way of delineating it is shown in the box overleaf.[25]

AUGUSTINE'S FREE WILL THEODICY

1. God created the universe, and everything in it was good.
2. Some of God's creation – namely *persons* – were given the good gift of freedom of the will (having freedom of the will in the universe is better than not having it, since a moral universe requires it, and a moral universe is better than a non-moral or amoral universe).
3. Some of these created persons – first angels, and then human beings – freely chose to turn from God's goodness; that is, they "sinned" and fell from their state of perfection (i.e. the "Fall" of humanity).
4. This turning of the will, or sinning, brought moral and natural evil into the universe.
5. Evil, though brought about by created persons, is not a thing or entity; it is a metaphysical deprivation, or lack, or privation, of the good (a *privatio boni*).
6. God will finally rectify evil when he judges the world, ushering into his eternal kingdom those persons who have been saved through Christ and sending to eternal hell those persons who are wicked and disobedient.

This has been the most utilized theodicy in the West since the fifth century of the common era, and it is still widely used today.[26] It has also been extensively criticized. Two objections are as follows.

Objections

For Augustine, God is entirely sovereign and not subject to the choices and whims of fallible and finite persons. But if God is sovereign, how did evil emerge in his universe? There appears to be a conflict between Augustine's free will defense on the one hand and his view of God on the other. For it seems that God, understood this

St. Augustine (354–430 CE) has been one of the most influential Christian philosophers, theologians, and Church Fathers in history. His spiritual pilgrimage led him from skepticism as a young adult to Bishop of Hippo in his later years. His work on human freedom spanned his career, and virtually every medieval philosopher of renown in the Christian West interacted with Augustine's work on free will and related issues such as divine foreknowledge, predestination, and grace. His most important philosophical works include the *City of God*, *On the Free Choice of the Will*, and his autobiography, the *Confessions*.

Theodicy: the word "theodicy" comes from two Greek terms – *theos* (God), and *dikei* (justice). A theodicy is an attempt to vindicate the goodness and justice of God given the reality of evil.

way, could have created persons who are spiritual saints and thus always choose the good. So why did they choose to sin?

Furthermore, how could an omnibenevolent being create a hell where countless persons will spend eternity in suffering and agony? There seems to be a conflict here between God's sovereignty and God's goodness.

Hick's Irenaean or soul-making theodicy

Based on the work of Irenaeus (c. 130–c.202 CE), an early Christian bishop, John Hick has developed a theodicy which is in stark contrast to the Augustinian type. Instead of God creating a paradise with perfect human beings who then fell into sin, the Irenaean theodicy has it the other way round. God created good but undeveloped persons, for moral maturity requires experiencing trials and hardships in life. The existence of evil, then, is not the result of perfect persons choosing to sin, but rather is a necessary element of the process of developing immature human (and perhaps other) persons into spiritually and morally mature beings, and evil is a part of God's soul-making strategy. The theodicy can be expressed as in the "An Irenaean (soul-making) theodicy" box overleaf.'

Objections

A number of objections have been offered to Hick's soul-making theodicy. One of them focuses on the apparent contrary evidence. Many people do not improve through the hardships that they endure; oftentimes the difficulties in one's life cause his life to end in utter tragedy. A quick glance at the evening news on virtually any day will provide ample demonstration of this point. A defender of the theodicy could respond that this present life isn't all there is, and God will have eons of time to work on an individual who responds poorly now. But of course this relies on the further belief in an afterlife – something not abounding with empirical evidential support.

Another objection to the soul-making theodicy is that it seems to be a rather brutish way for God to mature souls. To suggest that all of the suffering and pain – all of the horrendous evils – ever experienced throughout history was the result of God's grand cosmic intent, makes God appear somewhat less than the omnipotent, omniscient, and omnibenevolent being most theists take God to be.

AN IRENAEAN (SOUL-MAKING) THEODICY

1. God created the world as a good place (but not paradise) for developing human persons both spiritually and morally.
2. Through evolutionary means, God brought about human persons with freedom of the will and the capacity to mature in love and goodness.
3. Evil is the result of both the creation of a good soul-making world and of human choice to sin.
4. By placing human persons in this challenging environment, through their own free responses they have the opportunity to choose what is right and good and thus to gradually grow into the mature persons (exhibiting the virtues of patience, courage, and generosity, for example) that God desires them to be.
5. God will continue to work with human persons, even in the afterlife if necessary, by allowing them opportunities to love and choose the good, such that in the eschaton everyone will be brought into a right relationship with God.

A process theodicy

Process theology (and philosophy) was first developed by Alfred North Whitehead (1861–1947). It was further developed by Charles Hartshorne (1897–2000) and more recently by John Cobb, Jr. (1925–). It is based on the foundational premise that God and the world are in flux. While God is not the world (this is pantheism), God *participates* in the world (this is panentheism) – God and the world are in process together. God not only acts on the world, but is also acted on. All things, including God, are in the process of *becoming* rather than statically *being*. In this process of becoming, entities respond to each moment by making choices, and these choices are real and significant; they are never lost but are continually added to God's overall experience. God learns from such experiences, and thus is ever growing in knowledge and understanding. This view of God's knowledge is clearly in contrast to traditional theology in which God's omniscience is eternally complete and exhaustive.

Also, on the process view, God's omnipotence is rejected. God's power is not understood to be infinite, but limited as other free entities, such as human persons, also have the power to make their own choices. Furthermore, God's power is persuasive rather than coercive; God does not force creatures to do the good, but attempts to lure them in the right direction. Unfortunately, they cannot always be so lured, and sometimes they make the wrong choices; sometimes they do evil things. But all entities, including God, continue to evolve, and the hope is that eventually all evil will be eradicated as free creatures learn from prior experiences (their own and those of history) what is ultimately good and right.

A PROCESS THEODICY

1 God is not the transcendent creator who created the world *ex nihilo* (out of nothing), but is God-in-the-world; this is panentheism in which everything is *in* God but not everything *is* God.
2 God is neither omniscient nor omnipotent in the traditional sense; God's power is shared with other entities and God's knowledge increases as his experiences increase.
3 The universe is characterized by evolution, process, and change, some of which has been brought about by the self-determined free choices of entities including God and finite persons.
4 Some of the choices made by human persons are good and some are evil. There is the hope that evil will continue to be engulfed as all experiences are synthesized in God's own conscious life.

We can outline the process theodicy as in the box above.[27]

Objections

Various objections and criticisms have been offered to process thought and its attending theodicy, and we will briefly note three of them. First, the typical process critique of the traditional understanding of divine power has been called into question. While one strain of Calvinistic theology includes God's power as being exclusive and entailing absolute sovereign determination of all events, this is certainly not the only, nor even the most common, understanding of divine power. So this process critique is ill-placed against most traditional notions of omnipotence. On the other hand, the process critique of traditional theology which affirms human free will, and thus a limitation of sorts on God's power, is arguably weak. For example, in response to a free will theodicy, process philosophers have claimed that such a view allows that God could eliminate any particular free-will-oriented evil that happens, but he doesn't. Thus, God could stop a rapist before raping, cause a terrorist bomb to malfunction, or make certain that a thief is caught before escaping. Since God could do such things without interrupting free will but doesn't, they argue, God is not really good on this account. However, defenders of the free will theodicy respond by arguing that a type of free will which disallows one's actions to be effectual is not truly free will after all. So their objection isn't warranted.

A second objection has to do with the process denial of creation *ex nihilo*. On the process account, the world was not created by God out of nothing. There are various explanations for the existence of the world by process thinkers, but a common one is that it is eternal; it never began to exist. However, this view contradicts the standard big bang model of the universe which is currently widely held by cosmologists and astronomers. Of course the verdict on this issue is still out (for more on this topic, see Chapter 4).

A final objection is that the process theodicy does not really seem to be much of a theodicy. God is too impotent to eliminate the evils in the world as God has neither the knowledge nor the power to ultimately take care of the problem. Further, many see evil and suffering in the world as getting worse, not better. While God always does the best he can on the process view, it doesn't seem that he's doing very much, for evil abounds. Nor does it appear that God is improving in his ability to evolve a better world. Given this, without the eschatological hope of a final elimination of evil, the word "theodicy" here may be a misnomer.[28]

SUMMARY

In this chapter we examined various aspects of the problem of evil. After describing some significant terms and concepts in discussions of evil, I noted that there are a number of "problems," not just one, and I divided them into two categories: theoretical and existential. I then delineated three theoretical problems: logical, probabilistic, and Rowe's evidential argument. We examined each of these arguments as well as objections to them and responses to many of the objections. We looked at the free will defense and the "impossible to prove otherwise" response – two responses to the logical argument, and noted that they have proven rather effective in rebutting the argument.

Next, we noted the existential problem of evil and saw that while people often disbelieve in God due to the existential angst during times of experiencing evil, this is not an argument per se against theism. Thus, what's often needed in such cases is not rational argument but pastoral care. However, while pastoral care is often helpful and necessary, this obviously does not address the theoretical aspect of the problem. So, we next examined three theodicies – attempts to justify God given the evil in the world: the Augustinian, Irenaean, and process theodicies.

The problem of evil has been around for a very long time, and many people have put much thought into accounting for its (apparent) reality. No one has yet provided a solution that is universally satisfactory. Perhaps requiring such is to expect more than is within the realm of human possibility.

QUESTIONS FOR REVIEW/DISCUSSION

1. What is the problem of evil? Why is it a problem, and who is it a problem for?
2. Explain the logical problem of evil. Does the free will defense answer the theistic burden satisfactorily? Why or why not?
3. What is horrendous evil? What is its relevance to the problem of evil?
4. What is gratuitous evil? What is its relevance to the problem of evil?
5. Which of the theoretical problems of evil do you find most compelling? Are the solutions offered satisfactory? Explain.
6. Some Christian philosophers, including Marilyn Adams, have argued that an adequate response to evil should include a discussion of God becoming human (the incarnation of Christ) and suffering horrendous evil (through Christ's crucifixion), thus identifying with human pain and suffering. Do you think this idea would provide solace to one experiencing terrible evil? Why or why not?
7. What is the difference between a defense and a theodicy?
8. Explain the difference between Augustine's and Hick's theodicies. Can they both be consistently affirmed? Explain.
9. Is evil a problem for the atheist? Why or why not?
10. Explore the way a particular non-theistic worldview accounts for evil and suffering. What are some similarities with this way of understanding evil and suffering and theistic descriptions? What are some differences?

FURTHER READING

Adams, Marilyn M. (1999) *Horrendous Evils and the Goodness of God*. Ithaca, NY: Cornell University Press. (A comprehensive analysis of the problem of horrendous evil by a careful thinker.)

Adams, Marilyn M. and Robert M. Adams (1990) *The Problem of Evil*. New York: Oxford University Press. (A scholarly collection of essays from a variety of perspectives by leading philosophers.)

Bowker, John (1970) *Problems of Suffering in the Religions of the World*. Cambridge: Cambridge University Press. (An accessible and well-researched study on suffering in the major world religions.)

Davis, Stephen T., ed. (2001) *Encountering Evil: Live Options in Theodicy*. New edn. Louisville, KY: Westminster John Knox Press. (A revised edition of a classic work in theodicy from different philosophical and theological perspectives; includes essays, critiques, and rejoinders.)

Feinberg, John S. (2004) *The Many Faces of Evil: Theological Systems and the Problem of Evil*. 3rd edition. Wheaton, IL: Crossway. (Presents a philosophical/theological framework of theodicy.)

Hick, John (1978) *Evil and the God of Love*. 2nd edition. New York: Harper & Row. (Presents the soul-making theodicy discussed in this chapter; a classic in philosophy of religion.)

Howard-Snyder, Daniel, ed. (1996) *The Evidential Argument from Evil*. Bloomington, IN: Indiana University Press. (Includes sixteen essays on evil by eminent philosophers and theologians.)

Hume, David (1955) *Dialogues Concerning Natural Religion*. Parts 10 and 11. Ed. H. D. Aiken. New York: Hafner Publishing. (A classic work in philosophy of religion; includes a discussion among three fictional characters concerning the nature of God, and raises the issue of evil and suffering).

Lewis, C. S. (1962) *The Problem of Pain*. New York: Macmillan. (Lewis focuses on the value of pain and suffering as God's "megaphone" to rouse a morally deaf world.)

Ling, Trevor (1977) *Buddhism and the Mythology of Evil: A Study in Theravada Buddhism*. Oxford: Oneworld. (Examines myths of evil in Buddhist depictions of human existence and flourishing.)

Mackie, J. L. (1982) *The Miracle of Theism*. Oxford: Clarendon Press. (See especially his chapter on the problem of evil.)

Martin, Michael (1990) *Atheism*. Philadelphia, PA: Temple University Press. (Includes a wide-ranging critique of theistic responses to the problem of evil; note especially Chapters 14–17.)

Peterson, Michael L. (1998) *God and Evil: An Introduction to the Issues*. Boulder, CO: Westview Press. (The best general introduction to the topic in print.)

Pike, Nelson (1963) "Hume on Evil," *Philosophical Review* 72 (2): 180–97. (An important examination of Hume's remarks on the problem of evil.)

Plantinga, Alvin (1977) *God, Freedom and Evil*. Grand Rapids, MI: Eerdmans. (A classic account of the free will defense.)

Shankara ([8th century] 1975) *Crest-Jewel of Discrimination*. Trans. Swami Prabhavananda and Christopher Isherwood. Hollywood, CA: Vedanta Press. (The clearest exposition of Advaita Vedānta Hinduism; the introduction contains a section on evil.)

WEBSITES

http://plato.stanford.edu/entries/evil/
A helpful and concise entry from the *Stanford Encyclopedia of Philosophy* on the problem of evil written by atheist Michael Tooley.

http://www.infidels.org
A website operated by the Internet Infidels, an organization dedicated to defending and promoting a naturalistic worldview; contains a number of articles on the problem of evil.

http://www.leaderu.com
Leadership University is a web-based organization that contains a number of articles in support of the theistic worldview, including articles on the problem of evil.

http://www.qsmithwmu.com/an_atheological_argument_from_evil_natural_laws_(1991).htm
A preprint of an article by atheist philosopher Quentin Smith from the *International Journal for the Philosophy of Religion*, 29 (1991): 159–74.

http://www.ac.wwu.edu~howardd/god,evil,andsuffering.pdf
A preprint of an article by Christian theist philosopher Daniel Howard-Snyder from *Reason for the Hope Within,* ed. Michael Murray, GrandRapids, MI: Eerdmans, 1999, 76–115.

8 Science, faith, and reason

In a book condemning of religion entitled *The End of Faith*, author Sam Harris begins with an example intended to shock the reader:

> The young man boards the bus as it leaves the terminal. He wears an overcoat. Beneath his overcoat, he is wearing a bomb. His pockets are filled with nails, ball bearings, and rat poison.... The young man smiles. With the press of a button he destroys himself, the couple at his side, and twenty others on the bus... . The young man's parents soon learn of his fate. Although saddened to have lost a son, they feel tremendous pride at his accomplishment. They know he has gone to heaven and prepared the way for them to follow. He has also sent his victims to hell for eternity. It is a double victory.[1]

Harris notes that it is the young man's religion, or rather his religious beliefs, that lead him to engage in this kind of horrific and devastating behavior. He goes on to list atrocities and evils enacted by religious adherents from a variety of religions throughout the centuries. The problem, for Harris and a number of others, is that religion (in all its various forms) is both irrational and dangerous. Religion is based on blind faith, and as such it leads one over the ledge of reason and into the abyss of irrationality from which terrorism and violence naturally flow. Religious faith should be eradicated and replaced by reason, Harris maintains, and the domain of reason manifested at its best and highest form is science.[2]

But is this dichotomy between religion and science, with the former based on subjective blind faith and the latter based on objective reason and evidence, correct? Can religious beliefs ever be rationally justified? Should they ever be rationally justified? Furthermore, what is the appropriate relationship between science and religion? Are they in any way compatible? There is oftentimes a clash between faith and reason, between religion and science. But must that be so? These are some of the questions and issues we will explore in this chapter.

RELIGION AND SCIENCE

Both science and religion play fundamental roles in our world today. In Chapter 1 it was noted that roughly 85 percent of the population of the world affirms some form of religious belief; religion and its effects encompass the globe. Science and the effects of science are also ubiquitous. Whether in downtown London, the hills of southern Afghanistan, or the heart of the Brazilian rainforest, radios, cell-phones, satellite television and other inventions of science are often part of common daily life. It is also the case that many religious people are scientists and that scientific experimentation is sometimes used in religion. For centuries there has been a symbiotic relationship between these two domains. However, science and religion are also often at odds with one another. Galileo's dispute with the Roman Catholic

Church about whether the earth or the sun is stationary is a memorable case in point.[3] How are we to understand the relationship between science and religion?

Before examining this relationship, let's first attempt a brief description of science (a description of religion was offered in Chapter 1): *science involves the exploration, description, explanation, and prediction of occurrences in the natural world which can be checked and supported by empirical evidence.*[4] As it turns out, the claims made by those practicing science are sometimes at odds with religious claims. So how are science and religion to relate to each other? Various options have been proposed, and for our purposes we will narrow them down to three: conflict, independence, and integration.[5]

Conflict

One way of understanding the relationship between science and religion is to see them in conflict with one another. This conflict has been evident for centuries. Perhaps the most well known of the engagements has been the creation–evolution controversy. This clash was typified in 1860 when Bishop Samuel Wilberforce (1805–1873) asked biologist Thomas Huxley (1825–1895; known as "Darwin's Bulldog" for his advocacy of the theory of evolution) whether he claimed simian descent by way of his grandfather or grandmother. Huxley's reply was just as unscrupulous, stating that he would be much happier to have an ape for a grandfather than one who distorted the truth and confused matters.[6]

What led to the conflict is, arguably, a misunderstanding of the roles and legitimate constraints of both science and religion, and the misunderstanding comes from two domains. On the one hand are the scriptural literalists who maintain that the sacred scriptures (in this case it's the Bible) give a historically accurate account of the creation of the world, from the universe itself to specific plants, animals, and the first human beings. This creation story, they maintain, conflicts with the evolutionary account of the history of flora and fauna. They cannot both be true, and scripture trumps science. On the other hand are the scientific materialists who agree that the scriptural account and the evolutionary account are in conflict; they cannot both be true. They affirm, however, that naturalistic evolution is correct and no further religious story is needed to explain the origin or flourishing of living organisms.

There are numerous challenges to this conflict view. First, scientific materialism (sometimes referred to as *scientism*) – the view that the only viable way of acquiring knowledge is via the scientific method and the only reality is material – is much more a philosophical assumption than a scientific conclusion. How, for example, by following the scientific method, can one come to the conclusion that the scientific method is the only viable way of acquiring knowledge? And how, for example, from following the scientific method, can one know that the only reality is material? Following the dictates of science leads to neither conclusion.

Second, many theologians and religious studies scholars have concluded that the sacred scriptures should not to be taken as scientific textbooks. It is wrongheaded to understand them as providing, say, geological information (whether the earth is thousands or billions of years old), astronomical information (whether the sun is stationary or mobile), or biological information (whether humans evolved from lower animal forms or not). Along with Galileo, these thinkers maintain that God and God's creation are revealed in both "the book of nature" and "the book of scripture" – books which could not conflict since they are both from God. Perhaps neither science nor religion can provide us with a full and complete map of every domain, for they each have their own separate spheres of reality. This leads to the next option.

Independence

A second option for understanding the relationship between science and religion is independence; it is to view them as completely independent forms of thought and practice which never come into contact. This view tends to provide a more irenic relationship between science and religion, for since they are totally disparate realms they are never at odds. There are different expressions of independence, but two prominent ones are Protestant neo-orthodoxy and linguistic analysis. We will look briefly at each in turn.

Karl Barth (1886–1968), a central figure in the Protestant neo-orthodox movement in the twentieth century, maintained that God is transcendent and unknowable until God provides a self-disclosure. This disclosure does not occur through scientific investigation and discovery. Rather, it comes about through divine revelation – a revelation which occurs through the initiation of God's Spirit. The scriptures may provide the catalyst for this divine encounter, but this does not mean they are to be interpreted literally. They are fallible human recordings of revelatory events which provide religious insights as the Spirit moves in an individual. Science, for

Karl Barth (1886–1968) was a Swiss Reformed theologian and one of the most influential Protestant Christian thinkers of the twentieth century. He developed a "theology of the Word" in which religious knowledge and understanding is conferred by faith – a faith offered only by Christ, under the sovereignty of God. His theology is sometimes referred to as neo-orthodoxy by critics. He was a prolific writer, with his magnum opus being the thirteen-volume *Church Dogmatics*.

Barth, provides helpful information about the empirical world, but it cannot provide religious knowledge. The subject matter of these domains is completely dissimilar, as are their aims and methods of inquiry.

A second way of expressing independence is to interpret science and religion as different languages which provide their own unique set of functions. In the mid-twentieth century a group of scholars, referred to as logical positivists, maintained that for a claim to be true and meaningful it had to be empirically verifiable. Religious ideas, then, were seen to be meaningless. For a number of reasons logical positivism was short-lived, but an emphasis on language analysis was highlighted by a later movement dubbed *linguistic analysis*.[7] For the linguistic analysts, religious language and scientific language have different aims and functions. The function of religious language is to "recommend a way of life, to elicit a set of attitudes, and to encourage allegiance to particular moral principles."[8] The primary function of scientific language, on the other hand, is prediction and control in the natural world. Religion and science each have their own "language game," as some would call it, and the two games can never interact or conflict.

While a clear benefit of the independence option, in both forms described above, is that it avoids the warfare inimical to the conflict option, it comes with a price. Ian Barbour (1923–) describes the cost:

> If science and religion were totally independent, the possibility of conflict would be avoided, but the possibility of constructive dialogue would also be ruled out. We do not experience life as neatly divided into separate compartments; we experience it in wholeness and interconnectedness before we develop particular disciplines to study different aspects of it.[9]

Independence assumes that religion has nothing to say about the natural world and that science makes no cognitive claims about the religious domain. But this seems to be false. For example, the three major theistic religions affirm a creation event in which God brought the universe into being, and they describe God as being actively involved in the created order (inducing plagues, healing the sick, parting the sea, etc.). Some of the arguments for God's existence also include empirical facts as the basis for belief in a supernatural creator or designer, as we saw in Chapters 4 and 5. Non-theistic religions also provide claims relevant to the natural, physical universe. Buddhist understandings of the dharma (e.g. truth or ultimate reality), for example, or Buddhist and Hindu notions of karma, are taken to be real aspects of the world which have physical, causal effects within the world. Science and religion do sometimes make claims which conflict.

Furthermore, the independence view bifurcates the world into disparate domains and tends to negate a unified, coherent interpretation of what is actually experienced in the world. Perhaps there is a way of integrating science and religion such that their unique aims and methods are respected while at the same time providing for a more unified picture of the world. This leads to our final option.

Integration

A third way of understanding the relationship between science and religion is one in which some form of integration is possible between them.[10] The integration approach takes seriously both the conflicts which occur between religion and science on the one hand and the unique role of each domain on the other. Different versions of integration have been attempted, and two leading views will be sketched below.

One attempt to integrate science and religion is natural theology. Natural theology is the attempt to infer the existence of God from evidences in nature, and we examined several arguments which endeavor to do this very thing in earlier chapters. As was noted there, recent findings in physics and other branches of science are providing fresh material for natural theologians, and from it new arguments for God's existence have emerged in recent decades. Whether such arguments are plausible is not of concern here. Rather, the point is that even though natural theology and natural science have unique aims, goals, and methods, their findings can lead them to the same object. For example, as we saw in Chapter 5, the cosmic constants of the physical universe may point to an intelligent designer of the universe – a designer posited by the theistic religions. Also, Richard Swinburne (1934–) has recently proposed Bayesian (probabilistic) arguments for God's existence and for the resurrection of Jesus.[11]

A second approach at integration involves those working toward a systematic synthesis of religion and science. Process philosophy, typically associated with the works of American philosophers Alfred North Whitehead (1861–1947) and Charles Hartshorne (1897–2000), is an example of the attempt to merge science and religion into a coherent, comprehensive metaphysical system consonant with advances in modern science (including relativity and evolutionary theories).[12]

For process thinkers, the ancient and medieval views of the static, substantial natures of things are replaced by dynamic events which follow an evolutionary

Alfred North Whitehead (1861–1947) was an English mathematician and philosopher and the founder of modern process thought. In 1929 his Gifford Lectures were published as *Process and Reality* – the work which founded process philosophy. Other important works include *Science and the Modern World* and *Religion in the* Making. He also co-authored the *Principia Mathematica* – one of the central works in modern logic – with Bertrand Russell.

trajectory. The primary characterization of process thought is that *everything* which exists is characterized by process. This is consistent with the Buddhist doctrines of interdependent arising and *Anatman* discussed in Chapter 3 in which there are no substantial entities, only interconnected events.

The process view of divinity is one in which God, too, is in process. Process thinkers reject the classical theistic model in which God is immutable, simple, omnipotent, omniscient, beyond space and time, and completely transcendent. Rather, God is dipolar – containing a primordial nature which orders the world and a consequent nature which interacts with the world and continually changes with it.

The integration approach offers exciting prospects for developing new ways of relating science and religion. The two domains do seem to overlap in significant areas, and advancing the dialogue will require recognition of the important role of each domain in human (and non-human) life. It will also require humility for, if history repeats itself, current scientific theories will not remain static but will continue to evolve as humanity grows in knowledge about the vast and splendid world in which we live.

RELIGIOUS BELIEF AND JUSTIFICATION

Just as there are several ways to express the relationship between science and religion, we can convey the relationship between faith and reason in two broad categories. On the one hand are those who maintain that reason can and should be used to justify or validate religious faith; we can call views of this sort *rational validation views of faith and reason*. Looking for evidences for God's existence, or for reincarnation or life after death, or attempting to justify one's beliefs about the dharma or the *dao*, are all examples of rational validation.

On the other hand are those who deny that reason and evidence should be used to justify or validate religious faith; we can call views of this sort *non-evidential views of faith and reason*. This is not to say that adherents of non-rational views deny that reason is necessary for understanding religious beliefs or practicing religious faith. Rather, they deny that holding religious beliefs is dependent upon having reasons or evidences for those beliefs being objectively true. In previous chapters we have examined different kinds of evidences which have been used by those affirming rational validation to support certain religious beliefs (such as that God exists). In the remainder of this chapter we will examine several different non-evidential views of faith reason.

Fideism

For fideists (from the Latin word *fides* which means faith), using reason to demonstrate or evaluate religions or religious beliefs is always inappropriate. Faith is not the kind of thing which needs rational justification, fideists maintain, and attempting to prove one's religious faith may even be an indication of a lack of faith.

Perhaps the most well-known fideist was the philosopher Søren Kierkegaard (1813–1855). Kierkegaard lived in a Christian milieu in Denmark in which the philosophical work of G. W. F. Hegel (1770–1831) was culturally influential and widespread. On the Hegelian account, world history unfolds according to divine reason and logic. An often-repeated Hegelian slogan is "the real is the rational, the rational is the real."[13] For Hegel, the Christian religion is a mythological representation of this divine, rational unfolding and Christianity is religious consciousness in its most developed state.

Kierkegaard saw his society as one in which being a Christian had become, due to Hegelian and other influences, simply being born into "Christendom." It was no longer an individual experience of choosing to live an inward life of devotion and passion, but rather had become a set of cultural beliefs that one may come to hold through rational arguments and evidences. But for Kierkegaard, true religion is not cold and calculating, regurgitating the right answers to logical, formulaic issues in systematic, impersonal fashion. Rather, it is passionate and obsessive, more akin to an intimate relationship between two young lovers.

He believed there are no solid proofs for religious faith, and that even if there were they would be unhelpful for developing real religious faith, for "certainty… lurks at the door of faith and threatens to devour it."[14] Furthermore, Christian dogma – such as the belief that an infinite God becoming a finite human being – includes paradoxes that are inimical to reason and logic, while real religious faith entails a "leap." One philosopher of history sums up Kierkegaard's view on the matter this way:

> God is not man, and man is not God. And the gulf between them cannot be bridged by dialectical thinking. It can be bridged only by a leap of faith, by a voluntary act by which man relates himself to God and freely appropriates, as it were, his relation as creature to the Creator, as a finite individual to the transcendent Absolute.[15]

Georg Wilhelm Friedrich Hegel (1770–1831) was a German idealist philosopher. He argued that history has a teleology – it is the rational development and production of Mind or Spirit, what he called the Absolute. His works include *Lectures on the Philosophy of Religion*, *Phenomenology of Spirit*, and *Science of Logic*.

Søren Kierkegaard (1813–1855) was a Danish philosopher and theologian and the father of existentialism. He often wrote under pseudonyms, such as Johannes Climacus, and argued that one is unwise and mistaken to attempt to base one's religious beliefs on reason and evidence. His major works include *Either/Or*, *Fear and Trembling*, and *Concluding Unscientific Postscript*.

Choosing faith involves suspending reason; it is affirming something higher than reason and making a life commitment. This affirmation and commitment comes about through the existential choices an individual must make on a regular, perhaps even constant, basis. In a frequently quoted passage, Kierkegaard puts the point concisely:

> Faith is precisely the contradiction between the infinite passion of the individual's inwardness and the objective uncertainty. If I am capable of grasping God objectively, I do not believe, but precisely because I cannot do this I must believe. If I wish to preserve myself in faith I must constantly be intent upon holding fast to the objective uncertainty, so as to remain out upon the deep, over seventy thousand fathoms of water, still preserving my faith.[16]

Kierkegaard was living and writing within the Christian tradition, but fideists can be found in all the major religious traditions. For example, the term *Sradda* in Theravada and Mahayana Buddhism is the acceptance of the Buddha's teachings which comes prior to one's right understanding or right thought. Entering the Eightfold Path involves a faith step – an acquiescence (without rational argumentation or evidence) to the teachings of the Buddha.[17]

One criticism of fideism is that, in a religiously pluralistic culture, how is one to decide which religion (or set of religious beliefs) one should commit to? This may not be an issue in a culture in which there is only one religiously live option. But what about in a religiously pluralistic culture in which there are multiple live options? How is one to choose? Fideists offer various replies. One is that the evidences offered for any particular religious tradition are subjective and difficult, if not impossible, to assess from the "outside." So the choice must come from within.[18] Another reply (this one offered by Kierkegaard himself) is that reason provides only approximate conclusions at best, while faith offers personal passion and subjective certainty.[19] This passionate certainty, rather than cool, calculated reasoning, more accurately captures the essence of religious faith. When it comes to faith, one must make a choice: commit to believe or not, irrespective of the evidence.

William James and the will to believe

Another view of faith and reason which is, in certain respects, similar to Kierkegaard's fideism, is that of the early twentieth-century philosopher and psychologist William James (1842–1910). In a famous essay entitled "The Will to Believe," James argued that (contrary to the title's possible suggestion that one should affirm beliefs by mere fiat of will) there are occasions in which we are forced to make a decision to believe even if solid evidence is lacking, and that in appropriate circumstances this decision to believe is better than not believing. In order to set the stage for James's view, it will be helpful to first sketch the position to which he was responding – a position set forth by the British mathematician and philosopher, W. K. Clifford (1845–1879).

In an important paper entitled "The Ethics of Belief," Clifford argued that a person shouldn't believe something unless he or she has good evidence for the belief. He begins the essay with an example. Suppose a ship owner realizes that his ship might need some repair before setting sail, but he convinces himself otherwise. He remembers that the ship had many successful voyages, and that he believes in Providence and the providential care of human persons. After further contemplation, he is able to remove any distrust he might have about those involved in the original construction of the ship, and he comforts himself with the thought that they surely built his vessel well. Tragically, soon after its voyage begins, the ship sinks and all perish.

Clifford argues that the ship owner is morally responsible for this catastrophe because his beliefs were not based on evidence. Wishful thinking or hope is not enough; solid evidence is necessary for belief. Clifford then offers the following principle: "It is wrong always, everywhere, and for anyone, to believe anything upon insufficient evidence."[20] Thus on Clifford's account, sometimes referred to as *evidentialism*, believing has moral implications: it is *immoral* to believe without sufficient evidence. Clearly this principle has ramifications for all beliefs, not the least of which are religious ones.

James argues against Clifford's position and for the view that there are occasions when having beliefs in the absence of evidence is fully justified. He argues that there are times in life when we all need to choose to believe even when there is little, if any, evidence available on which to base our decisions. Consider the following example.

> Suppose … that I am climbing in the Alps, and have had the ill-luck to work myself into a position from which the only escape is by a terrible leap. Being without similar experience, I have no evidence of my ability to perform it successfully; but hope and confidence in myself make me sure I shall not miss my aim, and nerve my feet to execute what without those subjective emotions would perhaps have been impossible. But suppose that, on the contrary, the emotions of fear and mistrust preponderate; or suppose that, having just read

> the *Ethics of Belief*, I feel it would be sinful to act upon an assumption unverified by previous experience, – why, then I shall hesitate so long that at last, exhausted and trembling, and launching myself in a moment of despair, I miss my foothold and roll into the abyss. In this case (and it is one of an immense class) the part of wisdom clearly is to believe what one desires; for the belief is one of the indispensable preliminary conditions of the realization of its object. There are then cases where faith creates its own verification. Believe, and you shall be right, for you shall save yourself; doubt, and you shall again be right, for you shall perish. The only difference is that to believe is greatly to your advantage.[21]

For James, there are practical or pragmatic consequences to our beliefs. And as the example above indicates, sometimes it is beneficial to act even where evidence is lacking.

There are also times when there are competing hypotheses from which to choose. How do we decide in cases like that? James calls deciding between hypotheses an "option," and he delineates several kinds:

1 **Living or dead**: a live option is one in which both hypotheses have some emotional (but not rational) appeal to the one making the choice; a dead option lacks such appeal. For example, for many Europeans and North Americans in the nineteenth century, the option, "be a Hindu or a Buddhist," was not a live one, whereas "be a Christian or an agnostic" was a live option.
2 **Forced or avoidable**: a forced option is one in which both hypotheses are mutually exclusive and there is no third possibility. For example, the option to "read this book or don't read it" is forced. An avoidable option is one in which the two hypotheses do not involve such a logical disjunction or dilemma; for example, if asked which of the two American political parties one supports, there is no forced option here. One may hold to a third party, or simply be ambivalent about either of them.
3 **Momentous or trivial**: a momentous option is one in which much hangs on deciding about the hypotheses. For example, if you were given the opportunity to join the next crew of the space shuttle as they travel into outer space, your option would be momentous; it is a unique and significant opportunity. On the other hand, being offered the choice of drinking coffee rather than tea is trivial (on some occasions, at least!).

A *genuine option* is one that is living, forced, and momentous. Religion, James maintains, is a genuine option for some people. When confronted with a genuine option, even given a lack of evidence, taking a step of faith may be the best decision. Since evidence is lacking in these "forced" decision-making situations, he maintains, in making this choice we must use our non-intellectual or "passional" nature. James puts it this way:

> We may define "faith" as the firm belief in something for which there is no evidence. Where there is evidence, no one speaks of "faith." We do not speak of faith that two and two are four or that the earth is round. We only speak of faith when we wish to substitute emotion for evidence.
>
> Bertrand Russell[22]

> Our passional nature not only lawfully may, but must, decide an option between propositions, whenever it is a genuine option that cannot by its nature be decided on intellectual grounds; for to say, under such circumstance, "Do not decide, but leave the question open," is itself a passional decision – just like deciding yes or no – and is attended with the same risk of losing the truth.[23]

With respect to religious beliefs, the stakes are sometimes so great that the risk of losing truth is worth it, even though error is a real possibility. Following Clifford's approach to believing only when evidence is available and certain would cause our lives to be epistemically penurious and bereft of the fullness we could otherwise experience.[24] There is risk in both Clifford's and James's approaches. Following Clifford, while we may avoid believing what is false, we risk believing what is true and useful. James describes Clifford's approach this way: "better risk loss of truth than chance of error – that is your faith-vetoer's exact position."[25] Following James, choosing to believe runs the risk of falling into error about fundamental issues. Nevertheless, he says, "If religion be true and the evidence for it still be insufficient, I do not wish … to forfeit my sole chance in life of getting upon the winning side."[26]

Pascal's wager

Another form of pragmatic belief was offered a few hundred years earlier by the French mathematician Blaise Pascal (1623–1662). Pascal presented a pragmatic wager, often referred to as a *wager argument*, for religious belief.[27] Using a cost–benefit analysis of the reasonableness of belief in God, and based on a type of early

> **Blaise Pascal** (1623–1662) was a renowned French mathematician, physicist, and philosopher. After a mystical experience in 1654, he devoted much of his time and energy to philosophy and theology and defending Christianity, including his famous wager. His notes were collected and published posthumously with the title *Pensées* (*Thoughts*).

decision and probability theory, Pascal argued that believing in God (for him it was the Christian God) is a better bet than not believing.

> Either God is or [God] is not. But to which view shall we be inclined? Reason cannot decide the question. Infinite chaos separates us. At the far end of this infinite distance a coin is being spun which will come down heads or tails. How will you wager? Reason cannot make you choose either, reason cannot prove either wrong... . [B]ut you must wager. There is no choice, you are already committed. Which will you choose then? Let us see: since a choice must be made, let us see which offers you the least interest. You have two things to lose: the true and the good; and two things to stake: your reason and your will, your knowledge and your happiness; and your nature has two things to avoid: error and wretchedness. Since you must necessarily choose, your reason is no more affronted by choosing one rather than the other... . But your happiness? Let us weigh up the gain and the loss involved in calling heads that God exists. Let us assess the two cases: if you win, you win everything, if you lose you lose nothing. Do not hesitate then; wager that [God] does exist.[28]

The wager, which Pascal develops further in his *Pensées*, can be delineated as follows. There are a limited number of options concerning belief in God:

1 Believe in God and God does exist.
2 Believe in God and God does not exist.
3 Do not believe in God and God does exist.
4 Do not believe in God and God does not exist.

If you choose to believe in God and God does exist, you have great gain. If you choose to believe in God and God does not exist, you have not lost much (if anything). If you choose to disbelieve in God and God does exist, you have no great gain (and you may have great loss). If you choose to disbelieve in God and God does not exist, you again have no great gain. So, even with little or no evidence, we have reason – self-interested reason – to believe in God. Our best gamble, Pascal maintains, is to believe.

Figure 8.1 represents the structure of Pascal's decision matrix.[29]

Options	**Outcomes**	
	God exists	***God does not exist***
1) Believe in God	great gain	no great gain
2) Do not believe in God	no great gain	no great gain

Figure 8.1 Pascal's decision matrix

> The heart has reasons of its own which the mind knows nothing of.
>
> Pascal[30]

Obviously not everyone will be convinced by the wager argument. Suppose, Pascal muses, someone is in a state of unbelief and maintains that he cannot be moved to belief, even when presented with the wager, and that evidences and proofs are also insufficient for moving him to a state of belief. What is such a person to do?

> I would have you understand your incapacity to believe. Labor to convince yourself, not by more "proofs" of God's existence, but by disciplining your passions and wayward emotions. You would arrive at faith, but know not the way. You would heal yourself of unbelief, yet know not the remedies. I answer you: learn of those who have been bound as you are. These are they who know the way you would follow, who have been cured of a disease you would be cured of. Follow the way by which they began, by acting as if you believe, taking holy water, having masses said, and so forth. Even this will naturally make you believe.[31]

Various criticisms have been raised against Pascal's wager. First, it can be argued that we cannot choose to believe much, if anything, directly, let alone belief in God. Beliefs just don't usually seem to be within our direct control. For example, suppose you were offered a large sum of money to believe that a pink elephant is right now sitting beside you. Can you do it? Of course you could lie and say so even if you had no such belief. But can you really choose to believe it? It doesn't seem so. The same follows for virtually all beliefs.[32]

A second objection is similar to the one raised earlier with fideism. Namely, how is one to decide which religion, among the plethora of religions, one should wager on? Why wager on the Christian God, as Pascal proposed? Why not bet on Krishna, or Allah, or the *dao*, or *nirvana*, or all of the above? Given the many different and unique religious options which exist, how are we to wager? Pascal provides little criteria for making an informed bet given the pluralistic milieu which now encompasses much of the globe.

Third, even if one could come to religious faith through such a calculating wager, is this an appropriate method for acquiring authentic religious faith? It seems a rather unfitting way to enter into the trusting relationship in God informed by the Christian tradition in which Pascal was ensconced. Perhaps the same could be said of the other great faith traditions as well. Furthermore, the wager seems to assume that the universe is structured along utilitarian or decision theoretic lines, and has the added imperfection of only being appealing to those who are psychologically inclined to pleasure happiness and avoid pain – a strange appeal if losing and gaining one's life is at the core of the Christian call to discipleship.[33]

Alvin Plantinga and Reformed epistemology

A more recent approach to faith and reason is called "Reformed epistemology" (the term "Reformed" refers to the Christian, Calvinist Reformation theological tradition). Three of its primary proponents are Alvin Plantinga (1932–), Nicholas Wolterstorff (1932–) and William Alston (1921–). Reformed epistemology is non-evidentialist as it asserts that evidence is not needed in order for one's faith to be justified. But unlike fideism its adherents maintain that belief in God can be a *rational* endeavor despite a complete lack of evidence. This is obviously contrary to the evidentialist approach in which it is *irrational* to believe a claim without evidence. It is also unlike evidentialism in that its adherents are generally opposed to a view called classical foundationalism.

Foundationalism is the view that a belief is rationally justified if it is based on proper foundations. *Classical foundationalism* is the view that all justified beliefs must either be properly basic or derivative of properly basic beliefs. For the classical foundationalist, properly basic beliefs are those which are:

- **Incorrigible**: beliefs relevant to one's own experience about which it is virtually impossible to be in error, such as the belief that one is in pain or that one seems to be seeing something as blue, for example, or
- **self-evident**: beliefs involving simple logical or mathematical truths which, when understood, are taken immediately to be true, such as the law of non-contradiction or 2 + 2 = 4, or
- **evident to the senses**: beliefs directly involving one or more of the five senses, such as the belief that one is seeing green grass or smelling a fresh rose.

Classical foundationalists include Thomas Aquinas (1225–1274), René Descartes (1596–1650), John Locke (1632–1704), and David Hume (1711–1776). While they may differ on its precise meaning, those affirming classical foundationalism agree that properly basic beliefs must include at least two of the three elements noted above.

As Plantinga and others have demonstrated, there are serious problems with classical foundationalism.[34] Perhaps the most serious objection is that it seems to be self-refuting. Consider its criteria for a belief's being rational and justified only if the belief is incorrigible or self-evident or evident to the senses. Is this claim itself incorrigible, self-evident or evident to the senses? It seems not. So it doesn't even meet its own criteria for rational justification: if one affirms the view, one cannot rationally do so.[35]

Plantinga has argued that while classical foundationalism should be rejected, the foundationalist position that rationally justified beliefs must be ultimately based on properly basic beliefs is generally correct.[36] The foundationalism he defends

Alvin Plantinga (1932–) is John A. O'Brien Professor of Philosophy at the University of Notre Dame. He is widely known for his work in epistemology, metaphysics, and philosophy of religion (most especially his free will defense, his reformulation of the ontological argument, and Reformed epistemology). He has written many important books, including *God, Freedom, and Evil*, *The Nature of Necessity*, and *Warranted Christian Belief*. In 2004–2005 he gave the prestigious Gifford Lectures at St. Andrews University entitled *Science and Religion: Conflict or Concord?*

is grounded in a Reformed theology which circumvents the need for evidence for fundamental religious beliefs. Certain religious beliefs, he argues, such as belief in God, are "properly basic." Now it is important to note that what Plantinga and other Reformed epistemologists mean by a properly basic belief is different from the classical understanding. While on the classical view properly basic beliefs are beliefs which are incorrigible, self-evident and evident to the senses, on the Reformed epistemology view they are beliefs which are reasonably and appropriately held even without evidence. Examples include mental beliefs, memory beliefs, and ascribing mental states to others: (1) I see a computer, (2)I skipped breakfast this morning, and (3) my wife is in pain. Beliefs such as these are basic and properly so, argues Plantinga, for even though they are not based on other beliefs, they are not groundless.

> Although beliefs of this sort are typically taken as basic, it would be a mistake to describe them as *groundless*. Upon having experience of a certain sort, I believe that I am perceiving a tree. In the typical case I do not hold this belief on the basis of other beliefs; it is nonetheless not groundless. My having that characteristic sort of experience ... plays a crucial role in the formation of that belief. It also plays a crucial role in its justification.

Furthermore, beliefs like these above can be fully justified:

> Let us say that a belief is *justified* for a person at a time if (a) he is violating no epistemic duties and is within his epistemic rights in accepting it then and (b) his noetic structure [that is, the sum total of a person's beliefs and the way those beliefs are related] is not defective by virtue of his then accepting it. Then my being appeared to in this characteristic way (together with other circumstances) is what confers on me the right to hold the belief in question; this is what justifies me in accepting it. We could say, if we wish, that this experience is what justifies me in holding it; this is the ground of my justification, and, by extension, the ground of the belief itself.[37]

Plantinga's next move is to claim that belief in God is similar to the beliefs that I see a computer or that I skipped breakfast or that one is in pain – it too is a properly basic belief. Consistent with Reformed thinkers such as John Calvin (1509–1564), Abraham Kuyper (1837–1920), and Karl Barth (1886–1968), Plantinga argues that within every rational human mind there is a natural awareness of divinity. All people everywhere, he maintains, no matter how barbarous, have a deep-seated conviction that God exists and is their Maker.[38] While sin (and perhaps bad education) may affect one's ability to hold the belief that God exists, for many people – especially many Jews, Christians, Muslims, and theistic Hindus – the belief in God is a properly basic one.

Plantinga's proposal has been challenged on a number of fronts. First, if belief in the Christian God can be properly basic, why can't just about any belief be at the ground of one's noetic foundation? This is known as the "Great Pumpkin Objection," based on the *Peanuts* comic strip in which Linus believes in the Great Pumpkin who allegedly shows up in a pumpkin patch to sincere believers every Halloween. On Plantinga's construal, what's to keep belief in the Great Pumpkin from being properly basic? His reply is that there is a relevant difference between belief in God and belief in the Great Pumpkin. The Reformed epistemologist maintains that there is a natural tendency in us to have the former but not the latter belief. So, one is within one's epistemic rights to include belief in God as properly basic, but from this it doesn't follow that "bizarre" beliefs, such as belief in the Great Pumpkin, cannot be excluded.

This leads to a second criticism. Even if belief in God is properly basic for some people (Reformed epistemologists, say), this is no guarantee that the belief is, in fact, true. Plantinga grants as much.[39] Nevertheless, this is no reason to reject the Reformed epistemologist's construal of properly basic beliefs, for while there is no certainty that such a belief is true, there is certainty that if a belief is properly basic, one is rational in holding it.

This leads to yet a third criticism. For the Reformed epistemologist, a belief which is properly basic for one individual may not be properly basic for another individual. Belief in God may be properly basic for a Christian; belief in *nirvana* may be properly basic for a Buddhist; belief in the *dao* may be properly basic for a Taoist; belief in Krishna may be properly basic for a Hindu; belief in magic spells may even be properly basic for adherents of voodoo; and so on. There is no universal set of properly basic beliefs; indeed, there is no universal rationality either. So are we not trapped within a particular system of beliefs, forever unable to adjudicate between systems? In rejecting evidentialism, there are no evidences available by which to make evaluative judgments about beliefs or belief systems – religious or otherwise.

Plantinga's reply is twofold. First, he concurs that using his method for determining properly basic beliefs may lead different people to different conclusions. But that's simply the way things are in philosophical discourse. For philosophers to come to agreement on fundamental issues – on any issue! – may be too much to ask. As the First Law of Philosophy states, for every philosopher, there exists an equal and opposite philosopher. So this isn't a problem for his method any more than for any method in philosophy.[40] Second, in his most recent works, Plantinga does begin to spell out criteria (not evidence) for determining properly basic beliefs and for deciding whether a belief is warranted. Getting into that discussion, however, is beyond the scope of this book.[41] Much more could be said about faith and reason within Reformed epistemology, but this must suffice for now.

SUMMARY

In this chapter we examined various relationships between science and religion, and faith and reason. We first noted three basic options for relating science and religion: conflict, independence, and integration. For centuries science and religion have been at odds, and those affirming the conflict view see this as unavoidable. For those holding the independence view, however, science and religion never actually conflict because they are about completely different realms which never commingle: religion is about heavenly matters; science is about earthly ones. But this view demands a division of reality into separate and incongruent spheres and so seems to exclude a cohesive interpretation of the world. A third approach attempts to bridge the divide by respecting the unique roles offered by science and religion while also recognizing the potential conflicts which seem to occur between them. It recognizes that scientific practice sometimes has implications for religious faith, and religious belief isn't necessarily devoid of scientific reasoning.

We next examined several basic options for relating faith and reason. We first saw that there are two very different approaches: rational validation and non-evidential views. Rational validation sees reason and evidence as significant components of religious faith. On this view, arguments for God's existence, for example, can play an important role in establishing or strengthening religious faith. Non-evidential views, on the other hand, deny that evidence is significant for belief. We examined four basic categories: fideism, James's will to believe, Pascal's wager, and Reformed epistemology.

The fideist maintains that using reason for evaluating religious faith is never appropriate. Religious faith needs no rational justification; reason can even run counter to such faith. In response to those who disagree with this view (called evidentialists), William James argues that there are occasions where believing without evidence is pragmatically useful. For some people, taking a step of faith into religion is their best option. Blaise Pascal goes even one step further in his pragmatism: our best bet, he argues, is to believe in God. We have much to gain from so believing, and much to lose if we choose to disbelieve. Reformed epistemologists agree with fideism that religious faith does not depend on evidence, but they are not anti-rationalists for they also agree that religious faith can be a reasonable enterprise. They argue that belief in God is properly basic for some people – that believing in God, for example, is just as rational for some as the belief that they had breakfast on some given morning.

Beliefs are profuse and ubiquitous. Some are advantageous, some – as we saw at the opening of the chapter – are dangerous. So how do we choose what and when to believe? Perhaps Joseph Runzo sums it up best:

> When all is said and done, the only final justification for any faith commitment we have is our deepest sense of what is valuable tempered by experience and a rational understanding of the real consequences of adhering to those values.[42]

QUESTIONS FOR REVIEW/DISCUSSION

1. Which of the three views of the relationship between religion and science do you find to be most accurate given the ways religion and science are generally understood and practiced today? First characterize the view and then explain why you believe it to be so.
2. Evolution and creationism are often considered to be diametrically opposed beliefs about the existence and development of flora and fauna. Do you believe they can be reconciled? If so, how? If not, why not?
3. Should reason be used to justify or validate faith? Why or why not?
4. In the Old Testament (Hebrew Bible) the story is told of Abraham being willing to offer his son Isaac on a sacrificial altar in response to God's request (Genesis, Chapter 22). Abraham is championed as a great man of faith because of his willingness to sacrifice his son. Recently a woman in the USA was arrested for drowning her children in her bathtub. She said that God told her to take her children's lives. What might be some reasons that Abraham is heralded as a giant of religious faith while this woman is castigated by many as an insane murderer? What are similarities and differences between these examples?
5. According to non-evidential views of faith and reason, there are times when we need to choose to believe even if there is insufficient evidence for the belief. But can we simply choose to believe anything directly? Note again the pink elephant example. If we cannot choose beliefs directly, how might we end up having beliefs – in particular religious ones?
6. If one did come to believe in God based on Pascal's wager, does this provide real faith in God – the kind of faith described in the religious tradition of which Pascal was a part? Or does it provide a kind of self-interested belief unfitting for religious faith? Explain your thoughts on the matter.
7. What is evidentialism? Explain why you agree or disagree with Clifford's evidentialist account as described in the text.
8. What is foundationalism? Are you a foundationalist? Explain.
9. An evidentialist objector may claim that since there is insufficient evidence for belief in God, it is irrational to believe that God exists. How would a Reformed epistemologist respond? How would you assess this response?
10. Are faith and reason mutually exclusive concepts? Can you have faith in something or someone while also having reasons for what you have faith in? Explain.

FURTHER READING

Barbour, Ian (1990) *Religion in an Age of Science: The Gifford Lectures*. Vol. 1. San Francisco, CA: Harper & Row. (A highly influential and insightful work on the integration of science and religion.)

Cobb, John B., Jr. and David Ray Griffin (1976) *Process Theology: An Introductory Exposition*. Philadelphia, PA: Westminster Press. (A helpful introduction to process theology by two leading process thinkers.)

Conee, Earl and Richard Feldman (2004) *Evidentialism: Essays in Epistemology*. Oxford: Clarendon Press. (A recent development and defense of evidentialism.)

Evans, C. Stephen (1998) *Faith Beyond Reason: A Kierkegaardian Account*. Grand Rapids, MI: Eerdmans. (Explains and defends a Kierkegaardian view of fideism.)

Golding, Joshua L. (2007) "The Wager Argument," in Chad Meister and Paul Copan, eds., *The Routledge Companion to Philosophy of Religion*. London: Routledge. (A concise overview of Pascal's wager.)

Harris, Sam (2004) *The End of Faith: Religion, Terror, and the Future of Reason*. New York: W. W. Norton and Company. (Argues that religious faith is based on irrational thinking, is dangerous and harmful, and that a rational, scientific view should replace a religious one.)

Hick, John (1966) *Faith and Knowledge*, 2nd edition. Ithaca, NY: Cornell University Press. (A precursor to analytic, non-evidentialist epistemology which was highly influential on Reformed epistemologists, although Hick has taken his epistemological ideas in a different direction than they have.)

James, William ([1902] 1961) *The Varieties of Religious Experience*. New York: Collier Books; repr. London: Collier Macmillan Publishers. (One of James's most influential works; includes insightful analyses of various types of religious experience.)

Kuhn, Thomas (1970) *The Structure of Scientific Revolutions*. Chicago, IL: University of Chicago Press. (Often hailed as one of the most influential books of the twentieth century; presents an understanding of scientific progress as consisting of various paradigm shifts which include social and psychological factors.)

McGrath, Alister (1998) *The Foundations of Dialogue in Science and Religion*. Oxford: Blackwell. (Explores the relation between science and faith at the level of method; utilizes Christianity as a case study)

Murphy, Nancy (1990) *Theology in the Age of Scientific Reasoning*. Ithaca, NY: Cornell University Press. (Argues for the rationality of religious (Christian) belief by demonstrating that theological reasoning is similar to scientific reasoning of a certain kind.)

Pascal, Blaise ([1670] 1995) *Pensées*. Rev. edition. Trans. A. J. Krailsheimer. New York: Penguin. (A masterful work of French prose in which Pascal analyzes several philosophical paradoxes, including faith and reason.)

Peacocke, Arthur (1984) *Intimations of Reality: Critical Realism in Science and Religion*. Notre Dame, IN: University of Notre Dame Press. (A renowned biochemist and theologian argues for a critical realist approach to understanding the relation between science and religion.)

Plantinga, Alvin and Nicholas Wolterstorff, eds. (1983) *Faith and Rationality*. Notre Dame, IN: University of Notre Dame Press. (A collection of important essays on faith and reason by seven leading Reformed epistemologists.)

Polkinghorne, John (2000) *Faith, Science and Understanding*. New Haven, CT: Yale University Press. (Explores the interaction of science and religion and focuses on what science can say about the processes of a universe in which God is active.)

Swinburne, Richard (2005) *Faith and Reason*. 2nd edition. Oxford: Clarendon Press. (Argues that one should practice that religion which has the best goals and is more probably true; proposes criteria for analyzing the probabilities of different religious creeds being true.)

Taliaferro, Charles (2005) *Evidence and Faith: Philosophy and Religion since the Seventeenth Century*. Cambridge: Cambridge University Press. (An excellent and accessible overview of philosophy of religion from the modern period to the present; focuses on developing views of faith and evidence.)

Trigg, Roger (1998) *Rationality and Religion: Does Faith Need Reason?* Oxford: Blackwell. (Examines the question of whether religious faith needs reason; considers the question in a pluralistic society.)

Ward, Keith (2006) *Is Religion Dangerous?* Grand Rapids, MI: Eerdmans. (Explores such questions as "Does religion lead to terrorism and violence?" and "Are religious beliefs irrational and immoral?")

WEBSITES

http://www.pbs.org/faithandreason
Web pages from PBS documentary entitled *Faith and Reason*, hosted by Margaret Wertheim.

http://plato.stanford.edu/entries/process-philosophy/
Stanford Encyclopedia of Philosophy entry on process philosophy by Nicholas Rescher, a leading process thinker.

http://www.science-spirit.org/
A website whose mission is to explore the integration of the scientific and spiritual aspects of our culture in a way that is accessible and relevant to everyday living.

http://www.columbia.edu/cu/cssr/
Website for The Center for the Study of Science and Religion, an interdisciplinary, collaborative forum for the examination of issues lying at the boundary of the scientific and religious ways of comprehending the world and our place in it.

9 Religious experience

Countless individuals claim to have had a religious experience of one sort or another. One study indicates that at least thirty percent of the global population has had such an experience.[1] For some, these experiences provide first-hand evidence or proof for the reality of what the experiencer (the one having the experience) believes in and perhaps even for his or her religion as a whole. For others, they are illusions or delusions, psychological experiences brought on by a number of different but purely natural factors. In this chapter we will explore the meaning and diversity of religious experience. We will examine arguments which claim that religious experience provides justification for religious beliefs and rebuttals to those arguments. We will also look at attempts to offer purely naturalistic explanations of religious experience.

THE NATURE AND DIVERSITY OF RELIGIOUS EXPERIENCE

Everyone has experiences, and each of these experiences is unique to the one having it, for I cannot experience your experiences and you cannot experience my experiences. Some of my experiences are similar to yours, however, and vice versa. For example, I am now having the experience of grasping the meaning of the words in this sentence. And so are you. But chances are we have each had experiences completely unlike what the other has had. There are also those who have had experiences that you and I cannot even fathom – some religious, some not. In this chapter we are focusing on religious experience. So what is a religious experience?

What is a religious experience?

In a broad sense religious experience refers to any experience of the sacred within a religious context, including religious feelings, visions, and mystical and numinous experiences.[2] A religious experience is intensely personal, and it often occurs in the midst of such religious practices as prayer, meditation, worship, chanting, or the performance of other religious ritual. Many times such experiences occur in a church, synagogue, mosque, temple, monastery, or other holy place. But religious experiences have been recorded in any number of circumstances and locations. There are three general features which are common to the phenomenon of religious experience:[3]

1 **Universality**: religious experience is a universal phenomenon. Studies and surveys demonstrate that a significant proportion of the human population, past and recent, including within highly secularized societies, have had religious experiences.
2 **Diversity**: there is a wide diversity of religious experiences, and each experience is in some sense unique to the individual who has it. While there are similarities among the religious experiences of adherents of the various religious traditions,

there are also differences, and this adds to the richness and variety of the experiences across the religious spectrum.

3 **Importance**: religious experience is important in unique and momentous ways, often resulting in a transformed or reoriented life, a re-evaluation of the way one thinks or lives, or even a change of world views.

Categories of religious experience

Different schemas have been offered to describe and classify the diverse types of religious experience. Here we will utilize a classification which distinguishes three categories of experience: regenerative, charismatic, and mystical.[4]

A *regenerative religious experience* is one in which the experiencer undergoes a life transformation – a conversion, if you will. In Evangelical Christian circles this is often referred to as being "born again" or being "born from above" (based on the Book of John in the New Testament in which Jesus says "… no one can see the kingdom of God without being born from above." [John 3:3]). Elsewhere this kind of experience is expressed as "experiencing religion," "experiencing salvation," or being "delivered from evil."[5] Through such experiences, individuals often find their lives to be changed, filled with meaning and newness, and full of love, joy, and hope.

John Hick (1922–), one of the most influential philosophers of religion of recent times, describes his own religious conversion experience:

> As a law student at University College, Hull, at the age of eighteen, I underwent a powerful evangelical conversion under the impact of the New Testament figure of Jesus. For several days I was in a state of intense mental and emotional turmoil, during which I became increasingly aware of a higher truth and greater reality pressing in upon me and claiming my recognition and response. At first this was highly unwelcome, a disturbing and challenging demand for nothing less than a revolution in personal identity. But then the disturbing claim became a liberating invitation. The reality that was pressing in upon me was not only awesomely demanding but also irresistibly attractive and I entered with great joy and excitement into the world of Christian faith… . An experience of this kind which I cannot forget, even though it happened forty-two years ago … occurred – of all places, on the top deck of a bus in the middle of the city of Hull.… As everyone will be very conscious who can themselves remember such a moment, all descriptions are inadequate. But it was as though the skies opened up and light poured down and filled me with a sense of overflowing joy, in response to an immense transcendent goodness and love. I remember that I couldn't help smiling broadly – smiling back, as it were, at God – though if any other passengers were looking they must have thought that I was a lunatic, grinning at nothing.[6]

William James (1842–1910) was an American philosopher and psychologist and one of the founders of Pragmatism. He engaged in the psychological examination of religion and wrote influential works on religious experience and mysticism. His major works include *The Varieties of Religious Experience*, *The Will to Believe and Other Essays in Popular Philosophy,* and *Pragmatism*.

Along with conversion and salvation, another facet of the regenerative experience is moral transformation. In this case, prior to the experience, the individual may feel a sense of sin, guilt, or the inability to do what he or she knows to be morally appropriate. Upon having the regenerative religious experience, she senses that sin and guilt have been removed and a new vision of goodness is seen and sought after; a new or renewed emphasis on moral duties ensues in one's life. In William James's influential work, *The Varieties of Religious Experience*, he includes a study on regenerative experience.

In this study, he is not focused on conversion from one set of religious beliefs to another, but on moral transformation; specifically a transformation in which "one aim grows so stable as to expel definitively its previous rivals from the individual's life."[7] We can find such transformational experiences in all of the major religious traditions. The Old Testament, for example, contains a number of accounts of personal (and national) moral regeneration.[8] More recently, an Islamic convert describes his transformational experience this way:

> In the blessed pages of the Holy Qur'an I found solution to all my problems, satisfaction to all my needs, explication for all my doubts. Allah attracted me to His light with irresistible strength, and I gladly yielded to Him. Everything seemed clear now, everything made sense to me, and I began to understand myself, the Universe and Allah. I was bitterly aware that I had been deceived by my dearest teachers, and that their words were only cruel lies, whether they were aware of it or not. My whole world was shattered in one instant; all concepts had to be revised. But the bitterness in my heart was amply superseded by the ineffable joy of having found my Lord at last, and I was filled with love and gratitude to Him. I still humbly praise and bless Him for His Mercy with me; without His help, I would have remained in darkness and stupidity forever.[9]

A second category of religious experience is *charismatic experience*. This is a type of experience in which special abilities, gifts, or blessings are manifested. One of the fastest growing elements in the Christian religion is Pentecostalism and the related charismatic movements.[10] According to recent studies, at least a quarter of

Pentecostals are Christians who belong to Pentecostal denominations and churches, including the Assemblies of God and the Church of God in Christ. Pentecostal-type revivals began in the 1800s in places such as England, India, and Russia, and then migrated to the United States in the early 1900s (most notably to the Azusa Street Mission in Los Angeles, California). Charismatics are Christians who either describe themselves as "charismatic Christians" (but do not belong to Pentecostal denominations) or who manifest any or all of the so-called charismatic gifts.

the world's two billion Christians are thought to be members of this facet of Christian faith which emphasizes such "gifts of the Holy Spirit" as healing, speaking in tongues, prophesying, and dreams and visions.[11] These charismatic gifts are described in the New Testament in I Corinthians and in the Acts of the Apostles (which also include references to the Old Testament where charismatic gifts are prophesied), but are not limited to the more spectacular ones noted above; they also include supernatural infusions of wisdom, knowledge, and faith, for example.[12]

Charismatic experiences are not limited to the Judeo–Christian tradition, however. In Buddhism, for example, the monk is often understood to be a charismatic and holy figure – not one who has received a gift from God, but rather one who has experienced the blessings of the *Dharma* (teachings of the Buddha and the fundamental constituents of the world).[13] Hinduism too has its *gurus* and *sadhus*, and Islam has its *sheiks* and *walis*. These spiritual leaders are often taken to have charismatic qualities, gifts, and powers.[14]

One of the most famous visionary experiences in the Christian tradition is that described by Saint Teresa of Avila (1515–1582):

> Our Lord was pleased that I should sometimes see a vision of this kind. Beside me, on the left hand, appeared an angel in bodily form, such as I am not in the habit of seeing except very rarely. Though I often have visions of angels, I do not see them… . In his hands I saw a great golden spear, and at the iron tip there appeared to be a point of fire. This he plunged into my heart several times so that it penetrated my entrails. When he pulled it out, I felt that he took them with it, and left me utterly consumed by the great love of God. The pain was so severe that it made me utter several moans. The sweetness caused by this intense pain is so extreme that one cannot possibly wish it to cease, nor is one's soul then content with anything but God. This is not a physical, but a spiritual pain, though the body has some share in it.[15]

Saint Teresa of Avila (1515–1582; also known as Saint Teresa of Jesus) was a Spanish mystic and Carmelite nun. She had frequent visions and ecstatic religious experiences. She became the first woman to be named a Doctor of the Catholic Church in 1970, and is one of only three women to be so honored. Her writings include her autobiography, *Interior Castle*, and *The Way of Perfection*.

What constitutes an authentic or inauthentic charismatic experience, and who is authorized to have such experiences or to authenticate them, is not always easy to discern as different religious traditions and sects have their own interpretations and evaluations of charismatic phenomena. What one person or group takes to be an authentic charismatic experience may be taken by others in or outside the group as inauthentic – as demon possession, the work of the devil, or merely psychological hocus pocus. Nevertheless, charismatic experiences have been widely accepted throughout the religious traditions both historically and in recent times.[16]

A third category is *mystical experience* which, as described by James, includes four distinct characteristics:[17]

- **Ineffability**: the experience cannot be adequately described, if at all.
- **Noetic quality**: the experiencer believes that she has learned something important from the experience.
- **Transiency**: the experience is temporary and the experiencer soon returns to a "normal" state of mind.
- **Passivity**: the experience occurs without conscious decision or control and it cannot be brought to happen at will.

Mystical experiences take different forms, but a common theme among many of them is identity or union with God in Western religion, or with Absolute Reality – Brahman or *nirvana* or the *dao* – in Eastern religion. A description of a mystical experience within the Advaita Vedānta school of Hinduism is given by Shankara (c. 788–c. 820):

> When the mind is completely absorbed in the supreme Being – the *Atman*, the Brahman, the Absolute – then the world of appearances vanishes. Its existence is no more than an empty word. ... There is neither seer nor seeing nor seen. There is but one Reality – changeless, formless, and absolute. ... The universe no longer exists after we have awakened into the highest consciousness in the eternal *Atman*, which is Brahman, devoid of any distinction or division. ... Even though his mind is dissolved in Brahman, he is fully awake, free from the ignorance of waking life. He is fully conscious, but free from any craving.[18]

It is here in mystical experience that the monism of some Eastern religions is also experienced in Western theistic religions. We find monistic mystical experiences described in Judaism (e.g. *The Zohar*[19]), Christianity (e.g. Meister Eckhart and Saint John of the Cross[20]), and Islam (e.g. Sufi school of Ibn al-'Arabi[21]). While the three Western religions are broadly theistic, they have developed within them monistic streams of thought. Regarding union with the divine, for example, Christian mystic Meister Eckhart (1260–1327) says, "If I am to know God directly, I must become completely He and He I; so that this He and this I become and are one I."[22] Given such bold monistic language, it is not surprising that there has been lively debate within the theistic traditions about whether these mystics and mystical streams should be understood as heretical.

There is a wide range of experiences which are classified as mystical. Besides the union with God/Absolute Reality experiences noted above, another kind of mystical experience is nature mysticism. In this sense, even an atheist can have a mystical "religious" experience:

> Although my "cosmic experience" was irrational in terms of our accustomed view of the world, I am not satisfied that it was simply an illusion, or delusion. It affected me in a very real way, reoriented my outlook and enriched and enlarged my consciousness in many ways. But it did pose a riddle – the kind of riddle one cannot attempt to solve without becoming keenly aware of the ultimate mystery of creation. In this sense, I would call my experience "religious."[23]

The Buddhist experiences of *sunyata*, or emptiness, developed in the Madhyamika (Middle Way) school of Buddhism, and *satori*, or enlightenment, developed in the Zen tradition, are also considered by many to be mystical experiences. D. T. Suzuki (1870–1966) describes the essence of Zen as involving satori, a way of "looking into the nature of things" and understanding reality (*satori* literally means "to understand"), which provides a "fresher, deeper, more satisfying aspect" of life. It is not easily attained, however, and it cannot be reached through logical reasoning or cognitive explanation; it must be directly experienced.[24]

Yet another kind of mystical experience is numinous experience. Rudolf Otto (1869–1937) describes numinous experience in the Latin as *mysterium tremendum*

Daisetz Teitaro (D. T.) Suzuki (1870–1966) was Professor of Buddhist philosophy at Otani University, Kyoto, and taught at American universities, including Columbia and Harvard. He was a leading proponent of Zen Buddhism in the West. His major works include *An Introduction to Zen Buddhism*, *Essays in Zen Buddhism*, and *Mysticism: Christian and Buddhist*.

et fascinans (an overpowering, mysterious, luring experience).[25] He notes that it sometimes comes "sweeping like a gentle tide, pervading the mind with a tranquil mood of deepest worship." It may also "burst in sudden eruption up from the depths of the soul with spasms and convulsions, or lead to the strangest excitements, to intoxicated frenzy, to transport, and to ecstasy." It has both its "wild and demonic forms" and its "hushed, trembling" manifestations. During numinous experiences the individual may be "overwhelmed" and feel an "absolute overpoweringness" or a sense of "fear" and "dread." But he may also feel an alluring "awe" which is "beautiful and pure and glorious."[26]

Furthermore, numinous experiences may be focused on some particular individual, such as Jesus or Krishna; or on some object, such as an icon or stone; or there may be no identified object whatsoever in the experience. But they commonly reflect an encounter with an "Other" – a separate self or will or power which forces itself upon the consciousness of the experiencer, unexpectedly and profoundly.

RELIGIOUS EXPERIENCE AND JUSTIFICATION

We have seen that there is a wide variety and diversity of religious experiences, and they have been reported and detailed by numerous religious adherents across the religious spectrum and throughout the ages. But despite their being a common feature of the religious traditions, there remains a problem. Religious experience is typically a private matter. Someone claims to have an experience in which she senses that she is one with the divine, say. Or someone else claims to experience God or an angel speaking to him. What are we to make of such claims? Or what if we had a religious experience ourselves? Is a person justified in inferring from a religious experience (either one's own or that of another) knowledge of an objective reality which is the object of that experience? As William James asks, "Do mystical states establish the truth of those theological affections in which the saintly life has its root?"[27]

Furthermore, can one be mistaken about such experiences? And how would he know? Some philosophers of religion reject religious experience as a ground for religious belief. This is not to say that they necessarily deny that individuals have had authentic religious experiences. Rather, they deny that one can properly infer from such experiences that their cause was God, or *nirvana*, or Ultimate Reality, etc., or that what the experience was about (if it contained cognitive content) is true or actually exists. With reference to religious experience providing support for the belief in God, C. B. Martin (1924–) makes the following claim: "There are no tests agreed upon to establish genuine experience of God and distinguish it decisively from the ungenuine."[28] So, he concludes, a religious experience cannot establish the objective reality of the perceptual object of the experience; all it can provide is evidence for the reality of specific psychological states. But is this in fact all that can be derived from religious experience? Furthermore, since virtually everyone agrees that at least some religious experiences are illusory, how are we to assess which ones are veridical and which are not?

William Wainwright (1935–) offers an argument from analogy for the justification of religious experience based on sense perception which runs as follows. I experience a tree, and I believe that a tree exists. I experience God, and I believe that God exists. Even though there are dissimilarities between tree experiences and God experiences, there are enough relevant similarities to warrant belief in God if we are warranted in having tree beliefs. Both of the experiences are *noetic* (that is, they both have to do with the content of the mind, including beliefs, desires, values, etc). They both have a perceptual object, he maintains, and they both include states of affairs which can be checked or verified in some sense.[29]

However, whether religious experiences do include a perceptual object is a debatable point. Mystical experiences, for example, are often taken by mystics to be ineffable. An ineffable experience by definition contains no expressible cognitive content. So, arguably, in that case it could not be used to ground a particular religious belief. Furthermore, it is questionable whether the procedures for verifying a sensory experience are similar at all to those of a religious experience. We will look more carefully at this objection below.

William Alston (1921–) has further developed Wainwright's line of argument.[30] He introduces doxastic practice (*doxa* is a Greek term which means belief) – the practice of forming beliefs which are based on experience – and points out that religious experience and sense perception are both doxastic practices. He grants that arguments for justifying religious experience are (non-viciously) circular. However, he notes that arguments for justifying the reliability of sense perception are afflicted with the same circularity problem. How can I verify that the tree I experience in front of me really is a tree? By using other sensory input (either my own or someone else's). How do I know that sensory perceptions in general provide reliable information? By checking them with other sensory perceptions (either my own or someone else's). But despite the circularity, the reliability of sensory perceptions is rarely questioned. Alston contends that if religious experiences relevantly resemble other perceptual experiences, such as sensory perceptions (and sometimes they do, he argues), then religious experiences should be no more suspect than other perceptual experiences.

In an attempt to address the issue from a different direction and to shift the burden of proof to the skeptic of the veridicality of religious experience, Richard Swinburne (1934–) has introduced a principle of rationality which he dubs the Principle of Credulity. According to this principle, when it seems (epistemically) to someone that something is the case, then in the absence of special considerations it probably is.[31] When I'm walking through the forest and see a squirrel in a tree just ahead me, for example, I am justified in believing that it is, in fact, a squirrel in the tree just ahead of me; unless, that is, I have special reasons to doubt my belief in this case. So too

Richard Swinburne (1934–) is Emeritus Nolloth Professor of the Philosophy of the Christian Religion, University of Oxford, and Fellow of the British Academy. He is a leading philosopher of religion and a member of the Eastern Orthodox Church. His major works include *The Existence of God, Faith and Reason*, and *The Evolution of the Soul*.

with religious experience. One could be mistaken in believing that something is the way it appears, but unless there is good reason to disbelieve it, we should not do so. Swinburne claims that rejecting this principle will land one in a "skeptical bog" in which a person must doubt everything that cannot be proven deductively.[32]

Not everyone is satisfied with Swinburne's principle. Michael Martin (1932–), for example, argues for a negative principle of credulity: if it seems (epistemically) to someone that something is not the case, then it probably is not the case.[33] There are plenty of individuals who have never had a religious experience, even though they have tried, so why should the burden of proof be shifted to the skeptic who doubts their veracity? He notes that while in ordinary life the experience of a chair is a good ground for believing in a chair, so too the experience of the absence of a chair is a good ground for believing that the chair is absent.[34]

In a move similar to Swinburne's Principle of Credulity, Jerome (Yehuda) Gellman attempts to demonstrate the evidential value of religious experience through a principle he calls BEE (Best Explanation of Experience) which has a corresponding STING (Strength in Number Greatness).[35] BEE is expressed this way:

> If a person, S, has an experience, E, which seems (phenomenally) to be of a particular object, O, (or of an object of kind, K), then *everything else being equal* the best explanation of S's having E is that S has experienced O (or an object of kind, K), rather than something else or nothing at all.[36]

As with Swinburne's Principle of Credulity, BEE is taken to be a fundamental principle of rationality which governs everyday rational discourse and which connects one's experience to reality. As such, its rationality is independent of further argumentation; it needs no further proof.

STING is then expressed as follows:

> If a person, S, has an experience, E, which seems (phenomenally) to be of a particular object, O, (or of an object of kind, K), then our belief that S's having experienced O (or an object of kind K) is the best explanation (everything else being equal) of E, is strengthened in proportion to the number of experiences of O there are and in proportion to the variability of circumstances in which such experiences occur.[37]

In other words, the more people have a particular kind of religious experience, the stronger the case for its being veridical. Utilizing BEE STING, Gellman argues that the large number of experiences of God provides warrant for holding certain beliefs about God (such as that God is loving).

In the next section we will examine several challenges to religious experience as justification for religious beliefs. At this point it is worth mentioning that some view the attempt to seek justification for religious beliefs from religious experience as inappropriately emphasizing the cognitive aspect of such experience. Consider Buddhism. For the Buddhist adherent, a primary goal is to be released from a state of craving and suffering and to attain *nirvana*, no-self or emptiness. The Buddhist does not ultimately seek knowledge about, or evidence or proof for, the existence of God or Ultimate Reality or *nirvana*. Rather, she is seeking the extinction of self and its attending cognitive processes. This is not to say that Buddhists cannot use individual or cumulative religious experiences within their tradition to validate their religious beliefs, but that such experiences are primarily directed toward liberation, not cognition.[38]

CHALLENGES TO RELIGIOUS EXPERIENCE AS JUSTIFICATION FOR RELIGIOUS BELIEFS

So it can be argued that religious experience provides justification for religious beliefs. But there are also arguments challenging this point. We will first look at three of these arguments and then hone in on naturalistic explanations of religious experience.

Lack of verifiability

One argument against the claim that religious experience provides justification for religious beliefs is that such experiences are not verifiable (they are not checkable as are other kinds of experiences). Compare a religious experience with some other perceptual experience – seeing a black swan, for example. If someone claims to see a black swan in their backyard, it's easy enough to check. Other perceptions can be used to verify whether the claim is true or not: others can see it, they can catch it, or perhaps they can be bitten by it. But what about when someone claims to have a religious experience? How can this kind of claim be verified? It seems that it cannot. So, it is argued that religious experience cannot provide justification for religious beliefs.[40]

In this discussion, a distinction is sometimes made between first-person psychological reports such as "I seem to see a black swan" with perceptual experiences such as "I see a black swan." With the latter kind of experiences a person can be

> The claim of any particular religion or sect to have complete or final truth of these subjects [of the veridicality of religious experience] seems to me to be too ridiculous to be worth a moment's consideration. But the opposite extreme of holding that the whole religious experience of mankind is a gigantic system of pure delusion seems to me to be almost (though not quite) as farfetched.
>
> C.D. Broad[39]

mistaken. I thought it was a black swan, but it turned out to be a brown Canada goose. With the former kind of experience a person cannot be mistaken. Even though it turned out to be a brown Canada goose, the claim that "I seem to see a black swan" is nonetheless true. These sorts of first-person, private reports are about the goings on of one's own mind and are referred to as *incorrigible* experiences – while I might be mistaken in what I *see*, I cannot be mistaken that I *seem to see* what I do.

The question then becomes whether religious experiences are corrigible or incorrigible. If they are incorrigible, as some critics claim, then the experiencer cannot be mistaken about them. However, in that case, they are merely subjective private experiences and so do not provide objective evidence or justification for their being about a reality outside the mind of the one having the experience.

Conflicting claims within the variety of religious experience

Another objection is that religious experiences are widely divergent, conflicting, and even contradictory. As we noted above, throughout the centuries religious believers have had various types of religious experiences, and many of them are clearly inconsistent with one another. The Advaita Vedāntin experience that all reality is one and undifferentiated, for example, contradicts the Islamic experience that Allah is the one true God, a divine reality who exists as a separate being from the person having the experience. Doesn't this inconsistency count against the reliability of the experiences? Don't these experiences invalidate or cancel one another out? [41]

In reply, it's important to distinguish between one's having and describing a religious experience on the one hand with one's explanation of that experience on the other. A person may be justified in her claim that she had an experience of what seemed to be God's love and forgiveness, say. This may indeed be a veridical, perceptual experience. But to then go on and explain the experience by invoking God's existence might well be an invalid step – an ill-founded inference from the subjective experience to the objective reality of the presentational object.

An analogy may help at this point. Suppose in witnessing a traffic accident I claim to have seen a red car hit the pedestrian while another observer claims to have seen a brown truck hit the person. We both had perceptual experiences of the accident. However, if I go on to explain the death of the individual who was hit by invoking the reality of the red car, I could be mistaken. So too with the person invoking the existence of the brown truck. The point is this: even though we may both be mistaken with respect to our descriptions of the cause of the individual's death (suppose it was actually a blue mini-van that hit the pedestrian), that doesn't necessarily count against the reality of the fundamental content of the experiences. In this case there was a vehicle which was involved in the accident, even though the two observers were mistaken in their descriptions of the object experienced.

This may be all well and good. But what about experiences which are entirely contradictory, such as those of the Advaita Vedāntin and Muslim described above? Aren't they so inconsistent as to cancel each other out? Furthermore, isn't it the case that religious adherents have experiences which tend to conform to their own religious outlooks? Muslims have experiences of Allah; Christians have experiences of Jesus; Buddhists have experiences of no-self; and so on? This leads to the next objection.

The circularity objection

A third objection to the claim that religious experience provides justification for religious belief is that such justification is circular: it depends on assumptions which are not self-evident to everyone and yet are then utilized as controls or limitations on the experience. Thus it seems that most religious experiences reflect the beliefs and values germane to the religion, or worldview, of the experiencer. A polytheistic Hindu living in Kolkata believes that there are many gods who watch over and protect those who are devoted to them, and so when his friend claims to have experienced the presence and love of Lord Vishnu (or when he has such an experience himself), he takes it to be veridical and to reflect the true nature of things. So too with experiences in other religions: the experiencers are having experiences in line with what they already believe.

In reply, religious or worldview constraints may not be as binding on individuals as some claim. There are, for example, various reports of adherents of one religion having religious experiences which are foreign to the individuals' own religious beliefs and yet which are not uncommon among those of another religion. Sometimes such experiences can even be the cause of one changing her religious beliefs and identity.[42]

But maybe there is a better way of understanding and explaining religious experience. Perhaps there is a scientific account which demonstrates that religious experiences are not veridical at all but rather illusions or even delusions. We look next at two such explanations.

SCIENTIFIC EXPLANATIONS OF RELIGIOUS EXPERIENCE

Some hold the view that scientific explanations of religious experiences discredit them or demonstrate that they are non-veridical or even delusional. But does this follow? There are two kinds of natural, scientific explanations of religious experience we will consider. The first one, introduced by Sigmund Freud, is a psychological explanation.

A psychological understanding of religious experience

There are many different psychological explanations of religious experience. One of the most well known was offered by Sigmund Freud (1856–1939). Freud argued that feelings of helplessness and fear in childhood foster a desire for fatherly, loving protection. This desire, or wish, for a protective figure carries on into adulthood and demands a greater, more powerful being than a human father. Two further desires are prominent as well: the substantiation of universal justice and a continuation of our own existence after death. These combined wishes are satisfied through the illusion of divine providence.[43]

Freud's wish fulfillment hypothesis of religious experience (and religion in general) was primarily directed toward theistic religion in which a heavenly father replaced an earthly one as provider and sustainer. But it can apply to all religions and religious experience: they are psychological projections which fulfill certain fundamental human needs and longings – nothing more.

A reply to this conclusion of a psychological hypothesis or explanation of religious experience is that it may well be true that one has a religious experience (or belief) which is caused by certain needs and desires. *But so what*? This does not disprove the content of the experience (or belief). Suppose, for example, that one believes in the existence of a personal and powerful God because of a deep-seated need for a heavenly Father. Does that prove that a personal and powerful God does not exist? Certainly not. Furthermore, it could be that such a personal and powerful God utilizes the familial relationship as a pedagogical tool for teaching people about God's nature. In fact, this is precisely what many Jews, Christians, and Muslims actually believe and how they interpret passages in their sacred scriptures which refer to God

Sigmund Freud (1856–1939) was an Austrian neurologist, psychologist, and the father of psychoanalysis. He is often considered one of the most influential thinkers of the twentieth century. His major works include *The Future of an Illusion*, *Totem and Taboo*, and *Moses and Monotheism*.

as Father, friend, etc. A similar kind of reply could be developed with respect to the other religions as well.

A neuroscientific understanding of religious experience

Recent advances in neuroscience have given rise to the view that religious experience may be the result of purely neurophysiological causes and thus are ultimately delusory. John Hick delineates five examples derived from recent research which cover the gamut of religious experience types:

1 Epileptic seizures and frontal lobe stimulation by the "Persinger helmet" [a transcranial magnetic stimulator] cause religious visions.
2 Psychotropic drugs cause various forms of religious experience.
3 "Pure" consciousness, consciousness of the Void, Emptiness, *sunyata*, is caused by consciousness continuing after the cutting off of all perceptual input.
4 The sense of unity with all reality is caused by closing down the awareness of the bodily boundaries of the individual.
5 The sense of the presence of God or of other supernatural beings is caused by a splitting of the "self-system" into two, one half seeing the other half as a distinct entity.[44]

The research currently being done on the human brain demonstrates that it may be possible to indentify neural correlates of religious experience – perhaps all types of religious experiences. Some draw the conclusion that this proves that the content of the experience is false, or that what the experience is about does not exist. But even if it can be shown that there are neuroscientific (or other natural) explanations for religious experiences, can we draw these conclusions? It seems not. William Wainwright explains why:

> Many philosophers think that an experience of *x* is veridical only if *x* is one of its causes. Thus, a visual experience of my desk is a perception of my desk only if the desk causes my experience. Suppose, then, that a scientifically adequate natural explanation of religious experience is discovered. Would it follow that (1) God or some other supernatural entity isn't its cause or, at least, that (2) there is no reason for thinking that a supernatural entity is its cause? It would not.
>
> Classical theists believe that scientifically adequate explanations can be provided for most natural phenomena. But they also believe that these phenomena are immediately grounded in God's causal activity. Hence, an adequate scientific explanation of religious experience wouldn't show that God isn't its cause. Nor would it show that God's causal activity isn't necessary for its occurrence.[45]

Furthermore, if one approaches the question of whether religious experience can justify religious belief from a naturalistic (atheistic) worldview, the range of possible answers is going to be quite different from the person who approaches it from a religious worldview. As Ninian Smart noted:

> Of course, if one has already made up one's mind that the universe has no transcendent source and no transcendent side to it, that the only reality is the observable cosmos, then no doubt it will be easier to think that religion [and religious experience] arises out of psychological and other urges.[46]

Finally, there may be independent reasons for believing in the existence of God or Absolute Reality and for believing that this reality is the grounding cause of religious experience.

SUMMARY

Whatever their cause, religious experiences have been a part of the fabric of the religious traditions from their earliest developments. They come in all variety of forms, yet they have several common features: they are universal, diverse, and momentous in the life of the experiencer, often resulting in a morally or spiritually transformed life.

One important question which arises from religious experience is whether this kind of phenomenon can provide justification for religious beliefs. A number of attempts have been made to demonstrate that it can, and we examined several of them: two arguments from analogy based on sense perception, the Principle of Credulity, and BEE STING.

There are also important challenges to the claim that religious experience can provide justification for religious belief, and we examined three of these. First, it can be argued that religious experiences are not verifiable, or checkable, as are other types of experiences. Second, the conflicting claims of the various experiences (conflicts both within and without the religious traditions) may cancel each other out. And third was the circularity objection in which it is argued that justification for religious belief depends on presuppositions which are not self-evident to everyone and yet which are then utilized as controls or limitations on the experience.

Next, we looked at two scientific explanations of religious experience: psychological and neuroscientific. According to Freud's psychological view, certain feelings for protection are satisfied through the illusion of divine Providence: a person projects the existence of God or Absolute Reality. More recently, neuroscientific advancements have demonstrated that religious experience may be the result of neurophysiological causes. As such, some conclude that religious experiences are ultimately delusory.

From whatever perspective they are studied or experienced, perhaps because of their unusual and sometimes outlandish manifestations, religious experiences continue to capture the attention of religious believers and skeptics alike, and they are likely to do so for a very long time.

QUESTIONS FOR REVIEW/DISCUSSION

1. Briefly explain the three categories of religious experience described in this chapter. Do you think the variety of religious experiences fall neatly within them? Is there overlap?
2. Do you personally know anyone who has had a religious experience, or have you had one yourself? If so, how did they (or how would you) describe it? Does any sort of justification of religious belief follow from it?
3. Search the literature for examples of nature mysticism and monistic mystical experience. Do you find there to be a close similarity, or even identity, between them? Reflect on your findings.
4. In what ways are Eastern religious experiences different from Western ones? In what ways are they similar? What are some possible reasons for their differences and similarities?
5. How might a person having religious experiences differentiate between real experiences of the divine or the Absolute on the one hand and delusion or hallucination on the other?
6. In *The Varieties of Religious Experience*, William James points out that certain intoxicants, such as alcohol, can induce a kind of mystical consciousness. If mystical states can be induced in this manner, what does this imply about *religious* mystical states, if anything?
7. As noted in the text, Michael Martin responds to the Principle of Credulity by arguing for a negative principle and notes that not experiencing a chair is good reason for believing that a chair is not present. How might a theist reply to this response?
8. Do you agree with the objection that religious experience is circular and so does not provide justification for religious belief? Why or why not?
9. Many individuals, throughout the centuries and from differing religious traditions, have had intense religious experiences. Given that many of the different religious traditions are contradictory in their views of the divine/ultimate reality, does this affect the veracity of the religious experiences? Explain.
10. If correlations between brain events and religious experience can be demonstrated in most types of religious experience, does this prove that the content of the experience is false, or that what the experience is about does not exist? If so, how? If not, what does it prove?

FURTHER READING

Alston, William (1991) *Perceiving God*. Ithaca, NY: Cornell University Press. (A widely recognized work on the epistemology of religious experience.)

Davis, Caroline Franks (1989) *The Evidential Force of Religious Experience*. Oxford: Clarendon Press. (Examines the nature of religious experiences from different religious traditions and their use as evidence for religious beliefs; includes a study of the role of models and metaphors in descriptions of religious experience.)

Dupré, Louis (1976) *Transcendent Selfhood: The Rediscovery of the Inner Life*. New York: Seabury. (Chapter 8 offers an important discussion of the nature of the self as informed by mysticism.)

Freud, Sigmund ([1927] 1989) *The Future of an Illusion*. Trans. James Strachey. New York: Norton and Norton. (A classic work on religion by one of the most important thinkers of the late nineteenth and early twentieth centuries.)

Gellman, Jerome I. (1997) *Experience of God and the Rationality of Religious Belief*. Ithaca, NY: Cornell University Press. (Argues that mystical experiences can provide a rational basis for belief in God's existence; also examines reductionist explanations of apparent experiences of God and finds them insufficient.)

Griffith-Dickson, Gwen (2000) *Human and Divine: An Introduction to the Philosophy of Religious Experience*. London: Duckworth. (Analyzes religious experience among the world's religions and philosophical traditions.)

Gutting, Gary (1982) *Religious Belief and Religious Skepticism*. Notre Dame, IN: University of Notre Dame Press. (A contemporary discussion of religious experience.)

Hood, Ralph W., Jr. (1995) *Handbook of Religious Experience*. Birmingham, AL: Religious Education Press. (Examines religious experience from many facets such as religious experience in different faith traditions, depth psychologies, psychological orientations, and specialty concerns, including feminist theory.)

James, William (1902) *The Varieties of Religious Experience*. New York: Modern Library. (A classic study on religious experience – perhaps the definitive work.)

Jantzen, Grace (1995) *Power, Gender and Christian Mysticism*. Cambridge: Cambridge University Press. (Focuses on how men of power defined and controlled the identity and role of the mystic.)

Katz, Steven T., ed. (1978) *Mysticism and Philosophical Analysis*. Oxford: Oxford University Press. (An important collection of articles by Steven Katz, Ninian Smart, Peter Moore, George Mavrodes, and others.)

Katz, Steven T., ed. (1983) *Mysticism and Religious Traditions*. Oxford: Oxford University Press. (Includes studies of Jewish, Islamic, Christian, Hindu, Confucian, and Taoist mysticism.)

Katz, Steven T., ed. (2000) *Mysticism and Sacred Scripture*. Oxford: Oxford University Press. (Explores the neglected topic of how the mystics and mystical traditions use and interpret sacred scriptures.)

Martin, C. B. (1959) *Religious Belief*. Ithaca, NY: Cornell University Press. (Examines religious belief, including mystical experience, and offers an unsympathetic appraisal.)

Martin, Michael (1990) *Atheism: A Philosophical Justification*. Philadelphia, PA: Temple University Press. (Chapter 6 contains a critique of the view that religious experience offers evidence or justification for religious beliefs.)

Momen, Moojan (1999) *The Phenomenon of Religion: A Thematic Approach*. Oxford: Oneworld. (A rich and informative work on the phenomenon of religion which includes an emphasis on religious experience.)

Otto, Rudolf (1923) *The Idea of the Holy*. Oxford: Oxford University Press. (A classic work on religious thought and experience; Otto explores the idea of God as transcendent and "wholly other.")

Proudfoot, Wayne (1985) *Religious Experience*. Berkeley, CA: University of California Press. (Argues that all religious experience is filtered through ones' own concepts, beliefs, and linguistic practices.)

Shankara ([eighth century] 1947) *Shankara's Crest-Jewel of Discrimination*. Trans. Swami Prabhavananda and Christopher Isherwood. Hollywood, CA: Vedanta Press. (The classic eighth-century Advaita text about the path to true understanding of Brahman and *Atman*; includes descriptions of the Advaita Vedāntin experience of one's unity with Brahman.)

Smart, Ninian (1991) *The Religious Experience*. 4th edition. London: Macmillan. (A comprehensive history of religious experience.)

Strong, John S. (1995) *The Experience of Buddhism*. Belmont, CA: Wadsworth. (Anthology which offers translations of Buddhist texts of philosophy and doctrine as well as accounts of Buddhist practices, rituals, and experiences.)

Underhill, Evelyn ([1911] 1993) *Mysticism*. Oxford: Oneworld. (A classic exploration of the mystical experience.)

Wainwright, William (1981) *Mysticism: A Study of Its Nature, Cognitive Value, and Moral Implications*. Madison, WI: University of Wisconsin Press. (A comprehensive study on mysticism from a sympathetic analytic philosopher.)

Yandell, Keith (1993) *The Epistemology of Religious Experience*. Cambridge: Cambridge University Press. (An analytic philosopher argues against the view that religious experience is ineffable and for the view that strong numinous experience provides evidence that God exists; a rather technical treatment of the topic, but well worth a careful read.)

Zeahner, R. C. (1967) *Mysticism: Sacred and Profane*. Oxford: Oxford University Press. (Analyzes religious and religious-type experiences from drug-induced experiences to the religious experiences of Christians, Muslims, and Hindus.)

Zeahner, R. C. (1994) *Hindu and Muslim Mysticism*. Oxford: Oneworld. (Traces the development of mystical thought within the formative periods of the Hindu and Muslim traditions.)

WEBSITES

http://www.lamp.ac.uk/aht/Research/research.html
Religious Experience Research Centre. Located at the University of Wales, Lampeter, this center is focused on the study of contemporary spiritual and religious experience. Includes fascinating personal stories of religious experience.

http://www.infidels.org/library/modern/theism/experience.html
Infidels.org website. This link focuses on religious experience from a critical, skeptical perspective and includes essays and further links on the subject.

http://www.religiousworlds.com/mystic/index.html
Mysticism Resources Page. A website which provides information on traditional and modern spiritualities, including various forms of mysticism.

http://etext.lib.virginia.edu/toc/modeng/public/JamVari.html
William James's classic *The Varieties of Religious Experience* in electronic text form; Electronic Text Center, University of Virginia Library.

10 The self, death and the afterlife

All of the major religious traditions offer hope for satisfying the fundamental longings of humanity – longings for peace, fulfillment, and real, sustained happiness. But of course such longings are not often satisfied in this life, so the religions provide a solution: while our deepest yearnings may not be fulfilled in the here and now, they will ultimately be so. This life is not the end; we will continue to exist (in some sense) beyond death.

This claim raises a number of questions. Do we really continue to survive after we die, or is death the very end of our conscious existence? What kinds of evidence are there for such a belief, if any? If we do survive death, what will this experience be like, and what is it that survives? Will our thoughts and beliefs and memories be as they are now, or will everything change? Will I know my family and friends in the afterlife, or will we all be transformed beyond recognition? If we have thought much about life after death, these are the sorts of questions we have probably pondered. How we answer them is largely determined by our worldview or religious tradition.

While each of the world religions provides a positive answer to the question of whether there is a continued existence after death, the answers provided by them are quite different. Before we explore some of the central questions surrounding life after death, it is important to first delve into the issue of what the self is, and of what personal identity consists, for our answers to these issues will significantly influence our understanding of how we view the afterlife.

CONCEPTIONS OF THE SELF

There are various conceptions of the self which have been held historically in the East and the West, and we can delineate four of the major ones in the following manner:

1 dualism
2 materialism
3 monistic pantheism
4 the Buddhist doctrine of no-self.

We will briefly examine each one in turn.

Dualism

There have been a variety of conceptions of the self historically, and in the West dualism has been the most widely held of them all. On one major dualist account, a person consists of two substances, a material substance (the body) and an immaterial or mental substance (the soul or mind). René Descartes (1596–1650) is perhaps the most widely recognized defender of substance, or mind–body, dualism. On his account, the soul is an unextended (non-spatial) substance, and it is contrasted with the body, an extended (spatial) substance. The soul and the body (somehow) relate to one another, but how an immaterial substance can interact with a physical substance is a mystery – a mystery which has often been castigated as the problem of the "ghost in the machine."[1]

Another form of dualism is the Thomistic view (derived from the work of Thomas Aquinas, 1225–1274) in which the soul is understood to be a complex structure that keeps in check various mental states (such as feelings, thoughts, and sensations), capacities, and structures. On this account the soul, while immaterial, is what animates, unifies, and develops the biological functions of the physical body. It is an individual's source of life as well as its ordering principle.[2]

In one form or another, many of those in the Western religions have been dualists as the Hebrew Bible, the New Testament, and the Qur'an all seem, on a straightforward read at least, to affirm the reality of body and soul.[3] Many of the major Western philosophers, such as Plato, Aquinas, and Descartes, also held to some form of dualism. In the East, too, there are Hindu conceptions in which a distinction is held between the individual soul (*atman*) and the physical matter (*prakriti*) which makes up the body. Furthermore, most dualists – both religious and non-religious – have affirmed life after death. For some, immortality involves an embodied state, and the Jewish, Christian and Islamic views of the resurrection of the body are cases in point. For others, life after death involves being reincarnated in another physical existence – perhaps as an animal or another person. Yet for other dualists, life after death is disembodied existence where the soul is forever separated from any future physical existence.

A number of arguments have been put forth in defense of dualism, including the following. First, there is the distinction between physical events on the one hand and mental events on the other. Consider your thought of London. Does this thought have a weight, shape, smell, or taste? It seems to not be the kind of thing which can be described in terms of physics, chemistry and biology. But the *brain event* which is correlated with your thought of London *is* the kind of thing which is described in terms of physics, chemistry and biology. Therefore, mental events and brain events are not identical; one is physical and the other is not – they are two separate things.[4] The dualist argues that this distinction between mental and physical things is most plausibly explained within the dualist framework.[5]

Second, and related to the first, is what's called the *knowledge argument*. The following is a well-known story by philosopher Frank Jackson which is intended to demonstrate the heart of the argument:

> Mary is a brilliant scientist who is, for whatever reason, forced to investigate the world from a black and white room via a black and white television monitor. She specializes in the neurophysiology of vision and acquires, let us suppose, all the physical information there is to obtain about what goes on

> when we see ripe tomatoes, or the sky, and use terms like 'red', 'blue', and so on. She discovers, for example, just which wavelength combinations from the sky stimulate the retina, and exactly how this produces via the central nervous system the contraction of the vocal cords and expulsion of air from the lungs that results in the uttering of the sentence 'The sky is blue'. ...What will happen when Mary is released from her black and white room or is given a color television monitor? Will she learn anything or not? It seems just obvious that she will learn something about the world and our visual experience of it. But then is it inescapable that her previous knowledge was incomplete. But she had *all* the physical information. *Ergo* there is more to have than that, and Physicalism [the doctrine that everything which exists can be completely described in terms of physical information] is false.[6]

Since there are different kinds of experiences (subjective and objective) and different kinds of information (physical and non-physical) which a person can have, there is a difference between the physical and the mental. So, the argument continues, some form of dualism makes more sense than materialism as a general account of the self.[7]

A third argument offered in defense of dualism comes from personal identity. Consider the following scenario. Suppose you took your automobile – whatever it is you might drive – to the repair shop. The mechanic tells you that there are a number of problems with it and that it will take him a week to get it repaired. Now suppose when you return a week later, you discover that he replaced every single part of the automobile with a new part – each fender, tire, bolt ... everything (an expensive endeavor, for sure)! Would this still be the same automobile you brought in a week earlier? It seems evident that it would not be the same one. As a matter of fact, it could be argued that even if just *one* part had been replaced it would not literally be the same automobile; it would be similar, but not identical.

So, when it comes to objects like automobiles, a change of parts (and especially essential parts) changes the identity of the object. But what about persons? Is it the same for us? If our "parts" change, are we still the same person? In one sense, all of our parts *have* changed since childhood (all, or at least most all, of the cells in the human body are regenerated/replaced every seven years), but are we not yet the same person? Is not that person in your childhood photos you? Substance dualists argue that we maintain absolute identity through change because our essence – our immaterial substantial soul – remains the same through bodily change.

Materialists have various responses to this argument. One response is to agree with the dualist that personal identity is not constituted by the physical parts of a person but rather by her memories or psychological states. Same memories or psychological states equal same person. Another response is to disagree with the dualist – to affirm that personal identity is constituted by the material parts which make up an individual, but to add that those parts are not the body as a whole but certain fundamental parts. For example, personal identity may be constituted by some part of the brain or central nervous system – some part which doesn't change over time but literally remains the same (it is debatable whether there are such parts). Or perhaps personal identity consists in a certain continuity of parts which remain interconnected over time. For example, even though many (perhaps most!) of the parts of my automobile have been replaced by my mechanic over the past five years, it is still the same vehicle. And its identity is the same because of the continuity and interconnectedness of many of its parts.

Materialism

The idea that there is no immaterial aspect of the self – no soul or immaterial mind – has not been a prominent view historically, at least in the West. However, in the last two centuries, it has been held by a considerable number of persons, especially among those in academic settings. A host of arguments are offered to support the materialist view of the self, one being that there seems to be no reason to believe that human persons are anything more than the matter of which they are constituted. Philosopher Paul Churchland expresses the view concisely:

> [T]he important point about the standard evolutionary story is that the human species and all of its features are the wholly physical outcome of a purely physical process… . If this is the correct account of our origins, then there seems neither need, nor room, to fit any nonphysical substances or properties into our theoretical account of ourselves. We are creatures of matter. And we should learn to live with that fact.[8]

Further arguments have been offered to support the materialist view, and most of them hinge on the claim that a physical brain is necessary for a functioning mind. On one materialist view, called the *identity theory*, all mental properties are identical to physical properties of the brain. The mind just is the activity of the brain, and so there is no need to posit some additional immaterial mind or soul to account for reason, emotion, will, or consciousness. Much of the evidence in support of this view comes from the apparent neural dependence of mental phenomena. For example, narcotics, alcohol, and other drugs affect one's mental abilities, as do various brain diseases. This makes sense if the mind is the activity of the brain, but not so, it is argued, if the mind is a separate immaterial substance. Dualists respond by claiming that there is a *causal connection* between brain states and mental states but from this, they maintain, it does not necessarily follow that mental states are *identical* to brain states. Identity theorists reply that there is no need to add an additional substance when the data can be explained with just the one.[9]

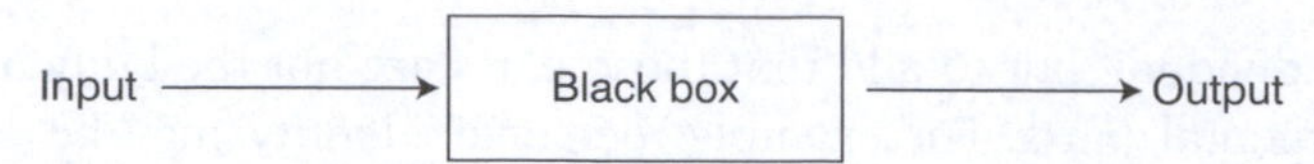

Figure 10.1 The mind as a black box

For a number of reasons which we cannot go into here, the identity theory has been in decline in recent years. Another materialist view has grown in prominence and is probably the dominant view today among philosophers of mind and cognitive scientists. This view is called *functionalism*.[10] Functionalists maintain (as do dualists) that it is impossible to identify particular mental states with particular brain states. However, it is possible to characterize mental states by reference to behavior. On the functionalist account, the mind is like a black box and can be explained in terms of inputs and outputs. Consider this analogy. I do not know how this computer on which I am typing works; I am totally unfamiliar with its internal structures, parts and inner workings. Nevertheless, I don't need to know such information. What counts is that given certain inputs, certain outputs follow. When I hit the letter "j" for example, a j shows up on the screen. To me, the computer is a black box.

Furthermore, computational functions can occur in different mediums. The earliest computers were made out of materials that were very different from what they are made of today, and their internal and external structures were quite different as well. Nevertheless, they could perform many of the same computations as modern computers (such as adding 2 + 2). On the functionalist account, the mind is a black box – it is like a living computer. In human persons, computational processes are fully realized in material structures, as they are in computers, and so no additional non-material entities (such as an immaterial mind or soul) needs to be posited to explain them.

For some materialists there is no life after death. Once the physical body dies, the person perishes forever. For other materialists, life after death is a real possibility. Recent Christian materialists, for example, maintain that there will be life after death when God raises the body back to life again in the eschaton.[11] We will examine the possibility of resurrection later.

Monistic pantheism

Another view of the self, which is held primarily by those in the Advaita Vedānta school of Hinduism, is monistic pantheism – "monism" (reality is a unified whole – there are no distinctions of things); and "pantheism" (all is divine). According to Advaita Vedānta, ultimate reality (which is typically referred to as "Brahman") is undifferentiated and beyond all qualities, including personhood. The universe flows from Brahman, whose very nature includes *maya* – an illusory aspect from which apparent differentiation and individuality emerged. Individual selfhood is an illusion,

> A jar made of clay is not other than clay. It is clay essentially. The form of the jar has no independent existence. What, then, is the jar? Merely an invented name!
>
> The form of the jar can never be perceived apart from the clay. What, then, is the jar? An appearance! The reality is the clay itself.
>
> This universe is an effect of Brahman. It can never be anything else but Brahman. Apart from Brahman, it does not exist. There is nothing beside Him. He who says that this universe has an independent existence is still suffering from delusion. He is like a man talking in his sleep.
>
> Shankara ([eighth century] 1947)

however, and a product of *maya*. The true self, or *Atman*, is in reality Brahman. This is reflected in the well-known Vedāntin phrase, "That art Thou."[12]

When one finally reaches enlightenment, or *moksha*, one escapes the clutches of this grand illusion and becomes aware of one's true Self as undifferentiated Brahman. A simile which is sometimes used here is that Brahman is like Space and individual selves are like space in jars. When the jars are destroyed the space in the jars merges back into Space. Enlightenment breaks open the jars, and individual identity is ultimately seen as being absorbed into undifferentiated Brahman.[13] Achieving *moksha* is an arduous task, however, and for the Vedāntin the process by which one attains it involves working off the negative effects of karma, typically through a succession of reincarnations.[14]

No-self

For a number of reasons Buddhists are not satisfied with the dualist, materialist, and Hindu views of the self. We saw back in Chapter 3 the Buddhist doctrine of *Anatman* (no-self). This view is based on the Buddhist metaphysic in which there is no "thing" that has independent existence; there are no individual substances. Similar to the Advaitin view noted above, a central truth of one school of Buddhism, the Mahayana school, is that the individual self does not exist and our belief that it does is merely an illusion. But contrary to the Advaitin view, there are various experiences, desires, feelings, and cravings which are real and are in continual flux.

Nevertheless, there is no self of which they are constituents. The following account of the Buddha's teachings on the matter is found in the sermon entitled "The Not-self Characteristic" as found in the Anatta-lakkhana sutta of the Pali Canon (Buddhists scriptures):

> The body, monks, is not self. If the body were the self, this body would not lend itself to dis-ease. It would be possible (to say) with regard to the body, "Let my body be thus. Let my body not be thus." But precisely because the body is not self, the body lends itself to dis-ease. And it is not possible (to say) with regard to the body, "Let my body be thus. Let my body not be thus."
>
> Feeling is not self.... Perception is not self.... Mental processes are not self.... Consciousness is not self. If consciousness were the self, this consciousness would not lend itself to dis-ease. It would be possible (to say) with regard to consciousness, "Let my consciousness be thus. Let my consciousness not be thus." But precisely because consciousness is not self, consciousness lends itself to dis-ease. And it is not possible (to say) with regard to consciousness, "Let my consciousness be thus. Let my consciousness not be thus."
>
> Thus, monks, any body [or consciousness, or feeling, or perception, etc.] whatsoever – past, future, or present; internal or external; blatant or subtle, common or sublime, far or near; every body [or consciousness, or feeling, or perception, etc.] – is to be seen as it actually is with right discernment as: "This is not mine. This is not myself. This is not what I am."[15]

An old Indian chariot analogy is often cited regarding the no-self view. A chariot is not the spokes, or the wheels, or the frame, or the axle; it's none of the individual parts. Neither is it the individual parts taken together. Yet neither is it something other than the parts. It turns out to be merely the sound of the word "chariot." So too with individual selves.[16]

Buddhists grant that grasping the no-self teaching may not be easy; here too it may well require working off the negative effects of karma and multiple reincarnations to come to this realization.

So we have four distinctive conceptions of the self, and they each provide unique views about death and the afterlife. For the materialist, life after death is possible if the body can be raised from the dead or in some way be reconstituted. For the dualist, physical death is not necessarily the end of the self either, for the soul may well continue to exist in the afterlife, either embodied or disembodied. For the Hindu pantheistic and Buddhist no-self conceptions, reincarnation and karma are of fundamental importance for understanding what happens after the body dies. We will look next at reincarnation and karma.

REINCARNATION AND KARMA

There are interesting similarities between the religions of the East and the West regarding death and the afterlife. For example, they both offer an eternal hope beyond the grave – hope for ultimately satisfying (or, as we will see below, extinguishing) the longings experienced in this life. But there are also significant differences between them. Perhaps the most striking difference is the widespread belief among those in the East in karma and reincarnation.

In its popular formulations, reincarnation is the view that the conscious self transmigrates from one physical body to the next after death. Each human being has lived former lives, perhaps as another human being or perhaps as another kind of organism, such as an animal. Some people claim to have memories of experiences from previous lives. For example, there is the famous case of an Indian boy named Parmod Sharma. As a young boy, Parmod began remembering specific details about his life as a man named Parmanand. He told his mother that she didn't need to cook meals for him any longer because he had a wife in Moradabad (a town about ninety miles away from Parmod's home). He then began speaking about many of the specifics of his life as a businessman who owned several shops – even offering the company names, including a biscuit and soda shop called "Mohan Brothers" – and described details about his wife and family. Not only did he claim to be married, but he had five children, four sons and a daughter!

Word got out about Parmod's story, and eventually reached the ears of a family in Moradabad who fit his descriptions to a tee. Turns out the family did own a biscuit shop called "Mohan Brothers" and one of the brothers, Parmanand, died eighteen months prior to Parmod's birth. Parmanand had left a widow and five children, four sons and a daughter. This story and thousands of others like it have been investigated and many of them published.[17] While a number of them turn out to be explainable by cryptoamnesia, or hidden memories, many of them cannot.

Reincarnation is an essential doctrine for both Hindus and Buddhists. But one might wonder how reincarnation makes sense within a Buddhist view of no-self. Indeed, there is much debate among Buddhist scholars on this subject.[18] One of the more influential answers is that at the death of consciousness (or the dissolution of the *skandhas* – mental events or bundles[19]), a new consciousness arises. This is called "rebirth," a term which better captures the meaning of the event than "reincarnation." This new consciousness is not identical to the former, but neither is it completely different from it. There is a causal connection between them as they form a part of the same causal continuum. For many Buddhists, the reason for the widespread belief in an individual self is ignorance (*avidya*). In order to move beyond ignorance and experience enlightenment, or *nirvana*, one must understand this no-self teaching as well the Four Noble Truths and the Noble Eightfold Path described back in Chapter 3.

Reincarnation is usually connected with the doctrine of *karma*, the idea that we reap the good and bad consequences of our actions, either in this life or in another. Those who affirm reincarnation and karma often point to a difficulty they see with the Western view: it seems exceedingly unfair that one child is born healthy into a wealthy, loving family whereas another child is born sickly into a poor, cruel environment. If there is a Creator God who brought these two persons into the world, such a God seems to be unloving and unjust. However, if the two children are

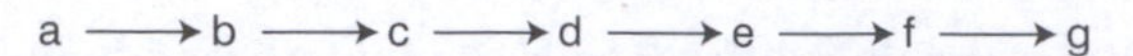

The letters a, b, c, etc., represent the life circumstances of a particular individual; the arrows represent the causal flow of circumstances from one's previous life to the next.

Figure 10.2 The karmic law of cause and effect

reaping the consequences of actions they performed in previous lives, this seems to provide a justification for the inequalities. The effect of one's karma determines the circumstances of our present and future lives; we reap what we sow.

Another reason sometimes offered for the belief in reincarnation is that many people claim to have experienced a previous life, and sometimes they can even document events which have occurred hundreds or thousands of years prior to their birth.[20] Even the more common déjà vu experiences are cited as evidence of reincarnation.

A number of objections have also been raised against reincarnation. For one, does it really offer a plausible explanation for the inequalities found in this life? According to the karmic law of cause and effect, my present life circumstances are explained by my actions in a previous life. And my life circumstances in that life are explained by my life circumstances in a life previous to that one. And so on indefinitely. So the solution we hoped for regarding inequalities seems to never come to an end; it ends up being relegated to the dustbins of the infinite past. Furthermore, does it really seem fair that when a person who has lived a long life dies and is reincarnated, she must start all over again as a baby with her maturity, life experiences, wisdom, and memories completely gone?

So we have examined four views of the self. On the materialist view, a person is the physical matter of which he or she is composed. On such a view, life after death would be possible if the matter was somehow brought back to life (on the identity theory) or if the mental processes of the brain were somehow transferred to a different medium after death (on the functionalist account). For the dualist, life after death could involve either an embodied or disembodied existence, and we will examine arguments for and against these possibilities below. Reincarnation and karma typically accompany the pantheist and no-self views. On both accounts there is life after death, but the afterlife involves a series of reincarnations and a radical transformation of what the individual understands herself to be: divine for the pantheist and impermanent non-substantiality for the Buddhist.

ARGUMENTS FOR IMMORTALITY

There are a number of arguments put forth by those who believe in immorality.[21] We will limit our examination to four.

Near-death experiences

The first argument we shall examine is based on near-death experiences (NDEs) which have allegedly been had by tens of millions of people.[22] NDEs are common patterns of events associated with impending death. They include a multitude of sensations such as fear, serenity, the presence of light, traveling through a tunnel, a heightened spiritual awareness, leaving the body and looking down on one's body, and meeting other persons or supernatural beings.

Astonishingly, virtually everyone who has had an NDE has concluded that there is life after death based on what they saw or felt.[23] Of course these experiences could be illusions or delusions or hallucinations, but the following elements of the experiences lend support to their veracity:

1 they are widely experienced by persons from diverse backgrounds and belief systems
2 there are common characteristics to the experiences
3 the experiences are sometimes quite specific with information otherwise unavailable to the person (such as locating objects in the room during surgery which were not present while the patient was alive/awake; describing an event in another location which occurred during surgery, etc.).

Besides NDEs, millions of people have described having other types of out-of-body experiences (OBEs) as well, including reincarnation and astral projection. While the evidence for NDEs and OBEs is not conclusive, such experiences provide some warrant for the belief in a soul which is separate from the body. If the soul exists and can be separated from the body, then life after death is a reasonable inference.

Resurrection

Some religions – most notably Judaism and Christianity – include the belief that our physical bodies will, in the eschaton, be resurrected from the dead. On the historic

> My recent [near-death] experiences have slightly weakened my conviction that my genuine death, which is due fairly soon, will be the end of me, though I continue to hope that it will be. They have not weakened my conviction that there is no god. I trust that my remaining an atheist will allay the anxieties of my fellow supporters of the Humanist Association, the Rationalist Press, and the South Place Ethical Society.
>
> A. J. Ayer[24]

Christian account, one bodily resurrection has already occurred: Jesus of Nazareth. Easter, of course, is the Christian celebration of this unique event. The Apostle Paul actually uses Jesus' resurrection as evidence for our own future bodily resurrection.[25]

There is much debate in the recent literature in philosophy of religion and biblical studies on the meaning of and evidence for the resurrection of Jesus.[26] Many biblical scholars – both those who believe that Jesus was resurrected from the dead and those who do not – agree with the following:

1 Jesus died on a cross and was placed in a tomb.
2 Jesus' body was gone from the tomb soon after his death (or at least the disciples believed this).
3 Jesus' disciples believed he was resurrected from the dead and appeared to and spoke with them.
4 Key Jewish leaders, including Saul of Tarsus (who became the Apostle Paul) and Jesus' brother James, were converted to belief in and worship of Jesus shortly after his death.

The question then becomes what best explains this data. Gary Habermas, Stephen Davis, and William Lane Craig are notable scholars who argue that Jesus' literal, bodily resurrection provides the best explanation of the historical facts. Michael Martin, Antony Flew, and Robert Price are notable scholars who argue that a naturalistic account provides the best explanation of the historical facts about Jesus body after his death. They maintain that there are reasonable, non-miraculous explanations for the emergence of the belief in Jesus' resurrection after his death, and so there is no reason to affirm a supernatural one.

The resurrection debate continues, but one solid conclusion we can reach is this: if there is reason to believe that Jesus was raised from the dead (and this is hotly contested), then this would provide evidence for life after death.

The nature of God

For most theists across the religious spectrum, including such towering historical figures as Thomas Aquinas (1225–1274), Avicenna (980–1037), and Madhva (1238–1317), God is understood to be infinitely good, loving, wise, and just. As such, God is not the kind of being who would create human beings with the longings and aspirations we all have, such as life after death, on the one hand, and then let them go eternally unsatisfied on the other. So, the argument goes, we can rest assured that there will be life after this life; God will make it so. Furthermore, if you love someone, you would not want them to cease to exist. Since God loves us with a perfect love, he would not want us to cease existing. So God will ensure our eternal existence.

Sri Madhvacarya, also known as **Madhva** (1238–1317) was the founder of the Dvaita or dualist school of Hindu Vedānta philosophy. He believed and argued that the Vedāntan canonical texts (the sacred Hindu scriptures including the Vedas and the Bhagavadgita) teach that there is a real, fundamental difference between the self (*Atman*) and ultimate reality (Brahman). This is in contrast to the Advaita Vedānta school in which *Atman* is identified with Brahman.

These assurances, of course, are not as certain as we might hope them to be. For as we will see below, even if God exists, there could be good reasons why a loving, just, and omnibenevolent God would not desire that we live on endlessly.

The nature of the soul

Both ancient and modern philosophers have argued for immortality based on the indestructible nature of the soul. Plato (428–347 BCE), for example, in his book *Phaedo* argues that if we practice philosophy in the right way we can be cheerful in the face of death, for the soul of the one who rightly practices philosophy is immortal since it is pure and simple (that is, has no parts) and divine-like. As such, it cannot be scattered or destroyed.[27] More recently, J. M. E. McTaggart (1866–1925) has also offered an argument for the immortality of soul based on its simplicity.[28] He argues that the soul is probably immortal since 1) it is not constituted by separable parts, and so cannot be destroyed through a separation of its parts (as material objects are destroyed), and 2) it probably cannot be annihilated since there is no evidence that anything is ever annihilated (even material objects don't just cease existing).

However, even if it is the case that we have an immaterial soul which does not consist of parts, one might ask why it could not simply cease existing with the death of the body? Perhaps like a magnetic field which is destroyed with the destruction of the magnet, so too the soul is destroyed with the destruction of the body.

ARGUMENTS AGAINST IMMORTALITY

There are also a number of arguments against immortality, and we will consider three of them.

The dependency of consciousness on the brain

One of the central arguments against immortality can be put this way:

1 In order for a human being to be immortal, the individual human self must survive physical death.
2 To be an individual human self entails being (able to be) conscious.
3 For an individual human self to be conscious, he or she needs a live, physical brain.
4 But the physical brain dies when the physical body dies.
5 Therefore, the individual human self dies when the body dies.
6 Therefore, a human being cannot be immortal.

The main premise in question for our purposes is 3, and several kinds of evidence are cited in support of it. First, and as we saw earlier in this chapter, since drugs and brain diseases affect mental abilities and consciousness, this provides strong empirical evidence that brain activity and consciousness depend on the brain (or are identical to the workings of the brain). Similarly, brain damage also affects consciousness and mental capabilities. Beyond this, various mental abilities are locatable in the brain. For example, the prefrontal cortex is the area of the brain in which the operations of consciousness, thinking, learning, and imagination occur. Taken together, these facts offer strong support that for an individual human self to be conscious, he or she needs a live, physical brain. Since dead persons lack a live, physical brain, there cannot be conscious life after death.

One response to this argument is that while having a live, functional physical brain may be a *sufficient* condition for consciousness, it is not a *necessary* condition. A number of dualists, for example, maintain that the soul continues to exist in a conscious state even after the death of the body.[29] Another response is to agree that individual human selves do need a live, physical brain to be conscious, and that will not be conscious following the death of the body (unless, say, God gives them a new body). However, they will be conscious once again when they are bodily resurrected from the dead (as noted above, bodily resurrection is a Jewish and Christian view).

Personal identity

Another argument against life after death directed at the dualist has to do with personal identity. If souls continued to exist in a disembodied state after the death of the physical body, then what would identify them as unique, individual entities? I can identify my friend Jim as the unique individual he is by pointing to him, or describing his physical characteristics, or perhaps by noting the way he behaves when in certain situations. But if Jim had no physical body, how could he possibly be identified as Jim? How could he be distinguished from, say, my other friends Terry, Tim and Cris? What would it be that made him the unique person he was when embodied?

A dualist could respond by claiming that even if it were not possible for one to identify a disembodied soul, or to distinguish one soul from another, it does not follow that such disembodied souls could not exist. While there might be an epistemic (knowledge) problem, it does not follow that there is an ontological (being) problem. Furthermore, since many monotheists believe that immortality will be embodied, it could be the resurrected body which constitutes the criterion for re-identification after death (from an external, third-person perspective) while the immaterial soul would constitute the survival criterion (from an internal, first-person perspective).

Eternal misery

One final argument against life after death does not entail a materialist view of the self as do those above. This argument can be utilized by materialists or dualists, by theists, pantheists or atheists. The argument runs this way. Even given the existence of a loving, kind, and gracious God, post-mortem existence may not be desirable; in fact, it may be boring or tedious or even downright horrifying. In this regard Grace Jantzen makes the following point:

> A paradise of sensuous delights would become boring, it would in the long run be pointless and utterly unfulfilling. We can perhaps imagine ways of making a very long feast meaningful; we do, after all, cope with lengthy terrestrial social occasions by choosing interesting conversational partners, and making the dinner occasions not merely for food and drink but also for stimulating discussion and for giving and receiving friendship the value of which extends beyond the termination of the dinner. But if the feasting literally never came to an end, if there were no progress possible from the sensuous enjoyment of paradise to anything more meaningful, then we might well wish, like Elina Macropolis, to terminate the whole business and destroy the elixir of youth.[30]

So eternal life might well be boring, pointless and unfulfilling. Heaven could be hell.

While Jantzen doesn't argue that there is no life after death, she does argue that it cannot be inferred from the claim that God is loving. She continues:

> Christian theologians increasingly recognize that it is not the case that the whole earth, every primrose, every songbird, all the galaxies of all the heavens, exist for the benefit of humanity alone. Yet it is true that God brought about the existence of all these things and delights in them; then it is also true that some of the things he delights in perish forever… . Just as that which is morally valuable is valuable for its own sake and not for the reward it can bring, so also trust in God, if it is worthwhile at all, is worthwhile even if it cannot go on forever. A relationship with another human being does not become pointless just because at some point

> it will end with the death of one of the partners; why should it be thought that a relationship with God would be pointless if one day it too should end?[31]

So eternal sensuous delights won't do it for us. What could a never-ending life be like such that it would be truly and eternally enjoyable – something we would desire forever? Perhaps there is no answer. Maybe Emily Dickinson got it right: "That it will never come again is what makes life so sweet." Perhaps even if God gave us a soul, there is no never-ending afterlife, for it would be just too miserable.

Charles Taliaferro responds to Jantzen's argument by making a distinction between a *time-enclosed good*, which he defines as "any good project, thing, event, state or process which is good but its good value is not preserved if it is temporally unlimited in extent" (e.g. eating a tasty meal), and a *non-time-enclosed good*, which he defines as "any good project, event, state or process which is good and its good value is not lost if it is temporally unlimited in extent."[32] He claims that for an afterlife to be truly good, it cannot consist of a singular time-enclosed good. But there is no reason to believe that an afterlife cannot include an indefinite variety of time-enclosed and non-time-enclosed goods. If God is omniscient and omnipotent, it seems God could certainly create an indefinite number of such goods. Taliaferro further argues that if we have reason to believe God deeply loves us, then we have reason to believe that God will preserve our lives, especially since as persons we possess a value which is not exhausted over time.

SUMMARY

In this chapter we have examined different conceptions of the self and the afterlife. We first focused on four unique conceptions of the self: dualism, materialism, monistic pantheism, and the Buddhist doctrine of no-self. For the materialist, life after death, if there is such life, would entail the continued existence (or the reconstituted existence) of the individual physical body. For the dualist, life after death could involve either an embodied or disembodied existence and the individual would exist in the afterlife as the very same person because he or she has the very same soul. For the monistic pantheist and no-self views, reincarnation and karma play a fundamental role both in this life and the next. For the pantheist the self is ultimate, undifferentiated reality. However, it may take many lifetimes to come to this realization. For the adherent of the no-self view, there is no substantial self, and (as with the pantheist) it may take many reincarnations to finally and fully recognize this fundamental truth.

We next examined arguments for and against personal immortality. We first looked at several arguments for immortality: near death experiences, resurrection, the nature of God, and the nature of the soul. While there are evidences for immortality, none of them offer conclusive proof. We then looked at several arguments against immortality: the dependency of consciousness on the brain, personal identity, and eternal misery. The evidences against immortality are impressive, but here too they are inconclusive.

Who we are and what happens to us after death are perennial questions that human beings have pondered for millennia. Reflecting on such questions will, no doubt, continue to be a part of the human intellectual experience in this life and, perhaps, even beyond.

QUESTIONS FOR REVIEW/DISCUSSION

1. Which view of the self do you find most persuasive? What are your reasons?
2. Do you agree with the materialist argument that since there is neural dependence on mental activity (being drunk affects one's ability to reason, for example) there is no need to posit some additional immaterial mind or soul to account for reason, emotion, will, or consciousness? Why? How might a dualist respond?
3. Explain the knowledge argument. Do you find it persuasive? Why or why not?
4. Do you believe in life after death? State your reasons for believing what you do about this matter.
5. What are some reasons for believing in reincarnation and karma? Evaluate one or two of those reasons.
6. Which argument against immortality do you believe is the strongest? Why? Evaluate the premises of this argument.
7. Of the four arguments for immortality presented in this chapter, the first two include empirical evidence and the latter two include religious/philosophical evidence. With respect to immortality, which type of evidence do you find most persuasive? Why?
8. Do some research on the evidence for near-death experiences (see Further reading and Websites below). Does this evidence make it more plausible to believe in life after death? Why or why not?
9. Do you agree with the claim that eternal life would end up being boring and pointless? What kinds of activities might keep it forever interesting and meaningful?
10. If there is no life after death, does this lead to a nihilistic view of life? Explain.

FURTHER READING

Baker, Lynne Rudder (2000) *Persons and Bodies: A Constitution View*. Cambridge: Cambridge University Press. (Defends a constitution view of human persons and offers a detailed account of the relation between persons and their bodies.)

Churchland, Paul M. (1992) *Matter and Consciousness: A Contemporary Introduction to the Philosophy of Mind*, rev. edition. Cambridge, MA: The MIT Press. (Presents pros and cons of various positions in the mind/body debate, including dualism, behaviorism, reductive materialism, functionalism and eliminative materialism; defends a materialist view of the mind.)

Cooper, John (2000) *Body, Soul, and Life Everlasting: Biblical Anthropology and the Monism-Dualism Debate*. Grand Rapids, MI: Eerdmans. (Utilizing the fields of theology, philosophy and science, Cooper defends what he calls "holistic dualism.")

Davis, Stephen T. (1993) *Risen Indeed: Making Sense of the Resurrection*. Grand Rapids, MI: Eerdmans. (Argues that the Christian belief in the bodily resurrection of persons is rational on historical, philosophical, and theological grounds.)

Edwards, Paul, ed. (1992) *Immortality*. New York: Macmillan. (An important collection of articles on the subject.)

Flew, Antony (1987) *The Logic of Immortality*. Oxford: Basil Blackwell. (A philosophical critique of the doctrine of immortality.)

Habermas, Gary and J. P. Moreland (2004) *Beyond Death: Exploring the Evidence for Immortality*. Eugene, OR: Wipf and Stock. (Explores the nature, evidence, and implications of immortality.)

Hasker, William (1999) *The Emergent Self*. Ithaca, NY: Cornell University Press. (Challenges materialist views of the mind and argues for an emergent individual.)

Hick, John (1987) *Death and Eternal Life*. New York: Harper and Row. Reissued by Macmillan. (An excellent, broad treatment of topics connected with death and survival; argues that philosophical and scientific objections to survival after death can be challenged.)

Le Poidevin, Robin (1996) *Arguing for Atheism: An Introduction to the Philosophy of Religion*. New York: Routledge. (An erudite but readable presentation by a leading philosopher; Chapter 10 focuses on death.)

Moody, Raymond (2001) *Life After Life: The Investigation of a Phenomenon – Survival of Bodily Death*. San Francisco, CA: HarperOne. (Originally published by Mockingbird Books in 1975, this is the first modern account of near-death experiences by the man who coined the term.)

Perry, John (1979) *Personal Identity and Immortality*. Indianapolis, IN: Hackett. (An insightful and entertaining dialogue on personal identity.)

Plato ([c. 386–380 BCE] 1997) *Phaedo*, trans. G. M. A. Grube. Indianapolis, IN: Hackett. (One of Plato's masterpieces in which he offers an argument for the immortality of the soul.)

Searle, John (1998) *Mind, Language and Society*. New York: Basic Books. (An accessible work on the mind and language by a leading philosopher; Chapter 2 argues for the mind as a biological phenomenon.)

Swinburne, Richard (1997) *The Evolution of the Soul*, rev. edition. Oxford: Oxford University Press. (An erudite and forceful defense of mind/body dualism.)

Taliaferro, Charles (1994) *Consciousness and the Mind of God*. Cambridge: Cambridge University Press. (Defends a non-materialistic view of persons and the reasonableness of viewing God as a non-physical, spiritual reality.)

Ward, Keith (1998) *Religion and Human Nature*. Oxford: Clarendon Press. (Examines the views of the world religions on the soul and its destiny; also offers a philosophical analysis of reincarnation and resurrection.)

Zaleski, Carol (1987) *Otherworld Journeys: Accounts of Near-Death Experiences in Medieval and Modern Times*. New York: Oxford University Press. (Compares recent near-death narratives with those of earlier historical periods.)

WEBSITES

http://plato.stanford.edu/entries/afterlife
A helpful and concise entry from the *Stanford Encyclopedia of Philosophy* on the afterlife by philosopher of religion William Hasker.

http://www.infidels.org/library/modern/lifeafterdeath/immortality/
An infidels.org site which includes a good number of articles on life after death, immortality, and related topics.

http://www.iep.utm.edu/p/person-i.htm
An informative entry on personal identity from *The Internet Encyclopedia of Philosophy* by philosopher Carsten Korfmacher.

http://www.mircea-eliade.com/from-primitives-to-zen/eschat.html
A compilation of sources from a variety of religious traditions on death and the afterlife.

http://www.iands.org/pubs/jnds/index.php
The online *Journal of Near-Death Studies* published by the International Association of Near-Death Studies.

http://www.healthsystem.virginia.edu/internet/personalitystudies/case_types.cfm
This site contains ongoing research into out-of-body experiences, near-death experiences, and reincarnation at the University of Virginia Health Science Center, Division of Personality Studies.

Glossary

Absolute
1. Not relative; 2. Ultimate reality ("The Absolute").

Actual infinite
A completed whole whose members cannot increase or decrease in number.

Advaita Vedānta
(Sanskrit term) A monistic (non-dual) school of Hindu thought which includes the view that only Brahman exists ("Advaita" means "non-duality" and "Vedānta" refers to the sacred Hindu scriptures, the **Vedas**).

Agnosticism
The view that one cannot be certain whether God exists; it is often contrasted with *theism* – belief in God – and *atheism* – disbelief in God.

Allah
"God" in Arabic – the exclusive God of Islam.

Anthropic principle
The term is used differently by atheists and theists. For *theists*, it is the view that the initial conditions and constants of the universe are finely tuned for human life – a view which suggests an intelligent designer of the universe. For *atheists*, it is the view that we should not be surprised that the initial conditions and constants of the universe are such that life is possible; for if they were otherwise, we would not be here to observe them.

A posteriori
Known or knowable on the basis of experience; knowledge that is based entirely on sense experience.

A priori
Known or knowable independent of, or prior to, experience; knowledge that is not based on sense experience.

Argument
A claim and the attending premise(s) which support the claim.

Atman
(Sanskrit term) The ultimate self, which is held to be identical to all "selves" and to Brahman.

Basic belief
A belief which is not based on other beliefs (non-inferential knowledge); for example, the belief that there are other minds besides one's own.

Big bang theory
A scientific theory attempting to explain the beginning of the universe; according to the current standard account, the universe (time, space, matter, and energy) exploded into existence as a **singularity** roughly 13 billion years ago and has continued to expand ever since.

Bodhisattva
One who has reached enlightenment but forfeits ***nirvana*** in order to help others reach enlightenment.

Brahma
The creator God of Hinduism. Brahma, Shiva (sustainer God), and Vishnu (destroyer God) comprise the Hindi triad of central cosmic deities.

Brahman
(Sanskrit term) In Hinduism, Ultimate Reality; the power underlying the cosmos; absolute divine reality. For **Advaita Vedānta** Hindus, Brahman is impersonal and identical with ***Atman***; for others, such as Ramanuja, Brahman is a separate and personal God.

Buddha
The "enlightened" or "awakened" one; the term is sometimes used to refer to the founder of Buddhism – Siddhartha Guatama (563–483 BCE) – and sometimes refers to other persons who have achieved a state of enlightenment.

Contingent
An *event* is contingent if it might not have occurred; a *proposition* is contingent if its denial is logically possible; a *being* is contingent if it could have not existed – if it is not logically necessary (the opposite of a **necessary being**).

Cosmological argument
An argument for the existence of God in which it is maintained that since there is a cosmos which exists, rather than just nothing, it must have been caused by something beyond it, namely God.

***Dao* (or *tao*)**
(Chinese term) "Way"; it has different meanings for different traditions: for the Confucians it refers to the life of virtue; for the Daoists it refers to the fundamental reality governing the universe.

Deductive argument
An argument in which if the premises are true, the conclusion must follow (put differently, to affirm the premises and deny the conclusion leads to a contradiction). Here is a standard example: All people are mortal; Socrates is a person; therefore, Socrates is mortal.

Deism
The belief that God exists, but such belief is based on reason rather than revelation or faith and also includes the view that the deity does not interfere with the creation.

Design argument
(or **teleological argument**) An argument for the existence of God based on the observation of (apparent) design, order, or purpose exhibited in the world.

Epistemology
The domain of philosophy that is primarily concerned with knowledge – its origins, nature, extent, and justification.

Evolution
The theory that all living things have evolved from pre-existing forms through purely natural processes, most notably through the mechanism of natural selection.

Fideism
The view that religious belief should be based on faith rather than reason.

Foundationalism
The view in epistemology that knowledge and belief rest on the foundation of **basic beliefs**.

Free will defense
A response to the atheist's charge that the following two propositions entail a contradiction: 1) God exists, and 2) evils exists.

Incarnation
The enfleshment of God in human form; for Christians, Jesus Christ is the incarnation of God.

Invalid argument
An argument which is not **valid**.

Irreducible complexity
A system which consists of multiple interacting parts that contribute to the basic function of the system whereby the removal of any of its parts would cause the system to quit functioning; Michael Behe argues that such systems exist in living organisms, and that they could not have been produced gradually via minor, successive modifications of previous systems as any precursor would be by definition nonfunctional.

Kalam cosmological argument
A version of the cosmological argument for God's existence in which it is claimed that since whatever begins to exist needs a cause, and since the universe began to exist, the universe must need a cause; it is further argued that this cause must be a personal creator.

Many-worlds hypothesis
The view that there are a large number of universes, perhaps an infinite number of them, and the fundamental parameters of physics vary from universe to universe (also called the "many-universes hypothesis," the "multi-universe hypothesis," and the "world-ensemble hypothesis").

Moksha
(Sanskrit term) Liberation from **samsāra**; one of the central goals of Hinduism.

Natural theology
The view that the existence of God can be demonstrated through the use of reason unaided by special revelation (e.g. the design argument, the kalam argument, etc.).

Necessary being
A being which, if it exists, exists necessarily; that is, a being that cannot not exist.

Nirvana
(Sanskrit term which literally means *extinction*) In Buddhism, it is the complete extinction of suffering and the causes of suffering; it is the indescribable state of ultimate happiness and peace.

Noetic
(from the Greek word *nous* = mind/intellect) Relating to the mind or its contents (e.g. beliefs, desires, etc.).

Ontological argument
An a priori argument in which it is logically impossible that God does not exist.

Open theism
A fairly recent philosophical view about the nature of God's knowledge whereby God is omniscient but that omniscience does not entail exhaustive knowledge of future contingent events (such as future free human actions).

Oscillating universe
A model of the universe in which it goes through periods of expansion and contraction, in which gravity causes the universe to contract, and some mechanism (yet unknown) causes it to expand; this cycle continues indefinitely.

Panentheism
The view that God permeates the world but, unlike **pantheism**, God is not identical with the world.

Pantheism
The view that everything is God and God is everything; usually includes the notion that the "all" is ultimately impersonal. Derived from two Greek terms: *pan* ("all") and *theos* ("God").

Possible world
Used in conjunction with the modal notions of possibility, necessity, and contingency; the way the world might have been, whereby each of an infinite number of logically possible states of affairs is taken to be a "world" (the actual world is understood to be one of the many ways the world might have been). Also relates to the modal status of propositions: a possible proposition is one that is true in at least one possible world, a necessary proposition is one that is true in all possible worlds, and a contingent proposition is one that is true in some possible worlds and false in other possible worlds.

Potential infinite
A finite number which can continue to increase over time by adding yet another number, but which has no end.

Problem of evil
Includes a variety of arguments against belief in God given the existence of evil in the world; typical categories include logical, evidential, and existential arguments.

Process theism
A form of theism (originated by Alfred North Whitehead and further developed by Charles Hartshorne) in which God is interdependent with the world and is also affected by those in the world; God and the world evolve together.

Properly basic belief
A **basic belief** which one is warranted in holding.

Reincarnation
The view that a person is reborn after death in a different body, perhaps many times and in many different forms (also used as a synonym for transmigration, although the latter often includes rebirth of one's soul occurring in animals as well).

Religious experience
Any experience of the sacred within a religious context, including religious feelings, visions, and mystical and numinous experiences.

Resurrection
The view that an individual, after dying, is fully and completely brought back to life; the same body is involved in the process.

Samsāra
(Sanskrit term) The world of phenomenal experiences whereby the soul passes through a perpetual cycle of death and rebirth.

Second law of thermodynamics
Processes occurring in a closed system tend to move toward a state of thermodynamic equilibrium – a state of maximum disorder and minimum usable energy (i.e. entropy – a measure of the amount of energy in disordered form in a system – increases over time).

Singularity
The initial instant of time; on one model of the universe, this was a state of infinite density and infinite temperature.

Specified complexity
A feature of an event in which the following characteristics are exhibited: it is complex and not easily repeatable through chance (i.e. highly improbable), and it is specified in that it matches an independently identifiable pattern. Proponents of intelligent design theory maintain that specified complexity is a reliable indicator of design by an intelligent agent.

Teleological argument
(See **design argument**)

Theodicy
(From the Greek terms *theos* = god, and *dike* = justice) An argument aimed at justifying the goodness of God given the existence of evil in the world.

Trinity
The view in historic Christianity that within the nature of the one God there are three eternal and coequal persons: Father, Son, and Holy Spirit.

Upanisads
A revered portion of the **Vedas**.

Valid argument
An argument in which the conclusion follows deductively from its premises; the premises may be false, but if they are true the conclusion must also be true.

Vedas
Ancient sacred scriptures of India; the oldest scriptures of Hinduism.

Worldview
A collection of beliefs and ideas centered around the fundamental issues of life; the conceptual grid through which one views reality.

Notes

1 RELIGION AND THE PHILOSOPHY OF RELIGION

1 See Sigmund Freud, *The Future of an Illusion*, translated by James Strachey (1927), in *The Standard Edition of the Complete Psychological Works of Sigmund Freud,* Volume 21 (London: Hogarth Press, 1968).

2 The data in the world religions' chart was gleaned from the following sources: John Bowker, ed., *The Oxford Dictionary of World Religions* (Oxford: Oxford University Press, 1997); Wendy Doniger, ed., *Merriam-Webster's Encyclopedia of World Religions* (Springfield, MA: Merriam-Webster, 1999); Don David Barrett, George Kurian, and Todd Johnson, eds., *World Christian Encyclopedia* 2nd ed. (New York: Oxford University Press, 2001); *The World Factbook* of the US Central Intelligence Agency, found at https://www.cia.gov/library/publications/the-world-factbook/print/xx.html. The percentages were rounded up and thus add up to slightly more than 100%.

3 Diana Eck, *A New Religious America* (San Francisco, CA: HarperSanFrancisco, 2001).

4 There are many different definitions of religion in the literature; doubtfully any of them capture all and only the religions. For a helpful collection and overview of definitions of religion, see Charles Taliaferro, *Contemporary Philosophy of Religion* (Oxford: Blackwell, 1998), 21–24.

5 See the following website for a variety of societies and journals devoted to the study of religion and the philosophy of religion: http://users.ox.ac.uk/~worc0337/phil_topics_religion.html.

6 The terms realism and non-realism, even religious realism and non-realism, have different meanings as they are used in the philosophy of religion literature. For example, religious realism is sometimes taken to be the view that religious claims are informative with respect to non-empirical issues. In this case, Sigmund Freud would not be a religious realist. As will be seen in what follows, I am not using the word this way.

7 Taken from Don Cupitt's website: http://www.doncupitt.com/realism/aboutnonrealism.html. Accessed 22 May 2008.

8 Sigmund Freud, *The Future of an Illusion*, 31.

9 See Freud, *The Future of an Illusion*.

10 See Richard Dawkins, *The Selfish Gene*, new ed. (New York: Oxford University Press, 1989), 192. For an explanation and defense of memetic theory by a leading proponent, see Susan Blackmore, *The Meme Machine* (Oxford: Oxford University Press, 2000).

11 Richard Dawkins, *The Selfish Gene*, 192.

12 Richard Dawkins, *The God Delusion* (New York: Houghton Mifflin, 2006), 199–200.
13 Richard Dawkins, *The God Delusion*, 188.
14 For Dennett's reflections on memes and religion, see his *Breaking the Spell: Religion as a Natural Phenomenon* (New York: Viking, 2006), 226–34.
15 For an interesting biography covering the life and work of this great philosopher, see Ray Monk, *Ludwig Wittgenstein: The Duty of Genius* (New York: Penguin Books, 1990).
16 Wittgenstein's notion of language games is described in his *Philosophical Investigations* (New York: Macmillan, 1953).
17 *Philosophical Investigations*, 11, #23.
18 *Philosophical Investigations*, 3, #2.
19 *Philosophical Investigations*, 15–21.
20 See Ludwig Wittgenstein, *Culture and Value*, edited by G. H. von Wright (Oxford: Blackwell, 1980), 82ff.
21 It should be noted that there is not a consensus that Wittgenstein was a non-realist. In fact, as he abhorred the notion of theories in philosophy on general, by his lights the realism/non-realism debate may well be a moot point. For more on this see D. Z. Phillips, *Wittgenstein and Religion* (New York: St. Martins Press, 1993).
22 For an insightful analysis of the realism/non-realism debate and a defense of realism, see Peter Byrne, *God and Realism* (Burlington, VT: Ashgate, 2003).

2 RELIGIOUS DIVERSITY AND PLUARLISM

1 Dalai Lama, *Ethics for the New Millennium* (New York: Riverhead Books, 1999), 219–31.
2 I would encourage every institution of higher learning to offer courses on the world's religions. I would even suggest that they be included in the required, core curriculum.
3 Keith Yandell, *Philosophy of Religion* (New York: Routledge, 1999), 56.
4 It should be noted that the majority of laypeople in Hindu and Buddhist religions do not seek *nirvana* or *moksha* in this life; instead, they are often fervently dedicated to obtaining merit for future lives and to fulfilling duties to family, ancestors, and the wider society.
5 There are, of course (as with each of these traditions), different strains of Judaism and not all of them would adhere to these elements and practices.
6 Roman Catholics and Protestants disagree on the role of the sacraments. For an irenic presentation of the differences, see Norman Geisler and Ralph MacKenzie, *Roman Catholics and Evangelicals: Agreements and Differences* (Grand Rapids, MI: Baker, 1995).
7 I have combined Runzo's and Netland's approaches into one. For their own presentations, see Joseph Runzo, "Religious Pluralism," in Paul Copan and Chad Meister, eds., *Philosophy of Religion: Classic and Contemporary Issues* (Oxford: Blackwell, 2008), and Harold Netland, "Inclusivism and Exclusivism," in Chad Meister and Paul Copan, eds., *The Routledge Companion to Philosophy of Religion* (London: Routledge, 2007).
8 I am using the phrase salvation/liberation to denote the soteriological goal of the major religious traditions rather than spelling out the various descriptors (e.g. enlightenment, awakening, etc.).
9 This table was inspired by Joseph Runzo's diagram in his excellent work, *Global Philosophy of Religion* (Oxford: Oneworld, 2001), 31.
10 Harold Netland notes different aspects of exclusivism in "Inclusivism and Exclusivism," in Chad Meister and Paul Copan, eds., *The Routledge Companion to Philosophy of Religion* (London: Routledge, 2007), 226–36.

11 For a properly basic-type response, see Alvin Plantinga, "Pluralism: A Defense of Religious Exclusivism," in *The Philosophical Challenge of Religious Diversity* (New York: Oxford University Press), 172–92.
12 See, for example, Jerry Walls, *Hell: The Logic of Damnation* (Notre Dame, IN: University of Notre Dame Press, 1992), Chapter 4.
13 See William Lane Craig, "'No Other Name:' A Middle Knowledge Perspective on the Exclusivity of Salvation Through Christ," in Phillip L. Quinn and Kevin Meeker, eds., *The Philosophical Challenge of Religious Diversity* (New York: Oxford University Press, 2000), 38–53.
14 See, for example, Ronald H. Nash, *Is Jesus the Only Savior?* (Grand Rapids, MI: Zondervan, 1994).
15 "Religious Relativism," in Chad Meister, ed., *The Philosophy of Religion Reader* (London: Routledge, 2008), 71.
16 I am using the male pronoun here not because I believe that God is male; rather, because that is the way God has historically been referenced in the theistic religions in which personal pronouns are utilized.
17 Alvin Plantinga has demonstrated that holding to exclusivism does not violate *any* moral or epistemic obligations. See ibid.
18 John Hick, *An Interpretation of Religion: Human Responses to the Transcendent*, 2nd ed. (New Haven, CT: Yale University Press, 2004), xix.
19 John Hick, *Problems of Religious Pluralism* (New York: St. Martin's Press, 1985), 36–7.
20 Ludwig Wittgenstein, *Philosophical Investigations* 3rd ed. (Englewood Cliffs, NJ: Prentice Hall, 1973).
21 The duck rabbit image is ubiquitous on the internet.
22 Cf. Gavin D' Costa, "John Hick and Religious Pluralism," in Harold Hewitt, ed., *Problems in the Philosophy of Religion: Critical Studies of the Work of John Hick* (London: Macmillan, 1991).
23 Peter Byrne, *Prolegomena to Religious Pluralism* (London: Macmillan, 1995), 153.
24 Byrne also maintains that the different descriptions of the Transcendent should be understood in metaphorical rather than literal fashion. See Byrne, *Prolegomena*, 164.
25 John Hick offers a version of this criticism in his "Religious Pluralism," in Chad Meister and Paul Copan, eds., *The Routledge Companion to Philosophy of Religion* (London: Routledge, 2007), 216–25.
26 Peter Byrne, *Prolegomena*, 200.
27 Ibid., 200–1.
28 Byrne makes this point at ibid., 202–3.
29 For Runzo's impressive defense of religious relativism, see his "Religious Relativism," in Chad Meister, ed., *The Philosophy of Religion Reader* (London: Routledge, 2007).
30 Ibid.
31 Ibid.
32 Ibid.
33 These criteria were derived from the following works: Keith Yandell, "Religious Traditions and Rational Assessments," in Chad Meister and Paul Copan, eds., *The Routledge Companion to Philosophy of Religion* (London: Routledge, 2007), 204–15; "Religious Experience and Rational Appraisal," in *Religious Studies* 8 (June 1974): 173–87; Harold Netland, *Dissonant Voices: Religious Pluralism and the Question of Truth* (Grand Rapids, MI: Eerdmans, 1991), 151–95; and William J. Wainwright, *Philosophy of Religion*, 2nd ed. (New York: Wadsworth, 1999), 182–5. The principles gleaned from these works have been reformulated and emended for purposes of this chapter. For other works dealing with the religious system evaluation, see Keith Yandell, *Philosophy of Religion: A Contemporary*

Introduction (London: Routledge, 1999), Chapters 9–13; Paul J. Griffiths, *An Apology for Apologetics* (Maryknoll, NY: Orbis, 1991), Chapters 2–4; Ninian Smart, "Truth, Criteria, and Dialogue Between Religions," in Thomas Dean, ed., *Religious Pluralism and Truth: Essays in Cross-Cultural Philosophy of Religion (New York: State University of New York Press, 1994),* 67–71; and Harold Netland, *Encountering Religious Pluralism: The Challenge to Christian Faith and Mission* (Downers Grove, IL: InterVarsity Press, 2001), Chapter 9.

34 Aristotle, for example, makes such a claim in *Metaphysics,* IV.4, 1006a5–22; XI.5, 1061b33–1062a19.

35 See Gavin D' Costa, "Whose Objectivity? Which Neutrality? The Doomed Quest for a Neutral Point from Which to Judge Religions," *Religious Studies* 29, 84.

36 William Wainwright, *Philosophy of Religion*, 183.

37 Keith Yandell offers a philosophical critique of the Buddhist "bundle theory" of the self in his *Philosophy of Religion* (London: Routledge, 1999), 246–59.

38 Mary Baker Eddy, *Science and Health with Key to the Scriptures*, (Boston, MA: The First Church of Christ, Scientist, 1971), 480:23–4.

3 CONCEPTIONS OF ULTIMATE REALITY

1 While the East/West distinction is not quite accurate, I am nevertheless using it here to abridge the discussion.

2 It should be noted that for a person raised in the West, many of the concepts of the Advaitins seem peculiar if not downright outlandish and are often difficult to wrap one's mind around. Of course, for a person growing up in an Eastern tradition such as this would view certain Western religious concepts as equally strange and perplexing. Nonetheless, in the global community of which we are now a part, it is beneficial for us to strive for mutual understanding and respect despite such differences in beliefs.

3 Shankara, *Shankara's Crest-Jewel of Discrimination*, as quoted in Chad Meister, ed., *The Philosophy of Religion Reader* (London: Routledge, 2007).

4 Chandogya Upanisad 6.9.1-4.

5 The four main Yogas generally recognized in Hindu literature are Karma (work and action), Bhakti (devotion), Jnana (intellection), and Raja (meditation).

6 Sri Ramana's essay, "Who Am I?", can be found in totality at http://www.arunachala-ramana.org/publications/who_am_i.html. It is published by V. S. Ramanan, President, Board of Trustees, Sri Ramanasramam, Tiruvannamalai, S. India.

7 See, for example, Arvind Sharma, "Hinduism," in Arvind Sharma, ed., *Our Religions* (San Francisco, CA: HarperSanFrancisco, 1993), 14–15.

8 Masao Abe, "Buddhism," in Arvind Sharma, ed., *Our Religions* (San Francisco, CA: HarperSanFrancisco, 1993), 115.

9 From *Anguttara-nikaya*, iii, 134; Sarvepalli Radhakrishnan and Charles A Moore, eds., *A Sourcebook in Indian Philosophy* (Princeton, NJ: Princeton University Press, 1957), 273, 274, as quoted in Keith E. Yandell, *Philosophy of Religion* (London: Routledge, 1999), 111.

10 Ramanuja, "God as Infinite, Personal, and Good," in Chad Meister, ed., *The Philosophy of Religion Reader* (London: Routledge, 2008), 124.

11 Anselm, *Proslogian*, in *St. Anselm: Basic Writing* (La Salle, IL: Open Court, 1962), Chapter 5, 56–7.

12 See Immanuel Kant, "The Ideal of Pure Reason," in *Critique of Pure Reason*, trans. Norman Kemp Smith (New York: St. Martin's Press, 1965), 487–507.

13 Thomas Aquinas, *Summa Theologica*, trans. The Fathers of the English Dominican Province, vol. 1 (New York: Benziger Bros, 1947), 137.

14 Some philosophers have noted that "metaphysical impossibility" is a richer notion than "logical impossibility." Peter van Inwagen goes even farther and argues that the phrase "logical impossibility" is not meaningful. See, for example, his *The Problem of Evil* (Oxford: Oxford University Press, 2006), 22–3.
15 Richard Swinburne, *The Coherence of Theism* (Oxford: Clarendon Press, 1977), 149.
16 For a defense of the open theist's position on God's knowledge, see William Hasker, *God, Time, and Knowledge* (Ithaca, NY: Cornell University Press, 1989), esp. Chapter 10.
17 William Lane Craig makes this point in "The Middle-Knowledge View," in James K. Beilby and Paul Eddy, eds., *Divine Foreknowledge: Four Views* (Downers Grove, IL: InterVarsity Press, 2001), 133–4.
18 A very helpful presentation of differing positions (along with responses to objections) can be found in Gregory E. Ganssle, ed., *God and Time: Four Views* (Downers Grove, IL: InterVarsity Press, 2001).
19 For a contemporary defense, see Brian Leftow, *Time and Eternity* (Ithaca, NY: Cornell University Press, 1991).
20 See Brian Leftow, *Time and Eternity* (Ithaca, NY: Cornell University Press, 1991). See also William Lane Craig, "Timelessness and Omnitemporality," in Gregory E. Ganssle, ed. *God and Time: Four Views* (Downers Grove, IL: InterVarsity Press), 132–6.
21 For one version of this objection, see Nelson Pike, *God and Timelessness* (London: Routledge and Kegan Paul, 1970), Chapter 6.
22 Duns Scotus and William of Occam rejected the doctrine of divine timelessness. Recent philosophers defending God's being everlasting include Nicholas Wolterstorff and Richard Swinburne. See, for example, Swinburne's *The Coherence of Theism*, rev. ed. (Oxford: Clarendon Press, 1993), 217–29.
23 For a defense of God's being everlasting, see Nicholas Wolterstorff, "Unqualified Divine Temporality" and William Lane Craig, "Timelessness and Omnitemporality," both in Gregory E. Ganssle, ed. *God and Time: Four Views* (Downers Grove, IL: InterVarsity Press), 187–213 and 129–60 respectively.
24 For a defense of this position, see Paul Copan and William Lane Craig, *Creation Out of Nothing: A Biblical, Philosophical, and Scientific Exploration* (Grand Rapids, MI: Baker Academic, 2005).
25 For Craig's defense of this position, see his "Timelessness and Omnitemporality."
26 See, for example, Alan Padgett, "Eternity," in Chad Meister and Paul Copan, eds., *The Routledge Companion to Philosophy of Religion* (London: Routledge, 2007), 292–4; see also Padgett's *God, Eternity, and the Nature of Time* (London: Macmillan, 1992), 12–17 and 147–8.
27 Charles Hartshorne, *Omnipotence and Other Theological Mistakes* (Albany, NY: SUNY Press, 1984), 7.
28 For more on divine attributes, see Edward Wierenga, *The Nature of God: An Inquiry into Divine Attributes* (Ithaca, NY: Cornell University Press, 1989) and Thomas V. Morris, *Our Idea of God: An Introduction to Philosophical Theology* (Downers Grove, IL: InterVarsity Press, 1991).

4 COSMOLOGICAL ARGUMENTS FOR GOD'S EXISTENCE

1 For a very helpful overview of the wide variety of cosmological arguments, see William Lane Craig, *The Cosmological Argument from Plato to Leibniz* (Eugene, OR: Wipf and Stock Publishers, 2001, first published by Harper & Row, 1980).

2 This tripartite demarcation of cosmological arguments was first offered by William Lane Craig in his work, *The Cosmological Argument from Plato to Leibniz*. This is now the standard way of demarcating cosmological arguments.
3 See Plato's *Laws*, trans. by Thomas L. Pangle (Chicago, IL: University of Chicago Press), Book 10, for a version of the cosmological argument.
4 See Aristotle's *Metaphysics* in *The Complete Works of Aristotle*, edited by Jonathan Barnes (Princeton, NJ: Princeton University Press, 1984), Volume II, Book 12, and his *Physics*, Volume I, Books 7 and 8.
5 *Summa Theologica*, trans. by the Fathers of the English Dominican Province (Notre Dame, IN: Ave Maria Press, 1948), 1.2. Article 3.
6 Ibid.
7 Following Aquinas himself in his later writings, in this form of the argument we are avoiding the issue of temporal infinity and focusing on the logical dependence of contingent things on a non-contingent (or necessary) cause. I agree with those scholars who maintain that while Aquinas does refer to time in this argument, this reference is ultimately simply a rhetorical device and not a declaration of an actual state of affairs. For a concise and helpful summary of the first Four Ways, see Norman Geisler and Winfried Corduan, *Philosophy of Religion*, 2nd ed. (Grand Rapids, MI: Baker Books, 1988), 158–60.
8 We can simplify the argument even further:
   1. If contingent things exist, then a non-contingent (necessary) ground must exist to explain their existence.
   2. Contingent things exist.
   3. Therefore, a non-contingent (necessary) ground must exist to explain their existence.
9 William Lane Craig argues as much in his *Theism, Atheism, and Big Bang Cosmology* (Oxford: Clarendon Press, 1993) 9–30.
10 F. C. Copleston, "A Debate on the Existence of God," in John Hick, ed., *The Existence of God* (New York: Macmillan, 1964), 174.
11 Ibid., 175.
12 David Hume, *Dialogues Concerning Natural Religion*, ed., Richard H. Popkin, 2nd ed. (Cambridge: Hackett Publishing, 1998), Part IX, 56.
13 Indeed, some do hold to the view that there are no contingent beings, and for various reasons. One such reason offered is that the terms "contingent" and "necessary" are meaningless.
14 See Immanuel Kant, *Critique of Pure Reason*, trans. Norman Kemp Smith (New York: St. Martin's Press, 1965, reprint), A605–7, 508–10.
15 See Gottfried Leibniz, *Monadology and Other Philosophical Writings*, trans. R. Latta (Oxford: Oxford University Press, 1898). See also Samuel Clarke, *A Demonstration of the Attributes of God, the Obligations of Natural Religion, and the Truth and Certainty of the Christian Revelation* (Whitefish, MT: Kessinger Publishing, 2003).
16 Richard Taylor, *Metaphysics*, 4th ed. (Englewood Cliffs, NJ: Prentice Hall, 1963), 100–1.
17 For more on this objection, see William L. Rowe, "Cosmological Arguments," in Philip L. Quinn and Charles Taliaferro (eds.) *A Companion to Philosophy of Religion* (Oxford: Blackwell, 1997), 331–7.
18 For a history and defense of the kalam argument, see William Lane Craig, *The Kalam Cosmological Argument* (London: Macmillan, 1979).
19 See, for example, the chapter by atheist philosopher Quentin Smith entitled "The Uncaused Beginning of the Universe," in William Lane Craig and Quentin Smith, *Theism, Atheism, and Big Bang Cosmology*, 108–40.

20 This is a slightly modified version of William Lane Craig's argument spelled out in his book, *The Kalam Cosmological Argument*, 103.

21 Premise 1 is presupposing an A-Theory of time in which there is real temporal flow. But this view of time is debated. For a readable defense of it, see William Lane Craig, *Time and Eternity: Exploring God's Relationship to Time* (Wheaton, IL: Crossway Books, 2001). For several defenses of the B-Theory of time, see Nathan Oaklander and Quentin Smith, eds., *The New Theory of Time* (New Haven, CT: Yale University Press, 1994).

22 The field of mathematics which deals with actual infinites is called "set theory," and there is lively debate about whether actual infinite sets exist in reality or are mere ideas in the mind. For more on set theory, see Patrick Suppes, *Axiomatic Set Theory* (Mineola, NY: Dover Publications, 1972).

23 Nicholas Everitt, *The Nonexistence of* God (New York: Routledge, 2004), 63–5. A similar argument is offered by J. L. Mackie in his *The Miracle of Theism* (New York: Oxford University Press, 1982), 93.

24 William Lane Craig, "The Existence of God and the Beginning of the Universe," *Truth: A Journal of Modern Thought* 3 (1991), 88–9. This essay can also be found at the Leadership University website: http://www.leaderu.com/truth/3truth11.html.

25 For several concisely stated objections to this philosophical argument against a traversed infinity, see Richard Sorabji, *Time, Creation, and the Continuum* (Ithaca, NY: Cornell University Press, 1893), 219–24.

26 Paul Davies, *God and the New Physics* (New York: Simon & Schuster, 1983), 199.

27 See, for example, Gribbin's "Oscillating Universe Bounces Back," in *Nature*, 259: 15–16 (1976).

28 For some of this evidence, see *The Large-Scale Structure of Space–Time*, edited by Stephen Hawking and George Ellis (Cambridge: Cambridge University Press, 1975); Stephen Hawking, *A Brief History of Time* (New York: Bantam Books, 1988); William Lane Craig, "The Ultimate Question of Origins: God and the Beginning of the Universe," *Astrophysics and Space Science* (1999), 723–40; and Alan Guth and Marc Sher, "The Impossibility of a Bouncing Universe," *Nature*, 302 (1983), 505–7.

29 Stephen Hawking and Roger Penrose, *The Nature of Space and Time*, The Isaac Newton Institute Series of Lectures (Princeton, NJ: Princeton University Press, 1996), 20, as quoted in William Lane Craig and Walter Sinnott-Armstrong, *God? A Debate Between a Christian and an Atheist* (New York: Oxford University Press, 2004), 8.

30 For more on brane cosmology, see P. J. Steinhardt and N. Turok, *Science* 296, 1436–93 (2002) and Paul Steinhardt's introductory essay at http://wwwphy.princeton.edu/~steinh/cyclintro.pdf. For other alternatives to the big bang, see Joseph Silk, *The Big bang*, 3rd ed. (New York: Henry Holt and Company, 2001), 385–407.

31 For a defense of the metaphysical position of agent causation regarding the free will debate, see Timothy O'Conor, *Persons & Causes: The Metaphysics of Free Will* (Oxford: Oxford University Press, 2000).

32 Quentin Smith, "A Defense of the Cosmological Argument for God's Non-existence," in William Lane Craig and Quentin Smith, eds., *Theism, Atheism, and Big bang Cosmology*, 234–6. I've added numbers 5 and 6 based on the conclusions he derives from the first four premises.

33 William Lane Craig, *Theism, Atheism, and Big bang Cosmology*, 224.

34 Ibid., 227.

35 Ibid., 235.

36 See Richard Swinburne, *The Existence of God* (Oxford: Clarendon Press, 1979), 129–32. See also Richard Swinburne, *Is There a God?* (Oxford: Oxford University Press, 1996), 43–7.

37 Smith, op. cit., 250.

5 TELEOLOGICAL ARGUMENTS FOR GOD'S EXISTENCE

1 Robin Collins makes note of this in his essay entitled "The Teleological Argument," in Chad Meister and Paul Copan, eds., *The Routledge Companion to Philosophy of Religion* (London: Routledge, 2007), 351. He references the work of Ninian Smart, *Doctrine and Argument in Indian Philosophy* (London: Allen and Unwin, 1964), 153–4.
2 William Paley (1802) *Natural Theology: Or, Evidences of the Existence and Attributes of the Deity Collected from the Appearances of Nature*. 12th ed. (Charlottesville, VA: Ibis., ND), 1–2, 3, 17–18.
3 Even though Hume's book was published twenty-three years earlier than Paley's, for some reason Paley did not reference or take into account Hume's work. It appears that he was unaware of it.
4 David Hume, *Dialogues Concerning Natural Religion* (1779), 2nd ed., edited by Richard H. Popkin (Cambridge: Hackett, 1998), Parts VI and VII.
5 Ibid., Part VIII.
6 For more on this point, see Chapter 7.
7 For a clear presentation of the theory of evolution, see Ernst Mary, *What Evolution Is* (New York: Basic Books, 2001).
8 Neal Gillespie, *Charles Darwin and the Problem of Creation* (Chicago, IL: University of Chicago Press, 1979), 83–4.
9 F. R. Tennant makes such a point in his *Philosophical Theology*, vol. 2, *The World, the Soul, and God* (Cambridge: Cambridge University Press, 1956).
10 Charles Darwin, letters to Asa Gray (May 22 and Nov. 26, 1860), in Francis Darwin, *Life and Letters of Charles Darwin* (London: Charles Murray), 11:312, 378, as quoted in Ian Barbour, *Religion in an Age of Science: The Gifford Lectures*, vol. 1 (San Francisco, CA: HarperSanFrancisco, 1990), 155.
11 Robin Collins, "The Teleological Argument," in Paul Copan and Chad Meister, eds. *Philosophy of Religion: Classic and Contemporary Issues* (Oxford: Blackwell, 2008), 99.
12 Collins provides these parameters in his essay, "A Scientific Argument for the Existence of God: The Fine-Tuning Design Argument," in Michael J. Murray, ed., *Reason for the Hope Within* (Grand Rapids, MI: Eerdmans, 1999), 49.
13 See Paul Davis, *The Accidental Universe* (Cambridge: Cambridge University Press, 1982), 90–1. John Jefferson Davis, "The Design Argument, Cosmic 'Fine-tuning,' and the Anthropic Principle," *The International Journal of Philosophy of Religion* 22 (1987): 140.
14 John Leslie, *Universes* (New York: Routledge, 1989), 4, 35; *Anthropic Cosmological Principle,* (Oxford: Oxford University Press, 1985)322.
15 Paul Davis, *Superforce: The Search for a Grand Unified Theory of Nature* (New York: Simon and Schuster, 1984), 242.
16 Leslie, *Universes*, 39–40.
17 John Leslie, "How to Draw Conclusions from a Fine-Tuned Cosmos," in Robert Russell, Robert J. Russell, William R. Stoeger, and George V. Coyne eds. *Physics, Philosophy and Theology: A Common Quest for Understanding* (Vatican City State: Vatican Observatory Press, 1988), 299.
18 For a readable and interesting overview of the current state of cosmological theories and various hypotheses on which they depend, see Brian Greene, *The Elegant Universe* (New York: Vintage Books, 2003). See also John Gribbin, *The Search for Superstrings, Symmetry, and the Theory of Everything* (New York: Little, Brown and Company, 1998).

19 For an insightful analysis of the many-worlds hypothesis, see Robin Collins, "Design and the Many-Worlds Hypothesis" in William Lane Craig, ed., *Philosophy of Religion: A Reader and Guide* (New Brunswick, NJ: Rutgers University Press, 2002), 130–48.

20 See Robin Collins, "The Teleological Argument," 143–4. Regarding the many-universes hypothesis, philosopher Alvin Plantinga writes: "Well, perhaps all this is logically possible (and then again perhaps not). As a response to a probabilistic argument, however, it's pretty anemic. How would this kind of reply play in Tombstone, or Dodge City? 'Waal, shore, Tex, I *know* it's a leetle mite suspicious that every time I deal I git four aces and a wild card, but have you considered the following? Possibly there is an infinite succession of universes, so that for any possible distribution of possible poker hands, there is a universe in which that possibility is realized; we just happen to find ourselves in one where someone like me always deals himself only aces and wild cards without ever cheating. So put up that shootin' arn and set down 'n shet yore yap, ya dumb galoot.'" "Darwin, Mind and Meaning," originally published in the May/June 1996 issue of *Books and Culture*.

21 John Barrow and Frank Tipler, *The Anthropic Cosmological Principle*, 15.

22 Ibid., 1–2.

23 Richard Swinburne, *The Existence of God*, rev. ed. (Oxford: Clarendon, 1991), 138. For an excellent analysis of the anthropic principle, see William Lane Craig, "The Teleological Argument and the Anthropic Priniciple" in William Lane Craig and Mark S. McLeod, eds., *The Logic of Rational Theism* (Lewiston, NY: Edwin Mellen, 1990), 127–53.

24 David Hume, *Dialogues Concerning Natural Religion*, 2nd ed., edited with an introduction by Richard H. Popkin (Indianapolis, IN: Hackett Publishing, 1998), Part IV, 31.

25 Atheist philosopher J. L. Mackie expounds on Hume's critiques of the design argument in *The Miracle of Theism: Arguments for and Against the Existence of God* (New York: Oxford University Press, 1982), 133–45. Richard Dawkins makes a similar point as it applies to biological systems in his *Blind Watchmaker: Why the Evidence of Evolution Reveals a Universe Without Design* (New York: W. W. Norton and Company, 1987), 141.

26 William Dembski, *Intelligent Design: The Bridge Between Science & Theology* (Downers Grove, IL: InterVarsity, 1999), 223.

27 Of course, where the wheel lands is not really a matter of chance. For there are very specific laws of nature which determine where it will stop. We refer to it as "chance" because we do not know where, precisely, the laws of nature will cause the wheel to stop. It could be argued that only at the quantum level is there truly chance; or perhaps there is no chance whatsoever.

28 William A. Dembski, "Explaining Specified Complexity," first appeared in *Metanexus: The Online Forum on Religion and Science* (www.metanexus.net) and can also be found at Leadership U: www.leaderu.com/offices/dembski/docs/bd-specified.html.

29 Michael Behe, *Darwin's Black Box: The Biochemical Challenge to Evolution* (New York: The Free Press, 1996), 39.

30 For an up-to-date overview of bacterial flagella in a standard microbiology textbook, see Lansing M. Prescott, John P. Harley, and Donald A. Klein, *Microbiology*, 6th ed., (New York: McGraw-Hill, 2004).

31 For an updated version of Behe's argument on irreducible complexity, see his "Irreducible Complexity: Obstacle to Darwinian Evolution" in William A. Dembski and Michael Ruse, eds.. *Debating Design: From Darwin to DNA* (Cambridge: Cambridge University Press, 2004), 352–70 and "The Challenge of Irreducible Complexity" in *Natural History* 111 (April, 2002), 74. For a critique of the irreducible complexity argument, see Kenneth R. Miller. "The Flagellum Unspin: The Collapse of 'Irreducible Complexity'" in *Debating Design*, 81–97 and "The Flaw in the Mousetrap" in *Natural History* 111 (April, 2002),

75 (http://www.naturalhistorymag.com/). For further critique, see Niall Shanks, *God, Darwin, and the Devil: A Critique of the Intelligent Design Theory* (New York: Oxford University Press, 2004), especially Chapter 5, and Paul Draper, "Irreducible Complexity and Darwinian Gradualism: A Reply to Michael J. Behe," *Faith and Philosophy* 19 (2002), 3–21.

32 Robert O'Connor, "The Design Inference: Old Wine in New Wineskins," in Neil A. Manson, ed., *God and Design: The Teleological Argument and Modern Science* (London: Routledge, 2003), 69. In this essay O'Connor is responding to "complex specified information" (CSI), but the argument applies to the notions of specified complexity and irreducible complexity as well.

33 Miller, "The Flaw in the Mousetrap". For a more comprehensive critique, see his "The Flagellum Unspin".

34 Miller, "The Flaw in the Mousetrap," 75.

35 Behe responds to some of Miller's criticisms in his "Irreducible Complexity: Obstacle to Darwinian Evolution" in *Debating Design*. For an advanced philosophical critique of the design argument, see Elliott Sober, "The Design Argument," in *Debating Design*, 98–129. See also Michael Martin, *Atheism: A Philosophical Justification* (Philadelphia, PA: Temple University Press, 1990), Chapter 5 and J. L. Mackie, *The Miracle of Theism: Arguments For and Against the Existence of God* (Oxford: Clarendon Press, 1982), Chapter 8.

6 ONTOLOGICAL ARGUMENTS FOR GOD'S EXISTENCE

1 For an excellent presentation of different versions of the ontological argument as well as rebuttals to them, see Graham Oppy, *Ontological Arguments and Belief in God* (Cambridge: Cambridge University Press, 1995).

2 Anselm, *Proslogion*, in *St. Anselm: Basic Writings* (LaSalle, IL: Open Court Publishing, 1962), 47.

3 Ibid., 53–4.

4 See, for example, various interpretations as sketched by Graham Oppy in "The Ontological Argument," in Chad Meister and Paul Copan, eds. *The Routledge Companion to Philosophical Theology* (London: Routledge, 2007), 112–26. For a more in-depth analysis of various interpretations, see Oppy's *Ontological Arguments and Belief in God* and *Arguing About Gods* (Cambridge: Cambridge University Press, 2006), Chapter 2.

5 Bertrand Russell, "My Mental Development", in *The Philosophy of Bertrand Russell*, ed. Paul Arthur Schilpp, 3rd ed. (New York: Tudor Publishing Company, 1951), 10.

6 Gaunilo, *In Behalf of the Fool*, in *St. Anselm: Basic Writings*, 309.

7 Anselm, *Anselm's Apologetic*, in *St. Anselm: Basic Writings*, 316–17.

8 Stephen T. Davis argues that Gaunilo's rebuttal here in unsound. See his "The Ontological Argument" in Paul Copan and Paul K. Moser, eds. *The Rationality of Theism* (London: Routledge, 2003), 100–3.

9 See Immanuel Kant, *Critique of Pure Reason*, trans. N. K. Smith (London: Macmillan [1781], 1933), 500–7.

10 This is on one common understanding of Kant's objection.

11 For an overview of Anselm's argument along with various objections that have been raised against it, see Peter Millican, "The One Fatal Flaw in Anselm's Argument," *Mind* 113 (2004), 437–76.

12 For a helpful presentation of modal logic and the semantics of possible worlds, see Kenneth Konyndyk, *Introductory Modal Logic* (Notre Dame, IN: University of Notre Dame Press,

1986). See also Raymond Bradley and Norman Swartz, *Possible Worlds: An Introduction to Logic and Its Philosophy* (Indianapolis, IN: Hackett, 1979).

13 By interpreting the argument modally, Plantinga hopes to avoid Kant's objection that existence is not a real property.

14 Graham Oppy simplifies it even further: "Say that an entity is *maximally excellent* if it is omnipotent, omniscient, and morally perfect. Say, further, that an entity is *maximally great* if and only if it is maximally excellent in every possible world… . Then, Plantinga's argument runs as follows:

1 It is possible that there is a maximally great entity.

2 (Hence) there is a maximally excellent entity. (From 1)."

Graham Oppy, "The Ontological Argument," in Chad Meister and Paul Copan, eds. *The Routledge Companion to Philosophy of Religion* (London: Routledge, 2007), 120.

15 Alvin Plantinga, *God, Freedom, and Evil* (Grand Rapids, MI: Eerdmans, 1974), 112. In a later work he declared that he had set the standard for success too high and wrote the following: "the ontological argument provides as good grounds for the existence of God as does any serious philosophical argument for any important philosophical conclusion." In Alvin Plantinga, "Self-Profile," in James E. Tomberlin and Peter Van Inwagen, eds., *Alvin Plantinga*, Profiles 5 (Dordrecht: D. Reidel, 1985), 71.

16 For an accessible presentation of the ontological argument which includes a brief overview of the language of possible worlds, see William Lane Craig, "The Ontological Argument," in Francis J. Beckwith, William Lane Craig, and J.P. Moreland, eds., *To Everyone An Answer: A Case for the Christian Worldview* (Downers Grove, IL: InterVarsity Press, 2004), 124–37. The description here which uses conjuncts and their negations was derived from this overview. For a bit more technical but nonetheless helpful overview of the semantics of possible worlds, see E.J. Lowe, *A Survey of Metaphysics* (Oxford: Oxford University Press, 2002), Chapter 7. For a collection of essays which covers a variety of theories of possible worlds, see Michael J. Loux, ed., *The Possible and the Actual* (Ithaca, NY: Cornell University Press, 1979).

17 J. L. Mackie makes the following claim: "In its simplest form the problem is this: God is omnipotent; God is wholly good; and yet evil exists. There seems to be some contradiction between these three propositions…" in "Evil and Omnipotence," *Mind* 64 (1955): 200.

18 For two laconic but insightful overviews of some of these arguments, see Robin Le Poidevin, "The Impossibility of God?" in Paul Copan and Chad Meister, eds., *Philosophy of Religion: Classic and Contemporary Issues* (Oxford: Blackwell, 2008), 188–201 and Bede Rundle, "Problems with the Concept of God," in *The Routledge Companion to Philosophy of Religion*, 408–16.

19 This argument was offered by Anthony Kenny in his essay entitled "Omniscience, Eternity, and Time," in Michael Martin and Ricki Monnier, eds., *The Impossibility of God* (Amherst, NY: Prometheus Books, 2003), 212. For an insightful response to this and other coherence objections, see Charles Taliaferro, "The Coherence of Theism," in *Philosophy of Religion: Classic and Contemporary Issues*, 173–87.

20 For several helpful works for and against the coherence of theism, see Richard M. Gale, *On the Nature and Existence of God* (Cambridge: Cambridge University Press, 1991); Michael Martin, *Atheism* (Philadelphia, PA: Temple University Press, 1990); Richard Swinburne, *The Coherence of Theism* (Oxford: Clarendon Press, 1977); and Edward Wierenga, *The Nature of God* (Ithaca, NY: Cornell University Press, 1989).

21 J. L. Mackie raises this objection in his *The Miracle of Theism* (Oxford: Clarendon Press, 1982), 55–6. For discussions of the metaphysical issues associate with modal logic, see Michael Tooley, ed., *Necessity and Possibility: The Metaphysics of Modality* (London: Routledge, 1999); Graeme Forbes, *The Metaphysics of Modality* (Oxford: Oxford University

Press, 1985); David K. Lewis, *On the Plurality of Worlds* (Oxford: Blackwell, 1986); Alvin Plantinga, *The Nature of Necessity* (Oxford: Oxford University Press, 1974).

22 For another objection to Plantinga's use of modal logic in articulating the ontological argument, see Michael Tooley, "Plantinga's Defense of the Ontological Argument," *Mind*, 90, (1981), 422–7.

23 This reply to Martin is presented in Stephen T. Davis, "The Ontological Argument," in Paul Copan and Paul K. Moser, eds., *The Rationality of Theism* (London: Routledge, 2003), 108-10.

7 PROBLEMS OF EVIL

1 See R. J. Rummel, *Death by Government* (New Brunswick, NJ: Transaction Publishers, 1997), 13. I'm indebted to John K. Roth for bringing this information to my attention. The words of philosopher G. W. F. Hegel summarize the last century: history is "the slaughter-bench at which the happiness of peoples, the wisdom of states, and the virtue of individuals have been sacrificed." G. W.F . Hegel, *Reason in History*, trans. Robert S. Hartman (Indianapolis, IN: Bobbs-Merill, 1953), 27.

2 For more on the AIDS crisis, see UNAIDS at http://www.unaids.org/en/AboutUNAIDS/default.asp.

3 David Hume, *Dialogue Concerning Natural Religion* (Indianapolis, IN: Hackett, 1988), 63.

4 See Wittgenstein's *Philosophical Investigations* (Oxford: Blackwell, 1953), §3.

5 John Hick, *Evil and the God of Love*, rev. ed.. (New York: HarperSanFrancisco, 1977), 12.

6 Marilyn McCord Adams, "Horrendous Evil," in Chad Meister, ed., *The Philosophy of Religion Reader* (London: Routledge, 2007).

7 William Rowe, "The Problem of Evil," as quoted in *The Philosophy of Religion Reader*, 529.

8 Bruce Russell, "Why Doesn't God Intervene to Prevent Evil?" as quoted in Louis P. Pojman, ed., *Philosophy: The Quest for Truth*, 3rd ed.. (Belmont, CA: Wadsworth, 1996), 74.

9 Paul Draper, "Arguments from Evil," in Paul Copan and Chad V. Meister, eds., *Philosophy of Religion: Classic and Contemporary Issues* (Oxford: Blackwell, 2008).

10 Alvin Plantinga has offered two slightly different versions of the free will defense in his *God and Other Minds: A Study of the Rational Justification of Belief in God* (Ithaca, NY: Cornell University Press, 1967), 131–155 and *The Nature of Necessity* (Oxford: Clarendon Press, 1974), 164–95. For a fairly non-technical form of the argument, see *God, Freedom, and Evil* (Grand Rapids, MI: Eerdmans, 1977), 7–64; note esp. 29–34.

11 Alvin Plantinga, *God, Freedom, and Evil*, 30.

12 It should be noted that Plantinga includes in his argument the possibility of *transworld depravity* (the claim that there is at least one possible world in which a person has morally significant freedom and yet commits at least one morally wrong action) as a further supposition in order to ensure that it is logically impossible for there to be a possible world in which there is no evil. Thus, regardless of which world God has created, one or more individual persons can be counted on to actualize evil because they are suffering from transworld depravity. This move is consistent with the Christian doctrine of the Fall.

13 This type of argument has also been referred to as the "inductive," "a posteriori" and "evidential" argument. We will examine another kind of evidential argument in the next section.

14 The structure of this argument basically follows Plantinga's delineation in his *God, Freedom, and Evil*, 59–61. For another very helpful presentation of the argument in a variety of forms, see Michael L. Peterson, *God and Evil: An Introduction to the Issues* (Boulder, CO: Westview Press, 1998), Chapter 4.

15 See Plantinga, *God, Freedom, and Evil*, 34–44. For a more in-depth treatment, see Plantinga's *The Nature of Necessity* (Oxford: Clarendon Press, 1974), Chapter 9, esp. sections 4–6.
16 For more on the notion of possible worlds, as it relates to this issue, see Plantinga, *The Nature of Necessity*.
17 The force of this argument is heightened by Plantinga's concept of transworld depravity. This issue will not be discussed here. See his *God, Freedom, and Evil*, 45–53.
18 Ibid., 61.
19 See, for example, Stephen J. Wykstra, "The Humean Obstacle to Evidential Arguments from Suffering: On Avoiding the Evils of 'Appearance'," *International Journal for Philosophy of Religion* (1984) 16: 73–93.
20 See John S. Feinberg, *The Many Faces of Evil: Theological Systems and the Problem of Evil*, revised and expanded ed.. (Wheaton, IL: Crossway Books, 2004), 477–87.
21 One could object to this by citing Ivan Karamazov-type examples (such as children being thrown to dogs) in which it seems evident that not every instance of suffering/evil is connected to a higher good. However, a reply could be given that, even if this is so, in a general sense all evil/suffering will in the end be redeemed by God. Marilyn McCord Adams makes such a point by utilizing a Christocentric theological framework which takes seriously the suffering Son of God. She argues that there is good reason for Christians to believe that God will, in the end, engulf and defeat all personal horrors through integrating participation in the evils into one's relationship with God.
22 For the open theist, God's omniscience does not include knowledge of some future events, such as free human actions. So at the creation of the universe God was unaware of much of the evil which would occur in the future.
23 Plantinga, *God, Freedom, and Evil*, 64.
24 Feinberg, *The Many Faces of Evil-*, 454.
25 See his *On the Free Choice of the Will* (Indianapolis, IN: Hackett, 1993).
26 For a recent and impressive defense of the free will theodicy, see Richard Swinburne, *Providence and the Problem of Evil* (Oxford: Clarendon Press, 1998).
27 For a recent and insightful presentation of a process theodicy based on creation out of chaos, see David Ray Griffin, "Creation out of Nothing, Creation out of Chaos, and the Problem of Evil," in Stephen T. David, ed., *Encountering Evil: Live Options in Theodicy*, new ed. (Louisville, KY: Westminster John Knox Press, 2001), 108–25.
28 For an extensive critique of process theology, see Royce Gordon Gruenler, *The Inexhaustible God* (Grand Rapids, MI: Baker Books, 1983).

8 SCIENCE, FAITH, AND REASON

1 Sam Harris, *The End of Faith: Religion, Terror, and the Future of Reason* (New York: W. W. Norton and Company, 2004), 11.
2 The following works make the same basic point: Christopher Hitchens, *God is not Great: How Religion Poisons Everything* (New York: Twelve, 2007); Richard Dawkins, *The God Delusion* (New York: Houghton Mifflin, 2006); and Victor J. Stenger, *God: The Failed Hypothesis* (Amherst, NY: Prometheus Books, 2007).
3 For a helpful, balanced overview of Galileo's encounter with the Roman Catholic Church, see Maurice A. Finocciaro, *The Galileo Affair: A Documented History* (Berkeley, CA: University of California Press, 1989).
4 This description of science was derived from that offered by Carl Hempel in his *Philosophy of Natural Science* (Upper Saddle River, NJ: Prentice Hall, 1966).

5 Ian Barbour describes *four* models in his highly influential work, *Religion in an Age of Science: The Gifford Lectures*, Volume 1 (San Francisco, CA: HarperSanFrancisco, 1990). I am abbreviating his work here, with various modifications and divergences.
6 See Ashley Montagu, *Man's Place in Nature* (Ann Arbor, MI: University of Michigan Press, 1959), 2.
7 For a work which chronicles the development of logical positivism, see Alberto Coffa, *The Semantic Tradition from Kant to Carnap* (Cambridge: Cambridge University Press, 1991).
8 Ian Barbour, *Religion in an Age of Science*, 14.
9 Ian Barbour, *Religion in an Age of Science*, 16.
10 For an overview of various attempts at integration, see Arthur Peacocke, *Creation and the World of Science: The Bampton Lectures* (Oxford: Clarendon Press, 1979).
11 See Richard Swinburne, *The Existence of God*, rev. ed., (Oxford: Clarendon Press, 1991) and *The Resurrection of God Incarnate* (Oxford: Oxford University Press, 2003).
12 The chief proponents of process thought today are John Cobb, David Ray Griffin, and Shubert Ogden. For a helpful overview of process philosophy, see John B. Cobb, Jr. and David Ray Griffin, *Process Theology: An Introductory Exposition* (Philadelphia, PA: Westminster Press, 1976).
13 Developed in G. W. F. Hegel, *Phenomenology of Spirit*, trans. A. V. Miller (Oxford: Clarendon Press, 1970 [1807]).
14 Søren Kierkegaard, *Concluding Unscientific Postscript*, trans. D. F. Swenson and W. Lowie (Princeton, NJ: Princeton University Press, 1941), 30.
15 Frederick Copleston, *History of Philosophy*, Vol. II (New York: Image Books, 1994), 336.
16 Søren Kierkegaard, *Concluding Unscientific Postscript*, 182.
17 For examples of faith in the Mahayana tradition, see *The Lotus Sutra*, trans. Burton Watson (New York: Columbia University Press, 1993).
18 In a private conversation with a leading Christian non-rationalist, I asked him this question. His response was that if a person is considering joining the Christian religion, it would be best for him or her to go to church, read the Bible, and spend time around other Christians. Then, at some point, he or she must commit.
19 See his *Concluding Unscientific Postscript*, 30–3.
20 William K. Clifford, *The Ethics of Belief and Other Essays* (Amherst, NY: Prometheus Books, 1999); repr. Chad Meister, ed., *The Philosophy of Religion Reader*, 363.
21 William James, "The Sentiment of Rationality," in Alburey Castell, ed., *Essays in Pragmatism* (New York: Hafner Press, 1948), 27.
22 Robert E. Enger, ed., *Bertrand Russell's Best,* (New York: The New American Library, 1960), 34.
23 William James, *Essays in Pragmatism*, ed. Alburey Castell (New York: Hafner Press, 1948), repr. Chad Meister, ed., *The Philosophy of Religion Reader* (London: Routledge, 2008), 370.
24 James defines faith this way: "a belief in something concerning which doubt is still theoretically possible; and as the test of belief is willingness to act, one may say that faith is the readiness to act in a cause the prosperous issue of which is not certified in advance." William James, "The Sentiment of Rationality," in *The Will to Believe and Other Essays in Popular Philosophy*, (New York: Longmans, Green and Co., 1897), 90.
25 James, "Will to Believe," 106.
26 James, "Will to Believe," 106
27 See, for example, Joshua L. Golding, "The Wager Argument," in Chad Meister and Paul Copan, eds., *The Routledge Companion to Philosophy of Religion* (London: Routledge, 2007).
28 Blaise Pascal, *Pensées*, Trans. A. J. Krailsheimer (New York: Penguin Books, 1995), 2.2, 122–3.

29 This matrix was first presented by Ian Hacking in "The Logic of Pascal's Wager," *American Philosophical Quarterly* 9 (1972): 186–92.
30 Blaise Pascal, *Pensées*, 127.
31 Ibid.
32 One could, perhaps, by say taking a psychedelic drug and staring at lots of pictures of pink elephants, get around to believing there is a pink elephant in the room. But this would not be acquiring a belief under one's direct, voluntary control.
33 I am indebted to my colleague Cristian Mihut for noting this point.
34 For a critique of classical foundationalism by Plantinga, see his "Reason and Belief in God," in Alvin Plantinga and Nicholas Wolterstorff, eds., *Faith and Rationality* (Notre Dame, IN: University of Notre Dame Press, 1983), esp. 59–63.
35 For a helpful and accessible presentation of foundationalism and criticisms of it, see Louis Pojman, *What Can We Know: An Introduction to the Theory of Knowledge* (New York: Wadsworth, 1995), Chapter 6.
36 There is debate about whether Plantinga's view is a form of foundational or rather a form of coherentism.
37 Alvin Plantinga and Nicholas Wolterstorff, eds., *Faith and Rationality*, 79.
38 See ibid, 87–91.
39 Plantinga puts it this way: "But *is* [Christian belief] true? This is a really important question. And here we pass beyond the competence of philosophy, whose main competence, in this area, is to clear away certain objections, impedances, and obstacles to Christian belief. Speaking for myself and of course not in the name of philosophy, I can say only that it does, indeed, seem to me to be true, and to be the maximally important truth." *Warranted Christian Belief* (New York: Oxford University Press, 2000), 499.
40 See, for example, his "The Foundations of Theism: A Reply" in *Faith and Philosophy* 3.3 (1986), 298–313.
41 For more on Plantinga's explication and defense of warranted religious belief, see his magisterial trilogy: *Warrant: The Current Debate* (Oxford: Oxford University Press, 1993); *Warrant and Proper Function* (Oxford: Oxford University Press, 1993); and *Warranted Christian Belief* (Oxford: Oxford University Press, 2000).
42 Joseph Runzo, *Global Philosophy of Religion* (Oxford: Oneworld, 2001), 214.

9 RELIGIOUS EXPERIENCE

1 See David Hay, *Religious Experience Today* (London: Mowbray, 1990), Appendix, 79–84.
2 For a helpful and concise overview of religious experience, see Gwen Griffith-Dickson, "Religious Experience," in Chad Meister and Paul Copan, eds., *The Routledge Companion to Philosophy of Religion* (London: Routledge, 2007), 682–91. See also Jerome I. Gellman, "Mysticism and Religious Experience," in William J. Wainwright, ed., *The Oxford Handbook of Religious Experience* (Oxford: Oxford University Press, 2005), 138–67.
3 These three features have been noted by Moojan Momen in his rich and insightful book, *The Phenomenon of Religion: A Thematic Approach* (Oxford: Oneworld, 1999), 88.
4 The following classification is based on the insightful work of Peter Donovan, *Interpreting Religious Experience* (New York: Seabury Press, 1979), 3-20. I have, however, ignored his fourth category, paranormal experience, as such experiences are not typically or necessarily understood to be religious. For other helpful classification schemas, see Richard Swinburne, *The Existence of God*, rev. ed. (Oxford: Clarendon Press, 1979), 249–53, and Carolyn Franks Davis, *The Evidential Force of Religious Experience* (Oxford: Clarendon Press, 1989), Chapter 2.

5 For varieties of such experiences, see William James, *The Varieties of Religious Experience* (New York: The Modern Library, 1902), Lectures IX and X, 186–253.
6 John Hick, *John Hick: An Autobiography* (Oxford: Oneworld, 2002), 33–4. It should be noted that while Hick does not discount this early conversion experience, he no longer adheres to the Evangelical views he did at the time. He now refers to himself as a "critic of evangelical theology." For an expression of his current view of religious pluralism, see Chapter 2 of this book ("Religious Diversity and Pluralism").
7 William James, *The Varieties of Religious Experience,* Lecture IX, 191.
8 The Psalms are filled with such experiences.
9 From *Islam – Our Choice: Impressions of Eminent Converts to Islam* (Karachi: Ashraf Publications, 1977), as quoted in *Interpreting Religious Experience*, 18.
10 For an overview of Pentecostal and charismatic spirituality, see Steven J. Land, "Pentecostal Spirituality: Living in the Spirit" in Louis Dupré and Don E. Saliers, eds., *Christian Spirituality: Post-Reformation and Modern* (New York: Crossroad, 1996), 479–99.
11 For information on the global Charismatic growth, see the Pew Research at http://pewforum.org/surveys/pentecostal/. For an analysis of the changing face of Christianity from a global perspective, see Philip Jenkins, *The Next Christendom: The Coming of Global Christianity* (Oxford: Oxford University Press, 2002). For a somewhat critical analysis of the global charismatic movement, see Ian Cotton, *The Hallelujah Revolution: The Rise of the New Christians* (Amherst, NY: Prometheus Books, 1996).
12 See I Corinthians 12: 4-11 and Acts of the Apostles 2:4–42. For a study on the nature of religious experiences in the early Christian church, see James D. G. Dunn, *Jesus and the Spirit: A Study of the Religious and Charismatic Experience of Jesus and the First Christians as Reflected in the New Testament* (Santa Ana, CA: Westminster Press, 1975).
13 See Donovan, *Interpreting Religious Experience*, 12–13.
14 Ibid.
15 *The Life of Saint Teresa*, trans. J. M. Cohen (New York: Penguin, 1957), 210.
16 For an explication of pragmatic tests (entailing moral and spiritual fruits in human life) for determining an authentic religious experience, see John Hick, *The New Frontier of Religion and Science: Religious Experience, Neuroscience, and the Transcendent* (New York: Palgrave Macmillan, 2006), Chapter 4.
17 William James, *The Varieties of Religious Experience*, 370–2.
18 Shankara, *Crest-Jewel of Discrimination*, trans. Swami Prabhavananda and Christopher Isherwood (Hollywood, CA: Vedanta Press, 1975), 99–100, 105.
19 *The Zohar* is mystical commentary on the Torah (the first five books of the Old Testament) and is an important collection of works of Kabbalah, or Jewish mysticism. See Isaiah Tishby, ed. *The Wisdom of the Zohar: An Anthology of Texts* (3 vols.), translated from the Hebrew by David Goldstein (Oxford: Oxford University Press, 1989).
20 See, for example, *Meister Eckhart: Selected Writings* (New York: Penguin Classics, 1995) and Saint John of the Cross, *Dark Night of the Soul* (New York: Image Books, 1990).
21 Ibn Arabi was a thirteenth-century Arab Sufi mystic. See, for example, his *Contemplation of the Holy Mysteries* (Oxford: Anqa Publishing, 2008), which includes fourteen visions and dialogues with God.
22 As quoted in Evelyn Underhill, *Mysticism* (Oxford: Oneworld, 1993), 420.
23 A "religious" experience of an atheist as quoted in J. M. Cohen and J.-F. Phipps, *The Common Experience* (London: Rider & Co., 1979), 173–4.
24 For Suzuki's description of the eight chief characteristics of satori, see his "Satori/Enlightenment" in Chad Meister, ed., *The Philosophy of Religion Reader* (London: Routledge, 2008), 491–501.

25 For Otto's description of the *mysterium tremendum*, see his *The Idea of the Holy*, trans. John W. Harvey (Oxford: Oxford University Press, nd), Chapter 4.
26 Ibid., 12–23.
27 William James, *The Varieties of Religious Experience*, 407.
28 C. B. Martin, "A Religious Way of Knowing," in Antony Flew and Alistair MacIntyre, eds., *New Essays in Philosophical Theology* (London: Macmillan, 1955), 79.
29 For Wainwright's argument, see his *Mysticism: A Study of Its Nature, Cognitive Value, and Moral Implications* (Madison, WI: University of Wisconsin Press, 1981), Chapter 3.
30 See William Alston, *Perceiving God: The Epistemology of Religious Experience* (Ithaca, NY: Cornell University Press, 1991).
31 Richard Swinburne, *The Existence of God*, rev. ed. (Oxford: Clarendon Press, 1991), 254.
32 Ibid., 254.
33 The exact formulation is this: "If it seems (epistemically) to a subject S that x is absent, then probably x is absent." Michael Martin, *Atheism: A Philosophical Justification* (Philadelphia, PA: Temple University Press, 1990), 170.
34 Ibid., 170.
35 Jerome Gellman, *Experience of God and Rationality of Theistic Belief* (Ithaca, NY: Cornell University Press, 1997).
36 Ibid., 46.
37 Ibid., 52–3.
38 This point was insightfully noted in Michael Peterson, William Hasker, Bruce Reichenbach, and David Basinger, *Reason and Religious Belief*, 4th ed.. (Oxford: Oxford University Press, 2009), 33. For an accessible presentation of Buddhist religious experience, see Gui-Young Hong, "Buddhism and Religious Experience" in Ralph W. Hood, Jr., ed., *Handbook of Religious Experience* (Birmingham, AL: Religious Education Press, 1995), 87–121.
39 C. D. Broad, *Religion, Philosophy, and Psychical Research* (London: Routledge and Kegan Paul, 1953), 200–210.
40 C. B. Martin argues that religious experiences don't provide justification for religious beliefs because they cannot be verified like other perceptual experiences. See his *Religious Belief* (Ithaca, NY: Cornell University Press, 1959).
41 William Alston responds to this objection, which he calls "the problem of religious diversity," in his *Perceiving God: The Epistemology of Religious Experience* (London: Cornell University Press, 1991), Chapter 7.
42 See William James, *The Varieties of Religious Experience*, Lectures IX and X on conversion, 186–253.
43 It's important to note that in maintaining that religious experiences are illusions, Freud is not claiming that they are necessarily false. Rather, he is offering a psychological perspective of religious experience as being a human wish fulfillment. For Freud's wish fulfillment theory, see his *The Future of an Illusion*, trans. James Strachey (New York: Norton and Norton, 1961).
44 John Hick, *The New Frontier of Religion and Science*, presented in Chapter 7 and delineated on page 66.
45 William J. Wainwright, *Philosophy of Religion*, 2nd ed. (New York: Wadsworth, 1999), 133.
46 Ninian Smart, *Philosophers and Religious Truth*, 2nd ed. (London: SCM Press, 1969), 124.

10 THE SELF, DEATH, AND THE AFTERLIFE

1 British philosopher Gilbert Ryle first used the term "ghost in the machine" as a deprecating description for René Descartes' substance dualism. For more on this, see Ryle's *The Concept of Mind*, new ed. (Chicago, IL: University of Chicago Press, 2002).

2 For an explication and defense of this view, see J. P. Moreland and Scott B. Rae, *Body and Soul: Human Nature and the Crisis in Ethics* (Downers Grove, IL: InterVarsity Press, 2000), esp. 202–13.

3 This may be an overstatement, specifically regarding Jewish understandings of the self as reflected in the Hebrew Bible. See, for example, Neil Gillman, *The Death of Death: Resurrection and Immortality in Jewish Thought*, new ed. (Woodstock, VT: Jewish Lights Publishing, 2000).

4 For a sustained defense of substance dualism, see Richard Swinburne, *The Evolution of the Soul* (Oxford: Clarendon Press, 1986). See also J. P. Moreland, *Consciousness and the Existence of God* (London: Routledge, 2008).

5 It should be noted that mental events could either supervene or be epiphenomenal on physical events in ways that avoid substance dualism. It is arguable that even if mental events have causal powers over physical events, this could be explained within a property dualist position.

6 Frank Jackson, "Epiphenomenal Qualia," *Philosophical Quarterly* 32 (1982), 130.

7 It should be noted that the knowledge argument attempts to establish that conscious experience includes non-physical properties. It is not an argument for substance dualism, but rather an argument against the physicalist position which posits only physical properties.

8 Paul M. Churchland, *Matter and Consciousness*, rev. ed. (Cambridge, MA: MIT Press, 1988), 21.

9 For several significant arguments in support of the identity theory, see Churchland, *Matter and Consciousness*, 26–34.

10 It should be noted that functionalism is not necessarily wedded to materialism, although most functionalists are materialists. For a helpful overview of functionalism, see John Heil, *Philosophy of Mind*, 2nd ed. (London: Routledge, 2004), Chapter 7.

11 For a defense of such a view, see Trenton Merricks, "The Resurrection of the Body and the Life Everlasting," in Michael J. Murray, ed., *Reason for the Hope Within* (Grand Rapids, MI: Eerdmans, 1999), 261–86. For different Christian views on the mind–body issue, see Joel B. Green and Stuart L. Palmer, eds., *In Search of the Soul: Four Views of the Mind–Body Problem* (Downers Grove, IL: InterVarsity Press, 2005).

12 As Shankara puts it: "The scriptures establish the absolute identity of *Atman* and Brahman by declaring repeatedly, 'That are Thou.' The terms 'Brahman' and 'Atman,' in their true meaning, refer to 'That' and 'Thou' respectively." In Shankara, "Brahman is All," in Chad Meister, ed., *The Philosophy of Religion Reader* (London: Routledge, 2008), 172.

13 Shankara puts it this way: "As the space in a jar in universal space, so the Self is to be merged without division in the Self supreme…" *Crest-Jewel of Wisdom*, verse 288 (many ed.s).

14 For a detailed article on karma and reincarnation in Advaita Vedānta, see Arvind Sharma, "Karma and reincarnation in Advaita Vedānta," in the *Journal of Indian Philosophy* 18.3 (September) 1990, 219–36.

15 This translation of the Anatta-lakkhana sutta, Samyutta Nikaya XXII, 59, can be found at http://acc6.its.brooklyn.cuny.edu/~phalsall/texts/anatta.txt.

16 See the *Questions of King Menander* in the Pali Canon. See also Sarvepalli Radhakrishnan and Charles A. Moore, eds., *A Sourcebook in Indian Philosophy* (Princeton, NJ: Princeton University Press, 1957), 284–5.
17 For a full description of this story, see "Is Reincarnation Real? The Case of Parmod Sharma," on the *beliefnet* website at http://www.beliefnet.com/story/121/story_12133_1.html. For similar stories, see the research on out-of-body experiences, near-death experiences, and reincarnation at the University of Virginia Health Science Center, Division of Personality Studies which can be found at http://www.healthsystem.virginia.edu/internet/personalitystudies/case_types.cfm.
18 The Pali canon includes a host of references to rebirth. For more on rebirth in Buddhist philosophy, see Francis Story, *Rebirth as Doctrine and Experience*, new ed. (Kandy, Sri Lanka: Buddhist Publication Society, 2003).
19 On the Mahayana Buddhist view, there are five *skandhas* – mental events or bundles – which constitute what we often call the "ego."
20 For examples, see the University of Virginia Health Science Center, Division of Personality Studies website which can be found at http://www.healthsystem.virginia.edu/internet/personalitystudies/case_types.cfm.
21 The term "immortality," while literally meaning "not-dying," is typically used in reference to immoral souls. However, I have used the terms "immortality" and "life after death" interchangeably in this chapter.
22 In the recent classic work, *Life After Life: The Investigation of a Phenomenon – Survival of Bodily Death* (San Francisco, CA: HarperOne, 2001), Raymond Moody examines over one hundred case studies of people who experienced "clinical death" and were subsequently revived. For more research on NDEs as providing evidence for immortality, see Gary Habermas and J. P. Moreland, *Beyond Death: Exploring the Evidence for Immortality* (Eugene, OR: Wipf and Stock, 2004). For an interesting autobiographical account of a famous atheist's experience of life after death, see A. J. Ayer, "What I Saw When I Was Dead," *National Review*, October 14, 1988. It can be found online at FindArticles.com, 13 May 2008, http://findarticles.com/p/articles/mi_m1282/is_n20_v40/ai_6701958.
23 See Habermas and Moreland, *Beyond Death*.
24 A. J. Ayer, "What I Saw When I was Dead,", 39.
25 I Corinthians 15:12–23.
26 For a recent work on the pro-resurrection side, see Gary Habermas and Michael Licona, *The Case for the Resurrection of Jesus* (Grand Rapids, MI: Kregel, 2004). For a recent work on the skeptical side, see Robert M. Price and Jeffery Jay Lowder, eds., *The Empty Tomb: Jesus Beyond the Grave* (Amherst, NY: Prometheus Books, 2005).
27 For the central argument, see *Phaedo*, 100b–107a.
28 See J. M. E. McTaggart, *Some Dogmas of Religion* (London: Edward Arnold, 1906), 108–9. I am indebted to William Wainwright for pointing out this argument.
29 For a defense of a substance dualist view of the soul, see Richard Swinburne, *The Evolution of the Soul*, rev. ed. (Oxford: Oxford University Press, 1997).
30 Grace M. Jantzen, "Do We Need Immortality?" in *Modern Theology* 1:1 (1984), 34–5.
31 Ibid., 41–3.
32 See Charles Taliaferro, "Why We Need Immortality," in *Modern Theology* 6:4 (1990), 367–77, and reprinted in Chad Meister, ed. *The Philosophy of Religion Reader* (London: Routledge, 2008), 625–35.

Index

Note: Italicized page numbers followed by a "b" refer to shaded boxes within the text.

Related titles from Routledge

THE PHILOSOPHY OF RELIGION READER

Edited by Chad Meister

'...This ambitious collection represents the leading edge of the field.'
Michael J. Murray, Franklin and Marshall College, USA

This new Reader brings together a collection of classical and contemporary key writings, offering students a comprehensive and up to date overview of the field. Global in perspective, it includes selections from non-theistic sources, as well as those from the Western theistic traditions of philosophy of religion and philosophical theology. The Reader contains ten thematic sections chosen to reflect current trends in the field, including:

Religious Diversity
Arguments For and Against the Existence of God
Faith, Reason and Evidence
Science, Religion and Miracles
Religious Experience
The Problem of Evil
Death and the Afterlife

To aid student learning, editorial introductions begin each thematic section, and each selection is supported with a contextual introduction, essay questions for discussion and a list of annotated further readings.

ISBN13: 978-0-415-40890-5 (hbk)
ISBN13: 978-0-415-40891-2 (pbk)

Related titles from Routledge

ROUTLEDGE COMPANION TO PHILOSOPHY OF RELIGION

Edited by Chad Meister and Paul Copan

The Routledge Companion to Philosophy of Religion is an outstanding guide and reference source to the major themes, movements, debates and topics in philosophy of religion. Sixty-four entries by a team of renowned international contributors are organized into nine clear parts, which include:

Philosophical Issues in the World Religions: Hinduism, Buddhism, African Religions, Chinese Religion, Judaism, Christianity, Islam

Key Figures in Philosophy of Religion: Augustine, Shankara, Ibn Sina/Avicenna, Moses Maimonides/Rambam, Thomas Aquinas, David Hume, Immanuel Kant, Søren Kierkegaard, Friedrich Nietzsche, William James

Arguments For God's Existence: The Ontological Argument, The Cosmological Argument, The Teleological Argument, The Moral Argument, The Argument from Consciousness, The Wager Argument

Arguments Against God's Existence: The Problem of Evil, Problems with the Concept of God, The Problem of Religious Language, Naturalistic Rejoinders to Theistic Arguments, Why Is There a Universe At All, Rather Than Just Nothing?, The Sociobiological Account of Religious Belief

Recent Topics in Philosophy of Religion: Reformed Epistemology, Feminism, Continental Philosophy, Phenomenology of Religion, Religious Naturalism, Religious Experience, Religion and Science

The Routledge Companion to Philosophy of Religion is essential reading for anyone interested in philosophy, religion and related disciplines.

ISBN13: 978-0-415-38038-6 (hbk)
ISBN13: 978-0-203-87934-4 (ebk)